Evaluation in the Human Services

Yvonne A. Unrau
Illinois State University

Peter A. Gabor
The University of Calgary

Richard M. Grinnell, Jr.
Illinois State University

Contents

PART II: TOOLS OF EVALUATION

Chapter 5 Data Sources, Sampling, and Data Collection   113

Chapter 6 Measurement   143

Chapter 7 Case-Level Evaluations   179

Chapter 8 Program-Level Evaluations   209

PART III: ISSUES OF EVALUATION

Chapter 9 Politics, Ethics, and Standards   257

PART IV: UTILITY OF EVALUATION

Chapter 11 Developing a Data Information System   307

Chapter 12 Decision Making with Objective and Subjective Data 333

Preface

THE AUDIENCE OF THIS BOOK is social work students and students in other related human service programs. It is designed to be used as a main text in introductory evaluation courses, case management courses, or applied research courses. It is also suitable as a supplementary text in practice methods and administration courses that place an emphasis on accountability.

GOAL AND OBJECTIVES

Our goal was to write an accessible, straightforward introduction to evaluation. In addition, this book contains only the core material that students realistically need to know to appreciate and understand the role of evaluation in professional social work practice. Thus, unnecessary material is avoided at all costs. To accomplish this goal, we strived to meet three simple objectives:

— To prepare students to participate in evaluative activities within their organizations
— To prepare students to become beginning critical producers and consumers of the professional evaluative literature
— To prepare students for more advanced evaluation courses and texts

In a nutshell, our goal is to provide students with a sound conceptual understanding of how the ideas of evaluation can be used in the delivery of social services. In addition, this book will provide them with the beginning knowledge and skills that they will need to demonstrate their accountability.

Conceptual Approach

With our goal and three objectives in mind, we present a unique approach in describing the place of evaluation in the social services. Simply put, our approach is realistic, practical, applied, and most importantly, user-friendly.

Over the years, little has changed in the way in which most evaluation textbooks present their material. A majority of texts focus on *program-level* evaluation and describe project type, one-shot approaches, implemented by specialized evaluation departments or external consultants. On the other hand, a few recent books present *case-level* evaluation, but place most emphasis on inferentially powerful—but difficult to implement—experimental and multiple baseline designs.

As social work educators and evaluators, we are convinced that neither of these two distinct approaches adequately reflects the realities in the field or the needs of students and *beginning* practitioners. We describe how data obtained through case-level evaluation can be aggregated to provide timely and relevant program-level evaluation information. Such information, in turn, is the basis for a quality improvement process within the entire organization.

In short, we have blended the two distinct evaluation approaches to demonstrate how they complement one another in contemporary professional practice. The integration of case-level and program-level approaches is one of the unique features of this book; we are convinced that this integration will play an increasingly prominent role in the future.

We have omitted more advanced methodological and statistical material such as a discussion of celeration lines, autocorrelation, effect sizes, and two standard-deviation bands for case-level evaluation, as well as advanced statistical techniques for program-level evaluation.

Some readers with a strict methodological orientation may find some of the described approaches simplistic, particularly the material on the aggregation of case-level data. We are aware of the limitations of the approach described in this book, but we firmly believe that this approach is more likely to be implemented by beginning practitioners than are other more complicated, technically demanding approaches.

It is our opinion that the aggregation of case-level data can provide valuable feedback about services and programs and be the basis of an effective quality-improvement process. It is our view that it is preferable to have such data, even if it is not methodologically airtight, than to have no aggregated data at all.

Theme

The underlying theme of this book is that social work practitioners can easily use evaluation procedures in their practices and programs. We maintain that professional practice rests upon the foundation that practice activities must be linked to the client's objectives, which are linked to the program's objectives, which are linked to the program's goals, which are linked to the agency's goals, which represents the reason why the program exists in the first place. The evaluation process presented in this book heavily reflects these connections.

Pressures for accountability have never been greater. Organizations and practitioners of all types are increasingly required to document the impacts of their services not only at the program level, but at the case level as well. Continually, they are challenged to improve the quality of their services and they are required to do this with scarce resources. In addition, few social service organizations can adequately maintain an internal evaluation department or hire outside evaluators. Consequently, we place a considerable emphasis on monitoring, an approach that can be easily incorporated into the ongoing activities of the practitioner and agency.

In short, we provide a straightforward view of evaluation while taking into account:

— The current pressures for accountability in the social services
— The current available evaluation technologies and approaches
— The present evaluation needs of students as well as their needs in the first few years of their careers

ACKNOWLEDGMENTS

We would like to thank the following people for their thoughtful reviews of our book:

— Richard L. Edwards
  University of North Carolina at Chapel Hill
— Leon Ginsberg
  University of South Carolina
— Mike Jacobsen
  University of North Dakota
— John L. Stretch
  St. Louis University
— Maria Roberts DeGennaro
  San Diego State University

Last but not least, we would like to thank Carol Ing for contributing Chapter 10 to this volume.

A LOOK TOWARD THE FUTURE

The field of evaluation and quality improvement in the social services is continuing to grow and develop. We hope this book contributes to that growth. In revising this volume, readers' feedback will be most appreciated. If you have suggestions for improvement in the next edition, or other comments, we would like to hear from you.

If this book helps students to acquire basic evaluation knowledge and skills and assists them in more advanced evaluation and practice courses, our efforts will have been more than justified. If it also assists them to incorporate evaluation techniques into their practice, our task will be fully rewarded.

January 2001

Yvonne A. Unrau
Peter A. Gabor
Richard M. Grinnell, Jr.

Part I

Building Blocks of Evaluation

1

Chapter Outline

Introduction

PROFESSIONAL SOCIAL WORKERS have an influential role in helping to understand and ameliorate the numerous social and economic problems that exist in our society. The very nature of our profession puts us directly in the "trenches" of society; that is, we interface with people and their problems. We practice in such places as inner-city neighborhoods and hospices and work with people such as the homeless and the mentally ill. We therefore see and experience client problems and injustices firsthand. Of course, we are expected to help make things better, not only for our clients but also for the society in which we all live. Unlike card and palm readers, as illustrated in Box 1.1, contemporary social work practitioners are expected to have a substantial evaluation knowledge base to guide and support their interventions. This knowledge base is generally derived from a social work evaluation course such as the one that has required you to buy this book.

Unfortunately, the day-to-day helping tools that we use in our profession could benefit from a bit of improvement. We lack the know-how to stop family violence, to eradicate discrimination, and to eliminate human suffering, for example. Social work education teaches us both theory and research that, in turn, we are expected to translate into useful interventions to help our clients. One only needs to sit face-to-face with a client such as a gay adolescent who has been beaten by his peers because of his sexual preference to realize the limits of our profession's knowledge base in helping us to know what to do.

BOX 1.1_____

CAN A PSYCHIC CARD AND PALM READER
SOLVE HUMAN PROBLEMS?

Madame *X* is a psychic card and palm reader. She has practiced in our local community for several years and has gained the highest admiration of many people. She advertises in the local newspaper, claiming:

> With my advice and insight, I will guide and help you to a more successful life. I can help you with such things as love, business, health, and marriage. One visit will convince you that I can solve any of your problems—big or small.

A number of questions should immediately come to mind upon reading Madame X's self-proclaimed expertise: Can she really solve human problems? How does she do it? Is she effective in her problem solving? Is she more (or less) effective than others who also claim to solve such problems? A cynical social worker might even ask: What is the future of my social work practice if Madame X were to establish her practice in my community?

While it is doubtful that any of us would be threatened by Madame X's claims, her advertisement does serve to illustrate how the process and objectives of helping people can

mistakenly be reduced to simplicity or, in this case, mysticism. A person who is a true believer in psychic card and palm reading would probably ask very few questions of Madame X. Most of us, however, would want to know much more about her knowledge base. We would want to ascertain why she feels she can take the complex process of human problem solving and claim to "solve any of your problems—big or small" by reading cards or palms.

It is less likely that similar questions would be addressed to social workers. Society generally makes certain assumptions regarding the extent of our knowledge base, the competency of our practice skills, and the effectiveness of our social service programs. Society is more discriminating about Madame X than it is about social workers because it has greater expectations for the way we develop our knowledge base and practice skills. Social workers—like all professionals (e.g., lawyers, physicians, nurses, architects, police officers)—are expected to have a good knowledge base to guide their interventions.

Moreover, there is considerable public pressure on social workers to "fix" problems. We are expected to stop parents from abusing their children, to keep inner-city youth from dropping out of school, and to prevent discrimination in society. Additionally, we are expected to achieve positive outcomes with less than adequate financial resources. And all of this is occurring under a watchful public eye.

In contrast to the card and palm reader portrayed in Box 1.1, professional social workers are expected to know how to evaluate their practices. That is the position of both the Council on Social Work Education (CSWE) and the

BOX 1.2

COUNCIL ON SOCIAL WORK EDUCATION'S
BSW AND MSW CURRICULUM RESEARCH CONTENT

B6.0—BSW Curriculum Content

- The research curriculum must provide an understanding and appreciation of a scientific, analytic approach to building knowledge for practice and to evaluating service delivery in all areas of practice. Ethical standards of scientific inquiry must be included in the research content.
- The research content must include quantitative and qualitative research methodologies; analysis of data, including statistical procedures; systematic evaluation of practice; analysis and evaluation of theoretical bases, research questions, methodologies, statistical procedures, and conclusions of research reports; and relevant technological advances.
- Each program must identify how the research curriculum contributes to the student's use of scientific knowledge for practice.

M6.0—MSW Curriculum Content

- The foundation research curriculum must provide an understanding and appreciation of a scientific, analytic approach to building knowledge for practice and for evaluating service delivery in all areas of practice. Ethical standards of scientific inquiry must be included in the research content.
- The research content must include qualitative and quantitative research methodologies; analysis of data, including statistical procedures; systematic evaluation of practice; analysis and evaluation of theoretical bases, research questions, methodologies, statistical procedures, and conclusions of research reports; and relevant technological advances.
- Each program must identify how the research curriculum contributes to the student's use of scientific knowledge for practice.

National Association of Social Workers (NASW). The CSWE is the official "educational organization" that sets minimum curriculum standards for BSW and MSW programs throughout North America. The NASW is a parallel "practice organization" that works to enhance the professional growth and development of practicing social workers. In a nutshell, both organizations firmly believe in the relevance of evaluation to social work education (Box 1.2) and to social work practice (Box 1.3).

So how is it that social workers are to both provide effective client services and advance the profession's knowledge base—all at the same time? As can be seen in Box 1.3, we do this by evaluating our social work practices and programs over time. We commit to NASW's philosophy of quality improvement by continually and systematically looking for new ways to make client

BOX 1.3

NASW'S *CODE OF ETHICS*
(RESEARCH AND EVALUATION)

- Social workers should monitor and evaluate policies, and the implementation of programs, and practice interventions.
- Social workers should promote and facilitate evaluation and research to contribute to the development of knowledge.
- Social workers should critically examine and keep current with emerging knowledge relevant to social work and fully use evaluation and research evidence in their practice.
- Social workers engaged in evaluation or research should carefully consider possible consequences and should follow guidelines developed for the protection of evaluation and research participants. Appropriate institutional review boards should be consulted.
- Social workers engaged in evaluation or research should obtain voluntary and written informed consent from participants, when appropriate, without any implied or actual deprivation or penalty for refusal to participate; without undue inducement to participate; and with due regard for participants' well-being, privacy, and dignity. Informed consent should include information about the nature, extent, and duration of the participation requested and disclosure of the risks and benefits of participation in the research.
- When evaluation or research participants are incapable of giving informed consent, social workers should provide an appropriate explanation to the participants, obtain the participants' assent to the extent they are able, and obtain written consent from an appropriate proxy.
- Social workers should never design or conduct evaluation or research that does not use consent procedures, such as certain forms of naturalistic observation and archival research, unless rigorous and responsible review of the research has found it to be justified because of its prospective scientific, educational, or applied value and unless equally effective alternative procedures that do not involve waiver of consent are not feasible.

- Social workers should inform participants of their right to withdraw from evaluation and research at any time without penalty.
- Social workers should take appropriate steps to ensure that research participants have access to supportive services.
- Social workers engaged in evaluation or research should protect participants from unwarranted physical or mental distress, harm, danger, or deprivation.
- Social workers engaged in the evaluation of services should discuss collected information only for professional purposes and only with people professionally concerned with this information.
- Social workers engaged in evaluation or research should ensure the anonymity or confidentiality of participants and of the data obtained from them.
- Social workers should inform participants of any limits of confidentiality, the measures that will be taken to ensure confidentiality, and when any records containing research data will be destroyed.
- Social workers who report evaluation and research results should protect participants' confidentiality by omitting identifying information unless proper consent has been obtained authorizing disclosure.
- Social workers should report evaluation and research findings accurately. They should not fabricate results and should take steps to correct any errors later found in published data using standard publication methods.
- Social workers engaged in evaluation or research should be alert to and avoid conflicts of interest and dual relationships with participants, should inform participants when a real or potential conflict of interest arises, and should take steps to resolve the issue in a manner that makes participants' interests primary.
- Social workers should educate themselves, their students, and their colleagues about responsible research practices.

services more responsive, more efficient, and more effective. This is the goal of the quality improvement process in social services.

THE QUALITY IMPROVEMENT PROCESS

Quality improvement means that we continually monitor and adjust (when necessary) our practices and programs in order to enhance client service delivery. It is at the case level that we actually provide services to client systems such as individuals, couples, families, groups, organizations, and communities. At this level, each and every client system can be singularly evaluated. At the case level we customize evaluation plans to learn about specific details and patterns of change that are unique to a single client system.

In most instances, social workers see individual clients through the auspices of some kind of a social service program. As a result, we can think of social service programs as aggregations of individual client cases. When conducting program-level evaluations we are interested in the *overall* characteristics of all the clients and the *average* pattern of change for all of them served by a program. In a nutshell, case-level evaluations evaluate the effectiveness and efficiency of our individual services, while program-level evaluations evaluate the effectiveness and efficiency of the social service programs as a whole.

Both case- and program-level evaluations yield data that are then turned into information. The two words, *data* and *information,* are often used interchangeably. In this book, the term *data* signifies isolated facts, in numerical (i.e., numbers) or text (i.e., words) form, that are gathered in the course of an evaluation. For example, the number and demographic characteristics of people in a specific lower socioeconomic community or the written responses of clients who responded to a client service satisfaction questionnaire can provide numerical and text data.

How we interpret the data when they have all been collected, collated, and analyzed is called *information.* For example, *data* collected in reference to client referral sources gathered from a program's intake unit may indicate that the program accepts 90 percent of its referrals from other social service programs and only 5 percent of people who are self-referred. One of the many pieces of *information* (or conclusions or findings drawn from the data) generated by these data may be that the program is somehow more accessible to clients who were referred by other social service programs than to those who were self-referred.

The distinction between data and information is simple—data are the facts, while information is the interpretation that we give to theses facts. Together, data and information help guide various decision-making processes in an effort to produce more effective and efficient services to our clients.

Producing meaningful and useful data and information for quality improvement in service delivery is a process that involves both the art and science of social work practice. While we might think of evaluation as a close cousin of science, it also has close relations with art. Useful evaluation designs require creativity and ingenuity just as much as they need logic, procedural detail, and research principles. If evaluation is to help our profession, we must —in the best sense and at the same time—be both "caring and sensitive artists" *and* "rigorous scientists."

WHY SHOULD WE DO EVALUATIONS?

Our profession must provide reasons for the policies and positions that it takes. As we can see from Boxes 1.2 and 1.3, evaluation procedures are an integral part of competent social work practice. Just as practitioners must be prepared to explain their reasons for pursuing a particular intervention with a client, so must the profession have rationales for integrating evaluation in our social work practice.

Why should evaluation be included in practice? Why is it needed? What is it for? We have noted that the fundamental reason for conducting evaluations is to improve the quality of the services we offer clients. More specifically, evaluations also: (1) increase our knowledge base, (2) guide decision making, (3) demonstrate accountability of program and practice objectives, and (4) assure that clients' objectives are met.

Increase Our Knowledge Base

One of the basic prerequisites of helping people to help themselves is knowing what to do. Knowing how to help involves practitioners possessing both relevant practice skills and knowledge. Child sexual abuse, for example, has come to prominence as a social problem only during the past few decades, and many questions still remain unanswered. In short, the knowledge base about child sexual abuse is uncertain, giving us more questions than answers. For example, does child sexual abuse stem from individual pathology in the perpetrators, to dysfunctions in the family systems, or to a combination of the two?

If individual pathology is the underlying issue, can the perpetrator be treated in a community-based program or is institutionalization a more effective alternative? If familial dysfunction is the issue, should clients go immediately into family counseling or should some other form of help be offered? To address these and other questions, we need to acquire general knowledge from a variety of sources in an effort to increase our overall knowledge base in the area of sexual abuse.

To begin with, we would want to consult other experts in the same field—either through published literature or by networking through professional channels such as conferences and associations. The advent of the Internet has made professional contact and consultation much easier in recent years. Our aim is to start with the work of others in order to learn from their mistakes and triumphs and to avoid reinventing evaluation and practice wheels that already exist and are working.

Building on knowledge generated by others is a basic ingredient of professional social work practice. Sometimes prior knowledge is rich and detailed, but more often than not it is sparse and vague. Either way, social work practitioners can contribute to a particular knowledge base by providing fruitful insight and understanding from their direct experiences with clients in the field.

Through case- and program-level evaluations, we can learn a great deal from practitioners in the field. Whom do they serve? What do they do? Which of their interventions are most effective? For example, a practitioner may have found through evaluation efforts that family therapy offered immediately yields a greater margin of positive change only when the abuse by the perpetrator was affection-based (i.e., intended as a way of showing love). With aggression-based abuse (i.e., fulfils the power needs of the perpetrator), however, the practitioner may have found that individual therapy results in more beneficial change.

Findings based on evaluations are more credible than findings based on experiences alone. Indeed, if a number of evaluation studies produce similar findings, theories may be formulated about the different kinds of treatment interventions most likely to be effective with different types of perpetrators who abuse their children.

Once formulated, a theory has to be tested. This, too, can be achieved by means of evaluations using simple evaluation designs. It should be noted that in our profession, however, very few evaluations test theories, because the controlled conditions required for theory-testing are more readily obtained in an artificial setting.

The data gathered to increase our general knowledge base are sometimes presented in the form of statistics. The conclusions drawn from the data may apply to groups of clients (program-level evaluation) rather than to individual clients (case-level evaluation), and thus will probably not be immediately helpful to a particular practitioner or client in the short term. Many workers and their future clients, however, will benefit in the long term when evaluation findings have been synthesized into theories, those theories have been tested, and effective treatment interventions have been derived from the theories.

Guide Decision Making

A second reason for doing evaluations to improve the quality of our services is to gather data in an effort to provide information that will help decision makers at all levels. People who have vested interests in programs are called *stakeholders*, and they have a role in making many different kinds of decisions in social service programs—from administrative decisions about funding to a practitioner's decision about the best way to serve a particular client system (e.g., individual, couple, family, group, community, organization).

Six stakeholder groups benefit from evaluations: (1) state and federal policymakers, (2) administrators of social service programs, (3) practitioners who work within the programs, (4) funders of the programs, (5) the general public, and (6) the clients served by the programs.

Policymakers

To policymakers in governmental or other administrative bodies, any individual social service program is only one among many. On a general level, policymakers are concerned with broad issues. For example, how effective and efficient are programs serving women who have been battered, youth who are unemployed, or children who have been sexually abused? If one type of program is more effective than another but also costs more, does the additional service to clients justify the increased cost? Should certain types of programs be continued, expanded, cut, abandoned, or modified? How should money be allocated among competing similar programs? In sum, policymakers want comparative data about the effectiveness of different social service programs serving similar clients.

Administrators

An administrator of a program is mostly concerned with his or her own individual program. Administrators want to know how well the program operates as a whole, in addition to how well its components operate. Is the assessment process at the client intake level successful in selecting only those referred persons who are likely to benefit from the program's services? Does treatment planning provide for the integration of individual, dyadic, group, and family services in an order and time that consider the client's particular demographic characteristics? Does the discharge process provide adequate consultation with other involved professionals? Like the policymakers mentioned above, administrators may also want to know which interventions are effective and which are less so, which are economical, which must be retained, and which could be modified or dropped.

Practitioners

Line-level practitioners who deal directly with clients are most often interested in practical, day-to-day issues: Is it wise to include adolescent male sexual abuse survivors in the same group with adolescent female survivors, or should the males be referred to another service if separate groups cannot be run? What mix of role-play, educational films, discussion, and other treatment activities best facilitates client learning? Will parent education strengthen families? Is nutrition counseling for parents an effective way to improve school performance of children from impoverished homes?

Of greatest importance to a practitioner is the question: Is my particular treatment intervention with this particular client working? A periodic evaluation of an entire social service program (or part of the program) cannot answer questions about individual clients. However, as we will see later in this book, we can carry out case-level evaluations to determine the degree to which our clients are reaching their practice objectives.

Funders

The public and private funding organizations who provide money to run social service programs want to know that their money is being spent wisely. If funds have been allocated to combat family violence, is family violence declining? And, if so, by how much? Is there any way in which the money could be put to better use? Often, the funder will insist that some kind of an evaluation of a specific program must take place before additional funds will be provided. Administrators are thus made *accountable* for the funds they receive. They must demonstrate that their programs are achieving the best results for the money received.

General Public

Increasingly, taxpayers are demanding that state and federal government departments in turn be accountable to them. Lay groups concerned with the care of the elderly, support for families, drug rehabilitation, or child abuse are demanding to know what is being done about these problems: How much money is being spent and where is it being spent? Are taxpayers' dollars effectively serving *current* social needs? In the same way, charitable organizations are accountable to donors, school boards are accountable to parents, and so forth. These bodies require evidence that they are making wise use of the money entrusted to them. As we will see throughout this book, an appropriate evaluation can provide such evidence through the data it yields.

A simple program evaluation can also be used as an element in a public relations campaign. Programs want to look good in the eyes of the general public or other parties. Data showing that a program is helping to resolve a social problem may, for example, silence opposing interest groups and encourage potential funders to grant more money. On occasion, an evaluation can help highlight a program's strengths in an effort to improve its public image. In other cases, however, administrators may merely wish to generate support for what they believe to be a good and beneficial program.

Clients

Only recently have the people who use social service programs begun to ask whether the program's services meet their needs. Does the program aim to meet the needs of the people it serves? Are ethnic and religious issues being sensitively considered? Do clients *want* what program administrators and funding sources think they ought to want? In short, is the social service program actually in tune with what the clients really need?

A factor relevant to serving client needs is whether the clients' cultural group administers the program, to some degree. If a community is predominantly African American or Asian or Mormon, do people from these respective groups operate the program, to some extent? If not, how much input does the community have in setting the program's objectives and suggesting appropriate intervention strategies for achieving them? An evaluation study might look not only at how well the program's objectives are being achieved, but also at whether they are appropriate to the clients being served.

Demonstrate Accountability

A third reason for including evaluations in the quality improvement process is to demonstrate accountability. As previously mentioned, administrators are accountable to their funders for the way in which money is spent, and the funders are similarly accountable to the public. Accountability means that one is answerable for the actions and decisions he or she makes. Program-level evaluations helps us to be accountable by providing data that can help us explain an entire program, and case-level evaluations can help us evaluate our day-to-day client outcomes.

Demonstrating accountability, or providing justification of a social service program, is a legitimate purpose of an evaluation insofar as it involves a genuine attempt to identify a program's strengths and weaknesses. Sometimes, however, an evaluation of a demonstration project may be undertaken solely because the terms of the funding demand it. For example, a majority of state and federally funded social service demonstration projects are forced to have periodic evaluations or their funds will be taken away. Accountability in our profession can take five forms:

— Coverage Accountability: Are the persons served those who have been designated as targets? Are there any other beneficiaries who should not be served?
— Service Delivery Accountability: Are reasonable amounts of services being delivered?
— Fiscal Accountability: Are funds being used properly? Are expenditures properly documented? Are funds used within the limits set within the budget?

— Legal Accountability: Are relevant laws, including those concerning affirmative action, occupational safety and health, and privacy of individual records being observed?

— Professional Accountability: Are our professional codes of ethics and accreditation service standards being met? (see Boxes 1.2 & 1.3)

Assure That Client Objectives Are Met

A fourth and final reason for incorporating evaluations in the quality improvement process is to determine if clients are getting what they need from a social service program. Responsible practitioners are interested in knowing to what degree each of their individual client's practice objectives are being achieved; that is, they are interested in evaluating their individual practices.

Clients want to know if the services they are receiving are worth their time, effort, and sometimes money. Usually, these data are required while treatment is still in progress, as it is hardly useful to a particular client to conclude that services were ineffective after the client has left the program. A measure of effectiveness is needed while there is still time to try a different intervention.

FEARS ABOUT EVALUATION

Despite the many reasons to support including evaluation in social work educational programs and social service programs, some social work students, practitioners, or administrators avoid doing so. Many times, evaluation is resisted because of fears that are associated with the evaluation process. Social work students tend to fear research and thus, by association, also fear evaluation, which uses many research principles and concepts. Practitioners may fear that evaluation will take up valuable client time that cannot be spared. Administrators may fear that evaluation will reveal negative aspects about their programs. Simply accepting and including evaluation as an integral part of practice can alleviate these types of fears.

It is helpful to use the analogy of the academic examination to illustrate the nature of this fear. Colleges and universities offering social work degrees are obliged to evaluate their students so that they do not release unqualified practitioners upon an unsuspecting public. Sometimes, evaluation is accomplished through a single examination set at the end of a course. More often, however, students are evaluated in an ongoing way, through regular assignments and frequent small quizzes. There may or may not be a final examination, but if there is one, it is worth proportionately less and feared less.

Most students prefer the second, ongoing course of evaluation prepared by their instructor. A single examination on which the total course grade depends is a traumatic event—even more so if the examination were not prepared by the course instructor. In turn, a mid-term, worth 40 percent, is less dreadful; and a weekly, 10-minute quiz marked by a fellow student may hardly raise the pulse rate. So it is with the evaluation of anything—from social service programs to the practitioners employed within them.

Similarly, an evaluation of a social service program conducted once every five years by an outside evaluator can be a very frightening event. On the other hand, an ongoing evaluation conducted by the practitioners themselves as a normal part of day-to-day program operations becomes a routine part of service delivery.

As we have alluded to above, an evaluation can be *internally driven,* that is, initiated and conducted by staff members who work within the program itself. On the other hand, the evaluation can be *externally driven*—initiated by someone outside the program to be evaluated, which is often the program's major funding source.

The principal motive behind internal evaluations is to improve the quality of services to clients on an ongoing basis. A distinct advantage of internal evaluations is that the questions posed are likely to be highly relevant to staff members' interests, thus indirectly reducing their fears toward the evaluation process. This is hardly surprising; since staff members are responsible for conducting the evaluations and, with their firsthand knowledge of the programs in which they work, they are in advantageous positions to ensure that the evaluations address relevant issues.

While social workers may fear internal evaluations less, there is a drawback to them; that is, internally driven evaluations may be viewed as lacking the credibility that comes with independent, outside evaluations. However, because people outside a social service program commission externally driven evaluations, they tend to reflect outside interests and do not address questions that are most relevant to program staff—a condition that tends to foster fear. As well, outside evaluations often impose an onerous data collection burden on staff and tend to be disruptive to normal program operations.

Of course, one of the realities of an ongoing internally driven evaluation is that the workers have to carry it out. Some may fear it because they do not know how to do it: They may never have been taught the quality improvement process during their studies, and they may fear both the unknown and the specter of the "scientific." One of the purposes of this book is to alleviate the fear and misunderstanding that presently shroud the quality improvement process, and to show that evaluations can be conducted in ways that are beneficial and lead to the improvement of the services we offer clients.

SCOPE OF EVALUATIONS

The word *program* is broad in it meaning. It can refer to small, specific, and short-term efforts, such as a film developed for use during a training session on AIDS. It may also refer to a nationwide effort to combat family violence, and include all the diverse endeavors in that field, with different practice objectives and their corresponding intervention strategies. Or, it may refer to a specific treatment intervention used with a specific social worker and undertaken with a specific client.

Different types of social service programs call for using different methods of evaluations. Thus, we need to know the parameters of a program before deciding how best to include an evaluative effort within it. The scope of any evaluation has to be sensitive to the following program characteristics:

— Boundary: The program may extend across a nation, region, state, province, city, parish, county, or community; or it may be extremely limited—for example, a course presented in an individual program or school.

— Size: The program may serve a fixed number of individual clients, such as a maximum of 10 individuals seeking group therapy, or many clients, such as all people infected with the HIV virus.

— Duration: The program may be designed to last for half an hour—a training film, for example—or it may be an orientation course on child safety lasting for two days, a group therapy cycle lasting for 10 weeks, or a pilot project designed to help the homeless being evaluated after two years. Or, as in the case of a child protection program, it may be intended to continue indefinitely.

— Complexity: Some programs offer integrated components, combining, for instance, child protection services, individual therapy, family therapy, and educational services under one common umbrella. Such a program is obviously more complex than one with a simpler, singular focus—for example, providing nutrition counseling to pregnant adolescents.

— Clarity and Time Span of Program Objectives: Some programs have objectives that can readily be evaluated; for example, to increase the number of unemployed adolescents who secure full-time work within two months of completing a six-week training course. Others have objectives that will not become evident for some time; for example, to increase educational achievement of children born to low-income single mothers.

— Innovativeness: Some social service programs follow long-established treatment interventions, while others experiment with new innovations—sometimes designed for use with current social problems, such as AIDS.

QUALITY IMPROVEMENT APPROACHES

As we shall see in this book, there are many types of evaluations that can be done to improve the quality of the services we offer our clients. All evaluations, however, can be classified under either the project approach or the monitoring approach to quality improvement.

An evaluation whose purpose is to assess a completed social service program (or project) uses a *project* approach to quality improvement. Complementary to the project approach, an evaluation whose purpose is to provide feedback while a program is still under way has a *monitoring* approach to quality improvement; that is, it is designed to contribute to the ongoing development and improvement of the program as it goes along.

The Project Approach ⇒ Completed program

As we have seen, evaluations that enhance the quality improvement process in our profession may be carried out daily or they may not be initiated until the program has been in operation for a number of years. A one-shot evaluation illustrates the *project approach* to quality improvement. This approach tends to give rise to evaluations with the following characteristics:

— Externally Driven: The evaluation will almost certainly be externally driven, that is, it will be initiated by someone outside the program who more often than not will decide on the evaluation questions to be answered and the data to be collected that will presumably answer the questions.

— **Resistant Staff:** Program staff may react negatively to the evaluation, seeing it as unrelated, intrusive, irrelevant, and an extra burden. Additionally, they may fear the evaluation will be used in some way to judge them. When an evaluation is externally driven, staff may resist implementation of an evaluator's recommendations, even if the program's administration insists that changes be made.

— **Intrusiveness:** Evaluation procedures are very likely to be intrusive, no matter how hard the person doing the evaluation works to avoid this. Because the procedures are not a part of a program's normal day-to-day routine but must be introduced as additional tasks to be performed, staff have less time to spend on normal, client-related activities. This diversion of attention may be resented when workers feel obliged to spend more time with clients rather than participating in an evaluation process that was mandated "from above," or "from outside the program."

— **Periodic or No Feedback to Staff:** The data obtained from a project-type approach to quality improvement, even if shared with the practitioners, is usually not directly or immediately relevant to them or to their current clients. This is particularly the case if an evaluation is designed to answer questions posed by administrators or funders, and workers' practice concerns cannot be addressed in the same evaluation project.

If, as sometimes happens, the project-type approach does yield useful information (via the data collected) for the staff, and changes are made on the basis of these data, the next evaluation may not take place for a long time, perhaps for years. If the evaluator is not on hand to analyze the benefits resulting from the changes, staff members may not be sure that there *were* any benefits.

— **Large Recommended Changes:** The changes recommended as a result of a project approach to quality improvement can be major. Administrators and evaluators may feel that with an evaluation occurring only once every few years, it is an event that ought to yield "significant" findings and recommendations to justify it. Large recommended changes can involve program renovations (e.g., overhaul the staff structure of a program) versus program refinements (e.g., add or revise a component of staff training).

— **Not Practical in Applied Settings:** All evaluations must be based on well-established evaluation principles and methods. Project evaluations, however, are more likely to be based on the scientific rigor necessary to obtain cause-and-effect knowledge. We will discuss basic types of evaluation designs in subsequent chapters. For now, it is enough to point out that evaluation designs used to obtain higher levels of quality improvement recommendations may require that clients be randomly assigned to experimental or control groups without regard to their individual rights—a technique that does not consider clients' special needs (see chapter 9). Similarly, evaluation designs to measure client change may require that measurement be carried out both before and after the treatment intervention, without regard to clinical time restraints or the client's emotional condition.

Usually, rigorous experiments for the purpose of increasing knowledge are carried out in laboratory-type settings and not in practice settings. However, the same rigorous conditions may be suggested if the purpose is, for example, to evaluate the effectiveness and efficiency of a therapy group. The worker might argue that more time will be spent in the administration of the measuring instruments than conducting therapeutic work; the evaluator can easily reply that results will be valid only if experimental conditions are observed. The issue here is: Whose interests are the evaluation intended to serve? Who is it *for*—the social work practitioner or the external evaluator?

In a project approach to quality improvement the answer is that it is sometimes for the evaluator, or for the administrative, academic, or funding body that has employed the evaluator. It should be stressed that this is not always the case. Many project approaches use unobtrusive evaluation techniques geared to actual practice situations. If, however, the evaluation is undertaken only once in a number of years, intrusion can be considered warranted in order to obtain reliable and valid results.

— Difficult to Incorporate in Practice Settings: A final characteristic of a project approach to quality improvement is that the methods used by the evaluator are difficult for staff to learn and almost impossible for them to incorporate into their normal day-to-day practices. In fact, staff are not expected to learn anything about evaluation procedures as a result of the program being evaluated. Nor is it expected that the evaluation methods employed will be used again before the next major periodic evaluation. The evaluator carries out the project approach and, essentially, until the next time, that is that.

The reader may have noticed that all the preceding characteristics we listed for the project approach to quality improvement are rather negative; without a doubt, the project approach is intrusive and traumatic, fails to meet the immediate needs of the workers, and may engender resentment and fear—especially if program workers have never been involved in a previous evaluation. We now turn to a second approach to quality improvement that complements the project approach and is the focus of this book—the monitoring approach.

The Monitoring Approach   Ongoing Prog

The monitoring approach to quality improvement is based on reliable and valid evaluation methods that can be integrated into a social service program as a part of its normal operating routine. This approach measures the extent that a social service program is reaching its intended population and the extent to which its services match those that were intended to be delivered. In addition, this approach is designed to provide immediate and continuous feedback on client service and progress to practitioners.

The monitoring approach is nothing more than the continual collection, analysis, reporting, and use of program data. This ongoing and dynamic approach to evaluation is planned and systematic. Ideally, such a system would be integrated with the program's records system so as to avoid duplication and enhance efficiency. For example, data on the changes the program aims to effect can be collected at intake, at specified times during treatment, at termination, and at follow-up. In this way, a constant stream of systematic data are collected, analyzed, and reported in an effort to help the program focus client-orientated interventions as they come into (intake), go through (treatment), and leave (termination) the program, and go on with their lives (follow-up).

Evaluations resulting from a monitoring approach to quality improvement tend to have the following characteristics:

— Internally Driven: Continuous routine use of evaluation methods may have been initially suggested by an administrator or an outside consultant or funder. However, the evaluation methods are put into place and used by practitioners for their own and their clients' benefit without the request (or demand) from any outside source. The evaluation may thus be said to be internally driven.

— Cooperative Staff: When evaluation is a process instead of an event, practitioners are more likely to collaborate in its efforts since it is an accepted part of the daily routine of delivering high-quality services.

— **Integrated**: By definition, an intrusion is something unrelated to the task at hand that interferes with that task. Evaluation methods that are routinely used to improve services to clients are part-and-parcel in workers' daily tasks. Necessary client-centered changes for solving problems are usually agreed upon by line-level practitioners and are usually accepted without difficulty because they result from informed decision making; that is, decisions are made based on data that are available to all program staff. A monitoring approach gives workers the opportunity to identify problems and suggest tentative solutions based on program data.

— **Ongoing Continuous Feedback**: There are some activities in a social service program that need to be monitored on a continuing basis. For example, client referrals are received daily and must be processed quickly. In order to estimate remaining program space, intake workers need a list of how many clients are presently being served, how many clients will be discharged shortly, and how many clients have recently been accepted into the program. This continually changing list is an example of a simple evaluative tool that provides useful data. The resulting information can be used to compare the actual number of clients in the program with the number the program was originally designed (and usually funded) to serve.

In other words, the list can be used to fulfill a basic evaluative purpose: comparison of what is with what should be, of the actual with the ideal. It might be found, in some programs, that the arithmetic of intake is not quite right. For example, suppose that a program has space for 100 clients. At the moment, 70 are being served on a regular basis. In theory, then, the program can accept 30 more clients. Suppose also that the program has five social workers; each will then theoretically carry a maximum caseload of 20.

In the caseloads of these five workers there ought to be just 30 spaces. But for some reason, there are more than 30. The supervisor, who is trying to assign new clients to workers, discovers that the workers can muster 40 spaces between them. In other words, there are 10 clients on the computer who are theoretically being served, but who are not in any of the five workers' caseloads. What has happened to these 10 clients?

Investigation brings to light the fact that worker records and computer records are kept in different ways. Computer records reflect the assumption that every client accepted will continue to be served until formally discharged. However, the practitioner who has not seen Ms. Smith for six months, and has failed to locate her after repeated tries, has placed Ms. Smith in the "inactive" file and accepted another client in her place. The result of this disparity in record keeping is that the program seems to have fewer available spaces, and clients who might be served are being turned away.

Simply discussing inactive files at a staff meeting might solve the problem. What steps will be taken to locate a client who does not appear for appointments? How long should attempts at contact continue before the client is formally discharged? Which other involved professionals need to be informed about the client's nonappearance and the discharge? When and how should they be informed? Is it worth modifying the intake computer's terminal display to include inactive files, with the dates they became inactive and the dates they were reactivated or discharged? Once decisions have been made on these points, a straightforward procedure can be put in place to deal with the ongoing problem of inactive files.

— Minor Recommended Changes: When change is an expected and ongoing process that results from regular monitoring, program adjustments or modifications tend to be small. Of course, continual monitoring can suggest that fundamental changes are needed in the way that the program is conceptualized or structured, but such large changes are rare. Most often, monitoring gives rise to continual minor refinements of programs.

— Easy to Incorporate in Practice Settings: The monitoring approach, like the project approach to quality improvement, is based on well-established evaluation methods. The difference between them can lie in whom the evaluation is intended to serve: the line-level worker or the evaluator. When the workers themselves, for their own and their clients' benefit, undertake evaluation, there is no doubt about for whom the evaluation is intended to serve.

Advantages of the Monitoring Approach

Social workers who are interested in improving the quality of the services they offer via evaluations are well on their way to taking responsibility for providing the best possible service to clients through systematic examinations of their strengths and weaknesses via the quality improvement process. Becoming a self-evaluating social work professional (or program) has definite advantages not only for clients, but also for workers. Some of these advantages are:

— Increased Understanding of Programs: A social service program is often a complex entity with a large number of interlinked components. Practitioners' main concerns usually have to do with the effectiveness of their treatment interventions. How can the confused sexual identity of an adolescent who has been sexually abused best be addressed? What teaching technique is most effective with children who have learning disabilities? Is an open-door policy appropriate for group homes housing adolescents who are mentally challenged? Answers come slowly through study, intuition, hunches, and past experience, but often the issues are so complex that practitioners cannot be sure if the answers obtained are correct.

Many social workers stumble onward, hoping their interventions are right, using intuition to assess the effectiveness of their particular interventions (or package of interventions) with a particular client. We will discuss case-level evaluations in future chapters and show how the use of simple evaluation designs can complement a worker's intuition so that an inspired guess more closely approaches knowledge. However, no amount of knowledge about how well an intervention worked will tell the worker *why* it worked or failed to work. *Why* do apparently similar clients, treated similarly, achieve different results? Is it something about the client? About the worker? About the type of intervention?

It is always difficult to pinpoint a reason for unsatisfactory achievement of program objectives because there are so many possible overlapping and intertwined causes. However, some reasons may be identified by a careful look at the program stages leading up to the interventions. For example, one reason for not attaining success with clients may be that they were inappropriate for the program and ought never have been admitted in the first place. Or, perhaps the program's assessment procedures were inadequate; perhaps unsuitable clients were accepted because the referral came from a major funding body. In other words, perhaps the lack of client success at the intervention stage derives from screening problems at intake.

Social workers who have been involved with a do-it-yourself evaluation may become familiar with the program's intake procedures, both in theory and in reality. They may also become familiar with the planning procedures, discharge procedures, follow-up procedures, staff recruitment and training procedures, recording procedures, and so on. The worker will begin to see a link between poor client outcomes at one program stage and inadequacies at another, between a success here and an innovation somewhere else. In sum, practitioners may be able to perform their own tasks more effectively if they understand how the program functions as a living organism. One way to gain this understanding is to participate in a hands-on, do-it-yourself evaluation.

— Relevant Feedback: A second advantage of the monitoring approach to evaluation is that the workers within the program can formulate meaningful and relevant questions. They can use evaluation procedures to find out what they want to know, not what the administrator, the funder, or a university professor wants to know. If the data to be gathered are perceived as relevant, staff are usually willing to cooperate in the evaluation. And if the information resulting from that data *is* relevant, it is likely to be used by the practitioners.

It is our belief that all evaluative efforts conducted in our profession provide feedback loops that improve the delivery of services. Feedback provides data about the extent to which a program's goal is achieved or approximated. Based on these data, services may be adjusted or changed to improve goal achievement.

— Timely Feedback: A third advantage is that the workers can decide when the evaluation is to be carried out. Evaluation procedures can be undertaken daily, weekly, monthly, or only once in five years, as will be discussed in the following chapters. The point here is that data are most useful when they help to solve a current problem, less useful when the problem has not yet occurred, and least useful after the event.

— Self-Protection: Most social service programs are evaluated eventually, often by outside evaluators. If staff have already familiarized themselves with evaluation procedures and with the program's strengths and weaknesses, they are in a better position to defend the program when an externally driven evaluation occurs. In addition, because improvements have already been made as a result of self-evaluations, the program will be more defensible. In addition, the staff will indirectly learn about evaluation designs and methodology by monitoring their practices on a regular basis. Modifications recommended by an outside evaluator are hence likely to be less far-reaching and less traumatic.

An additional consideration is that staff members themselves are likely to be less traumatized by the idea of being evaluated: Evaluation is no longer a new and frightening experience, but simply a part of the routine—a routine that tries to improve the quality of services for clients.

— Practitioner and Client Satisfaction: A monitoring approach to a case-level evaluation can satisfy the worker that an intervention is appropriate and successful, and it can improve a client's morale by demonstrating the progress that has been made toward his or her practice objective. Moreover, data gathered at the case level can always be used at the program level. Improvement of the program as a whole can follow from an improvement in one worker's practice.

— **Professionalism:** A monitoring approach to evaluation is consistent with the expectations of professional conduct in social work. Social workers who use systematic methods to evaluate their work benefit from evaluation results through informed decision making. Evaluation results can be used to support critical program changes or defend controversial program actions. They can confirm or challenge workers' long-held beliefs about a mode of operation. Additionally, evaluation can reveal program flaws and deficiencies that require corrective action.

PROGRAM LEARNING

Social service programs are dynamic organizations and must be responsive to outside pressures as well as internal struggles. They have to do this while providing efficient and effective client services. It is within the context of social service programs that workers and evaluators alike learn about client life experiences, witness client suffering, observe client progress and regress, and feel societal pressure to produce great change with little resources. Integrating evaluation into program services (and social work practice), therefore, presents an immense opportunity to learn more about social problems, the people they affect, and how interventions work.

In order for organizational learning to occur, however, there must be an opportunity for continuous feedback—that is, for stakeholders to make sense out of data collected. All levels of staff have an influence on a program's growth and development. Figure 1.1 depicts an evaluation process that encourages learning, growth, and development in social service programs.

The most fruitful place to begin in the evaluation cycle is at the top right of Figure 1.1—Documenting Program Operations and Expectations. Before we begin the process of evaluation, however, it is critical to know the current circumstances within the program, a topic discussed in detail in the following chapter.

As we have already mentioned, stakeholders are central to the evaluation process. Thus, they are shown in the center of the evaluation cycle depicted in Figure 1.1. While it is ideal to obtain input from as many stakeholder groups as possible as we cycle through the evaluation process, sometimes we must settle for contributions from only of those who are interested and available to participate at a given point in time. Nevertheless, we must keep in mind that

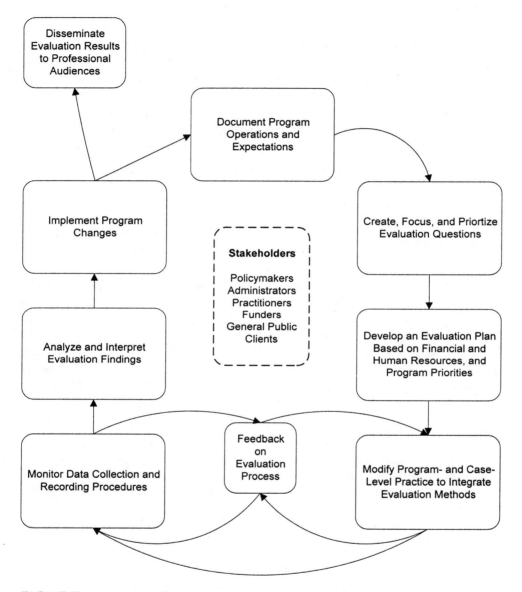

FIGURE 1.1   The Generic Evaluation Process

stakeholders provide a valuable resource for reactions to program development as the program goes through the entire evaluation cycle.

After program operations and expectations have been agreed upon and documented, an evaluation needs to create, focus, and prioritize specific evaluation questions. This phase of the cycle involves brainstorming these questions and selecting those that are of greatest concern. Do stakeholders want to know, for example, the profile of clients being served by the program? Do practitioners want to assess the efficiency of their referral system? Are funders wondering if clients are satisfied with the services they received? While an endless list of potential evaluative questions is possible, an evaluation can adequately address only a few them at best, given the fiscal and human constraints.

Eventually, a decision is made as to which questions the evaluation will focus upon. An evaluation plan is then created and modifications to case- and program-level practices are made, and data collection begins. Note that Figure 1.1 shows two smaller feedback loops in the evaluation cycle. These loops serve to gather data on how the evaluation process is proceeding. Are modifications to case-level practice working for practitioners? What obstacles do practitioners encounter in the data collection and recording procedures, if any? Staying tuned to the evaluation process increases the likelihood that errors and problems will be detected early on.

After data collection has occurred, an evaluation cycles through to analyzing data, forming recommendations, and ultimately implementing change. Figure 1.1 shows that program changes cycle back to the beginning—Documenting Program Operations and Expectations. Additionally, evaluation findings can be helpful to external audiences so that the program is actively involved in contributing to the knowledge base of our profession.

SUMMING UP AND LOOKING AHEAD

This chapter introduced the concept of quality improvement and explained how evaluation provides tools for the quality improvement process effort. We then presented a brief introduction to why our profession needs evaluations and discussed the various program characteristics that must be taken into account before doing an evaluation. Two approaches to quality improvement were introduced and a generic model for program evaluation was presented.

Now that we know how program evaluations can be useful for our profession, we need to understand what a social service program actually is—the topic of the following chapter.

KEY TERMS

Accountability: A system of responsibility in which program administrators account for all program activities by answering to the demands of a program's stakeholders and by justifying the program's expenditures to the satisfaction of its stakeholders.

Case-Level Evaluation: A form of appraisal that monitors change for individual clients.

Client Data: In evaluation, measurements systematically collected from clients of social service programs; ideally, data are collected in strict compliance with the evaluation design and procedures.

Client System: *An* individual client, a couple, *a* family, a group, *an* organization, or a community that can be studied with case- and program-level evaluation designs and with quantitative and qualitative research approaches.

Data: Isolated facts, presented in numerical or descriptive form, on which client or program decisions are based; not to be confused with information.

Data Sources: People or records that are the suppliers of data.

Evaluation: A form of appraisal using valid and reliable research methods. There are numerous types of evaluations geared to produce data which in turn produce information that helps in the decision-making process. Data from evaluations are used in the quality improvement process.

External Evaluation: An evaluation that is conducted by someone who does not have any connection with the program; usually requested by the agency's funding sources. This type of evaluation complements an internal evaluation.

Information: The interpretation given to data that have been collected, collated, and analyzed; information is used to help in the decision-making process; not to be confused with data.

Internal Evaluation: An evaluation that is conducted by someone who works within a program; usually an evaluation for the purpose of promoting better client services. This type of evaluation complements an external evaluation.

Monitoring Approach to Quality Improvement: An evaluation that aims to provide ongoing feedback so that a program (or project) can be improved while it is still underway; contributes to the continuous development and improvement of a human service program. This approach complements the project approach.

Monitoring System: The evaluation design, protocols, and procedures that ensure systematic, complete, and accurate data collection; also includes a schedule for reporting and disseminating findings.

Program: An organization that exists to fulfil some social purpose; must be logically linked to the agency's goal.

Program Data: In evaluation, measurements systematically collected about a program's operations. Ideally, the data are collected in strict compliance with the evaluation design and procedures.

Program Evaluation: A form of appraisal, using valid and reliable research methods, that examines the processes or outcomes of an organization that exists to fulfill some social purpose.

Program-Level Evaluation: A form of appraisal that monitors change for groups of clients and organizational performance.

Program Monitoring: A program activity comprised of the ongoing collection, analysis, reporting, and use of collected program data.

Project Approach to Quality Improvement: Evaluations whose purpose is to assess a completed or finished program (or project); complements the monitoring approach.

Quality Improvement Process: An ethical commitment to continually look for and seek ways to make services more responsive, efficient, and effective; a process that uses the data from all types of evaluations to improve the quality of human services.

Stakeholder: A person or group of people having a direct or indirect interest in the results of an evaluation.

STUDY QUESTIONS

1. In your own words, discuss why quality improvement is important to the social services.

2. What two general types of evaluations can be used in the quality improvement process? Provide an example of how each one is used when your social work program evaluates its efforts, via the Council on Social Work Education's mandate.

3. List and discuss the four reasons why social workers need to do evaluations. How do they interact with one another?

4. What are stakeholders? List and discuss the eight different types of stakeholders that any evaluation must pay attention to. List the various stakeholders for your social work program. Provide a rationale for why you listed each one. Who is the client stakeholder of your social work program? Why?

5. List and discuss the five forms of accountability. Provide a social work example of each one.

6. Are you fearful of evaluation? Why, or why not? Are you less or more fearful of evaluation since you read Chapter 1? If you are still fearful after reading Chapter 1 you need to read it again.

7. List and discuss the six program characteristics that must be taken into account when doing an evaluation. Provide an example of each one.

8. List and discuss in detail the two general approaches to quality improvement.

9. List and discuss the seven characteristics of the project approach to quality improvement. Provide an example of each one.

10. List and discuss the six characteristics of the monitoring approach to quality improvement. Provide an example of each one.

11. List and discuss the six advantages of the monitoring approach to quality improvement. Provide an example of each one.

12. In your own words discuss the relationship between evaluation and program learning.

13. Discuss how a social service program can do a project approach and a monitoring approach to evaluation at the same time.

14. Take a look at Box 1.3. Do you agree with NASW's principles? Why, or why not? Discuss how you believe this course will prepare you to abide by NASW's *Code of Ethics* when it comes to research and evaluation.

15. What are data? What is information? From your own experiences, provide an example of how information was derived from data.

REFERENCES AND FURTHER READINGS

Beck, R.A., & Rossi, P.H. (1990). *Thinking about program evaluation.* Thousand Oaks, CA: Sage.

Bisno, H., & Borowski, A. (1985). The social and psychological contexts of research. In R.M. Grinnell, Jr. (Ed.), *Social work research and evaluation* (2nd ed., pp. 83–100). Itasca, IL: F.E. Peacock Publishers.

Chambers, D.E., Wedel, K.R., & Rodwell, M.K. (1992). *Evaluating social programs.* Boston: Allyn & Bacon.

Council on Social Work Education. (2000). Baccalaureate and masters curriculum policy statements. Alexandria, VA: Author.

Gabor, P.A., & Grinnell, R.M., Jr. (1994). *Evaluation and quality improvement in the human services.* Boston: Allyn & Bacon.

Gabor, P.A., Unrau, Y.A., & Grinnell, R.M., Jr. (1997). *Evaluation and quality improvement in the human services* (2nd ed.). Boston: Allyn & Bacon.

Gabor, P.A., Unrau, YA., & Grinnell, R.M., Jr. (2001). Program-level evaluation. In R.M. Grinnell, Jr. (Ed.), *Social work research and evaluation: Quantitative and qualitative approaches* (6th ed., pp. 481–509). Itasca, IL: F.E. Peacock Publishers.

Grinnell, R.M., Jr. (2001). Introduction to research. In R.M. Grinnell, Jr. (Ed.), *Social work research and evaluation: Quantitative and qualitative approaches* (6th ed., pp. 1–19). Itasca, IL: F.E. Peacock Publishers.

Grinnell, R.M., Jr., & Siegel, D.H. (1988). The place of research in social work. In R.M. Grinnell, Jr. (Ed.), *Social work research and evaluation* (3rd ed., pp. 9–24). Itasca, IL: F.E. Peacock Publishers.

Hornick, J.P., & Burrows, B. (1988). Program evaluation. In R.M. Grinnell, Jr. (Ed.), *Social work research and evaluation* (3rd ed., pp. 400–420). Itasca, IL: F.E. Peacock Publishers.

National Association of Social Workers. (1999). *Code of ethics.* Washington, DC: Author.

Patton, M.Q. (1983). *Practical evaluation.* Thousand Oaks, CA: Sage.

Patton, M.Q. (1987). *Creative evaluation* (2nd ed.). Thousand Oaks, CA: Sage.

Patton, M.Q. (1990). *Qualitative evaluation and research methods* (2nd ed.). Thousand Oaks, CA: Sage.

Patton, M.Q. (1997). *Utilization-focused evaluation: The new century text* (3rd ed.). Thousand Oaks, CA: Sage.

Raymond, F.B. (1985). Program evaluation. In R.M. Grinnell, Jr. (Ed.), *Social work research and evaluation* (2nd ed., pp. 432–442). Itasca, IL: F.E. Peacock Publishers.

Royce, D., Thyer, B.A., Padgett, D.K., & Logan, T.K. (2001). *Program evaluation: An introduction* (3rd ed.). Belmont, CA: Brooks/Cole.

Rubin, A., & Babbie, E. (1997). Program-level evaluation. In R.M. Grinnell, Jr. (Ed.), *Social work research and evaluation: Quantitative and qualitative approaches* (5th ed., pp. 560–587). Itasca, IL: F.E. Peacock Publishers.

Schuerman, J.R. (1983). *Research and evaluation in the human services.* New York: Free Press.

Tripodi, T. (1983). *Evaluative research for social workers.* Englewood Cliffs, NJ: Prentice-Hall.

Tripodi, T., Fellin, P.A., & Meyer, H.J. (1983). *The assessment of social research: Guidelines for the use of research in social work and social service* (2nd ed.). Itasca, IL: F.E. Peacock Publishers.

Unrau, Y.A., & Gabor, P.A. (2001). Evaluation in action. In R.M. Grinnell, Jr. (Ed.), *Social work research and evaluation: Quantitative and qualitative approaches* (6th ed., pp. 510–526). Itasca, IL: F.E. Peacock Publishers.

Weinbach, R.W. (2001). Research contexts. In R.M. Grinnell, Jr. (Ed.), *Social work research and evaluation* (6th ed., pp. 41–54). Itasca, IL: F.E. Peacock Publishers.

2

Chapter Outline

What Is a Program?

T HE PREVIOUS CHAPTER PRESENTED how program evaluations are an essential part in the delivery of social services. However, we have not defined what a program is. It is difficult to do any kind of program evaluation without having a clear understanding of how programs are organized as they go about their day-to-day business—the topic of this chapter. When doing a program evaluation we must understand the context within which the program exists and the logic of how it is designed. We will start at the birthplace of all social service programs—social service agencies.

SOCIAL SERVICE AGENCIES

A *social service agency* is an organization that exists to fulfill a legitimate social purpose, such as:

— To protect children from physical, sexual, and emotional harm
— To enhance quality of life for developmentally delayed adolescents
— To improve nutritional health for housebound senior citizens

Agencies can be public—funded entirely by the state and/or federal government—or private—funded by private funds, deriving some monies from governmental sources and some from client fees, charitable bodies, private donations, fund-raising activities, and so forth. Regardless of funding source, agencies are defined by their: (1) mission statements, (2) goals, and (3) objectives.

Agency Mission Statements

All agencies have mission statements that provide unique written philosophical perspectives of what they are all about and make explicit the reasons for their existence. Mission statements sometimes are called *philosophical statements* or, simply, a *program's philosophy*. Whatever it is called, a mission statement articulates a common vision for the organization in that it provides a point of reference for all major planning decisions. Mission statements are like lighthouses in that they exist to provide direction. A mission statement not only provides clarity of purpose to persons within the agency, but it also helps them to gain understanding and support from those stakeholders outside the agency who are influential to the agency's success (see Chapter 1).

Mission statements are usually given formal approval and sanction by legislators for public agencies, and by executive boards for private ones. They can range from one sentence to ten pages or more and are as varied as the agencies they represent. Brief examples of agency mission statements are as follows:

— This agency strives to provide a variety of support services to families and children in need, while in the process of maintaining their rights, their safety, and their human dignity.

— The mission of this agency is to promote and protect the mental health of the elderly people residing in this state by offering quality and timely programs that will deliver these services.

— The philosophy of this agency states that clients are partners in their treatment, and all services should be short-term, intensive, and focus on problems in day-to-day existence.

— The philosophy of this agency is to protect and promote the physical and social well-being of this city by ensuring the development and delivery of services that encourage and support individual, family, and community independence, self-reliance, and civic responsibility to the greatest degree possible.

In short, an agency mission statement lays the overall global conceptual foundation for programs housed within it since each program (soon to be discussed) must be logically connected to the overarching intent of the agency as declared by its mission statement. Creating mission statements is a process of bringing interested stakeholders together to agree upon the overall direction and tone of the agency. The process of creating mission statements is affected by available words in a language, as well as the meaning given to those words by individual stakeholders. While mission statements are essential to the development of an agency's goal, we must exercise caution so as not to spend too much time wordsmithing at the expense of developing other parts of the agency's model.

Agency Goals

As should be evident by now, social service agencies are established in efforts to reduce gaps between the current and the desired state of affairs for a specific target population. While mission statements can be lengthy and include several philosophical declarations, agency goals are concise, and there is only one per agency. An agency goal is always defined at a conceptual level, and is not measured. Its main ambition is to guide us toward effective and accountable service delivery in two ways:

— First, directed by the agency's mission statement, the agency's goal acts as a single focal point to guide the entire range of the agency's activities in a specific direction.
— Second, an agency's goal functions as an umbrella under which all of its programs, program goals, program objectives, practice objectives, practice activities, and maintenance objectives within the agency are logically derived (to be discussed shortly).

Requirements for Goals

It is essential that an agency's goal reflects the agency's mandate and be guided by its mission statement. This is achieved by forming a goal with the following four components:

— The nature of the current social problem to be tackled
— The client population to be served
— The general direction of anticipated client change (desired state)
— The means by which the change is supposed to be brought about

Agency goals can be broad or narrow. Let us look at two generic examples:

Agency Goal—National: The goal of this agency is to enhance the quality of life of this nation's families who are dependent on public funds for day-to-day living (*current social problem to be tackled and client population to be served*). The agency supports reducing long-term dependence on public funds (*general direction of anticipated client change*) by funding innovative programs that increase self-sufficiency and employability of welfare dependent citizens (*means by which the change is supposed to be brought about*).

Agency Goal—Local: The goal of this agency is to help youth from low socioeconomic households in this city (*client population to be served*) who are dropping out of school (*current social problem to be tackled*) to stay in school (*general direction of anticipated client change*) by providing mentorship and tutoring programs in local neighborhoods (*means by which the change is supposed to be brought about*).

In general, an agency goal reflects the scope of the agency. National agencies are clearly broader in boundary and size than local ones, for example. Additionally, more complex agencies such as those serving multiple populations or addressing multiple social problems will capture a more expansive population or problem area in their goal statements. An agency's goal statements must be broad enough to encompass all of its programs. That is, each program within an agency must have a direct and logical connection to the agency that governs it. However small or large, an agency always functions as one entity, and the agency goal statement serves to unify all of its programs.

Agency Objectives

There is only one purpose of an agency's objective—to establish specific social service programs that directly link to the agency's overall goal. In short, no

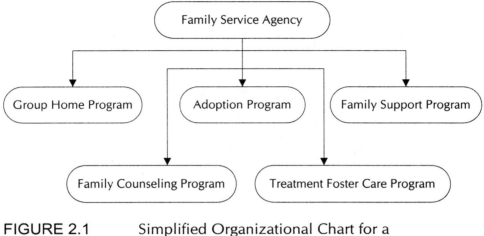

FIGURE 2.1   Simplified Organizational Chart for a
                    Family Service Agency

agency should have a program housed within it in which the services the program delivers cannot be directly connected to the agency's goal.

In the preceding local agency goal example, the agency defines itself as providing programs that help city youth stay in school. As such, the agency would not have nutritional programs for the elderly, marriage counseling programs, or any other programs that would not work toward the agency's overall goal, or its intended result, of keeping socioeconomically disadvantaged youth in the city in school.

SOCIAL SERVICE PROGRAMS

Whatever the current social problem, the desired future state, or the population it wishes to service, an agency sets up programs to help work toward its intended result—the agency goal. There are as many ways to organize social service programs as there are people willing to be involved in the task.

Mapping out the relationship among programs is a process that is often obscured by the fact that the term *program* can be used to refer to different levels of service delivery within an agency (see Figures 2.1, 2.2 and 2.3 for examples). In other words, some programs can be seen as subcomponents of larger ones, such as "Public Awareness Services," which falls under the Nonresidential Program for the Women's Emergency Shelter as depicted in Figure 2.3.

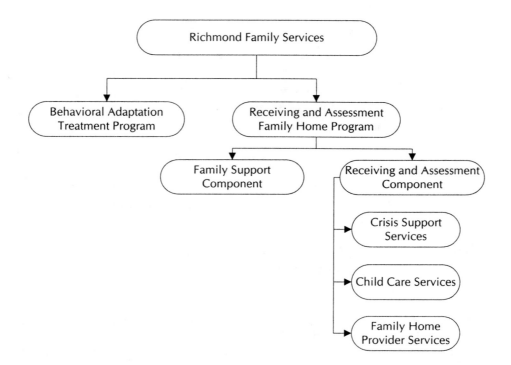

FIGURE 2.2   Organizational Chart of a Family Service
                      Agency (Highlighting the Receiving and
                      Assessment Component)

Figure 2.1 presents a simple structure of a family service agency serving families and children. Each program included in the Family Service Agency is expected to have some connection to serving families. Both the Family Support Program and the Family Counseling Programs have obvious connections, given their titles. The Group Home Program, however, does not, since its title reveals nothing about who resides in the group home or for what purpose. Since the Group Home Program operates under the auspices of "family services," it is likely that it temporarily houses children and youth who eventually will return to their families. Most importantly, the agency does not offer programs that are geared toward other target groups such as the elderly, or the homeless.

By looking at Figure 2.1, it can be easily seen that this particular family service agency has five programs within it that deal with the agency's target population—family and children: a group home program for children, a family counseling program, a child adoption program, a treatment foster care program, and a family support program.

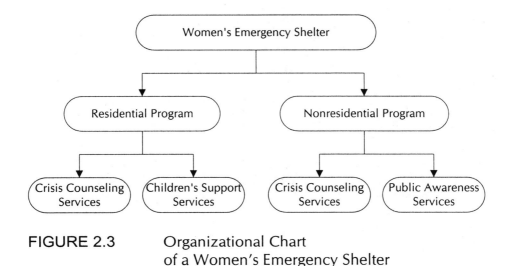

FIGURE 2.3   Organizational Chart
of a Women's Emergency Shelter

Figure 2.2 provides another example of an agency that also deals with families and children. This agency (Richmond Family Services) has only two programs, a Behavioral Adaptation Treatment Program, and a Receiving and Assessment Family Home Program. The latter is further broken down into two components—a Family Support Component, and a Receiving and Assessment Component. In addition, the Receiving and Assessment Component is further broken down into Crisis Support Services, Child Care Services, and Family Home Provider Services.

How many programs are there in Figure 2.2? The answer is two—however, we need to note that this agency conceptualized its service delivery much more thoroughly than did the agency outlined in Figure 2.1. Richmond Family Services has conceptualized the Receiving and Assessment Component of its Receiving and Assessment Family Home Program into three separate sub-components: Crisis Support Services, Child Care Services, and Family Home Provider Services. In short, Figure 2.2 is more detailed in how it delivers its services than is the agency represented in Figure 2.1. Programs that are more clearly defined are generally easier to implement, operate, and evaluate.

Another example of how programs can be organized under an agency is presented in Figure 2.3. This agency, a women's emergency shelter, has a Residential Program and a Nonresidential Program. Its Residential Program has Crisis Counseling Services and Children's Support Services, whereas the nonresidential program has Crisis Counseling Services and Public Awareness Services. This agency distinguishes the services it provides between the women who stay within the shelter (its Residential Program) and those who come and

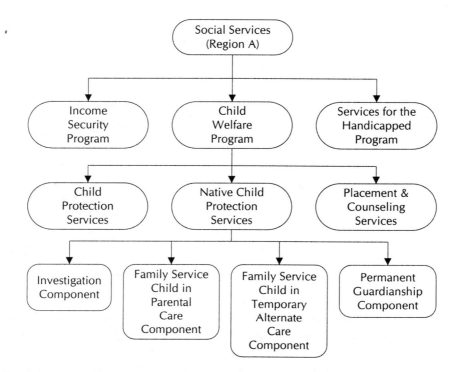

FIGURE 2.4   Organizational Chart of a State's Social
                    Service Delivery System (Highlighting
                    the Native Child Protection Services)

go (its Nonresidential Program). The agency could have conceptualized the services it offers in a number of different ways.

A final example of how an agency can map out its services is presented in Figure 2.4. As can be seen, the agency's Child Welfare Program is broken down into three services, whereas the Native Child Protection Services is further subdivided into four components: an Investigation Component, a Family Service Component, a Child in Parental Care Component, a Family Service Child in Temporary Alternate Care Component, and a Permanent Guardianship Component.

The general rule of ensuring that programs within an agency are logically linked together may seem simple enough that you might be wondering why we are emphasizing this point. The reality is that many social service programs are added to agencies on a piecemeal basis. That is, new programs are often born out of funding opportunities that come available for new, but unrelated, programs (to the agency's goal that is). With the opportunity to seize new funds sometimes comes funding restrictions that result in creating new programs that fit poorly with established services. While social service administrators must constantly seek new resources to provide better or additional services within their agency's programs, it is important that new programs do not compromise existing ones.

By simply glancing at Figures 2.1 to 2.4, it can be seen that how an agency labels its programs and subprograms is arbitrary. For example, the agency that represents Figure 2.2 labels its subprograms as components and its sub-subprograms as services. The agency that represents Figure 2.3 simply labels its subprograms as services—not as components, as was done in Figure 2.2. The main point is that an agency must structure and conceptualize its programs, components, and services in a logical way that makes the most sense to the agency's overall goal, which is guided by its mission statement and mandate.

While there is no standard approach to naming programs in the social services, there are themes that may assist with organizing an agency's programs. We present four themes and offer, as a general rule, that an agency picks only one (or one combination) to systematically map out its programs.

— **Function** (e.g., Adoption Program, Family Support Program)
— **Setting** (e.g., Group Home Program, Residential Program)
— **Target population** (e.g., Services for the Handicapped Program)
— **Social problem** (e.g., Child Sexual Abuse Program; Behavioral Adaptation Treatment Program)

Program names can include acronyms such as P.E.T. (Parent Effectiveness Training), or catchy titles such as Incredible Edibles (a nutritional program for children). Whatever the title, it is best that it reflects the primary purpose of a program. Including the target social problem (or the main client need) in the program's name simplifies communication of a program's purpose. In this way, a program's name is linked to its goal and there is less confusion about what services it offers.

Nondescript program names can lead to confusion in understanding a program's purpose. The Group Home Program in Figure 2.1, for example, suggests that this program aims to provide a residence for clients. In fact, all clients residing in the group home do so to fulfill a specific purpose. Depending on the goal of the program, the primary purpose could be to offer shelter and safety for teenage runaways. Or, the program aim might be the enhanced functioning of adolescents with developmental disabilities.

An Agency Versus a Program

What is the difference between an agency and a program? Like an agency, a program is an organization that also exists to fulfill a social purpose. There is one main difference, however; a program has a narrower, better-defined purpose and is always nested within an agency.

Sometimes an agency may itself have a narrow, well-defined purpose. The sole purpose of a counseling agency, for example, may be to serve couples who are sexually dysfunctional. In this case, the agency comprises only one program, and the terms *agency* and *program* refer to the same thing. If the clientele happens to include a high proportion of couples who are infertile, for example, it may later be decided that some staff members should specialize in infertility counseling (with a physician as a cocounselor) while other workers continue to deal with all other aspects of sexual dysfunction. In this case, there would then be two distinct sets of social work staff, each one focusing on different goals, and two separate types of clients; that is, there would be two *programs* (one geared toward infertility counseling and the other toward sexual dysfunction). Nevertheless, the *agency*, with its board, its senior administrator (executive director), and its administrative policies and procedures, would remain.

PROGRAM LOGIC MODELS

Programs are born via program logic models. Building or creating program logic models involves general and specific thinking about a program. The process begins by articulating a program's general intentions for solving identified problems—the conceptualization or idea of the program's purpose. It also involves setting specific plans for how the program is to accomplish what it sets out to do. A program for sexually aggressive children, for example, may aim to reduce the deviant sexual behavior of its young clients (i.e., the intention) by providing individual counseling (i.e., plan for achieving the intention). A major purpose of program logic models is to easily communicate a model of service delivery to interested stakeholders. They provide a blueprint for implementing a program's services, monitoring its activities, and evaluating both its operations and achievements.

Program logic models present plausible and logical plans for how programs aim to produce change for their clients. Therefore, implicit in every program model is the idea of theory—an explanation for how client change is brought

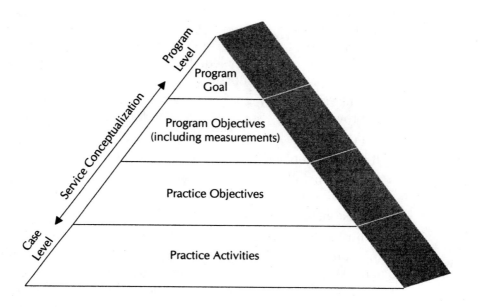

FIGURE 2.5   Program Logic Model Components for
                    Conceptualizing Treatment Services

about. The program for sexually aggressive children as described above suggests that such children will reduce sexual perpetration by gaining an understanding or insight through sessions with an individual counselor. Programs that articulate a theoretical approach such as psychoanalytic or behavior counseling make their program theory more explicit. Programs serving the same population offer an alternative theory of change when different interventions are used.

A program logic model has three major components that are used to clearly describe and organize thinking about program service delivery: (1) program goal, (2) program objectives, and (3) program activities. A graphic example of how these components relate to one another is presented in Figure 2.5.

PROGRAM GOALS

A program goal has much in common with an agency goal, discussed previously.

— First, like an agency goal, a program goal must also be compatible with the agency's mission statement. Goals must logically flow from the mission statement as they are announcements of expected outcomes dealing with the social problem that the program is attempting to prevent, eradicate, or ameliorate.

— Second, like an agency goal, a program goal is not measurable—it simply provides a programmatic direction for the program to follow.

— Third, a program goal must also possess four characteristics:

✓ It must identify a current social problem area.

✓ It must include a specific target population within which the problem resides.

✓ It must include the desired future state for this population.

✓ It must state how it plans to achieve the desired state.

— Fourth, a program goal reflects the hopes of social workers within the program. Workers in a program may expect that they will "enable adolescents with developmental disabilities to lead full and productive lives." The program goal phrase of "full and productive lives," however, can mean different things to different people. For example, some may believe that a full and productive life cannot be lived without integration into the community. They may, therefore, want to work toward placing these children in the mainstream school system, enrolling them in community activities, and finally returning them to their parental homes, with a view to making them self-sufficient in adult life. Others may believe that a full and productive life for these children means the security of institutional teaching and care and the companionship of similar children. Still others may believe that institutional care with limited outside contact is the best compromise.

Agency goal statements are meant to be sufficiently elusive that they can change with societal expectations over time. Another reason that goals have intangible qualities is that we want enough flexibility in our social service programs to adjust program conceptualization and operation as needed. Remember that, by establishing a program logic model, we are crafting a theory of client change. By evaluating the program, we test the program's theory—its plan for creating client change.

Unintended Program Results

Working toward a program's goal may result in a number of unintended results. For example, a group home for adolescents with developmental disabilities may strive to enable residents to achieve self-sufficiency in a safe and supportive environment. This is the intended result, or goal. Incidentally, however, the group home may produce organized resistance from neighbors—a negative unintended result. This resistance may draw the attention of the media and allow the difficulties in finding a suitable location for such homes to be highlighted in a sympathetic manner: a positive unintended result.

Meanwhile, the attitude of the community may affect residents to such an extent that they do not feel safe or supported and do not achieve self-sufficiency; that is, the program may not have achieved its intended result, or goal.

Program Goals Versus Agency Goals

Perhaps the group home mentioned above is run by an agency that has a number of other homes for adolescents with developmental disabilities. It is unlikely that all the children in these homes will be capable of self-sufficiency as adults; some may have reached their full potential when they have learned to feed or bathe themselves. The goal of self-sufficiency will, therefore, not be appropriate for the agency as a whole, although it might do very well for Group Home X, which serves children who function at higher levels. The agency's goal must be broader—to encompass a wider range of situations—and because it is broader, it will probably be more vague.

To begin, the agency may decide that its goal is "to enable adolescents with developmental disabilities to reach their full potential" as outlined in Figure 2.6:

— Group Home X, one of the programs within the agency, can then interpret "full potential" to mean self-sufficiency and can formulate a program goal based on this interpretation.

— Group Home Y, another program within the agency serving children who function at lower levels, may decide that it can realistically do no more than provide a caring environment for the children and emotional support for the family. It may translate this decision into another program goal: "To enable adolescents with developmental disabilities to experience security and happiness."

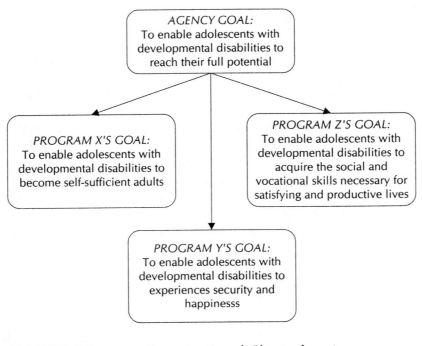

FIGURE 2.6   Organizational Chart of an Agency
with Three Programs

— Group Home Z, a third program within the agency, may set as its
program goal "To enable adolescents with developmental disabilities to
acquire the social and vocational skills necessary for satisfying and
productive lives."

Figure 2.6 illustrates the relationship among the goals of the three group
homes to the goal of the agency. Note how logical and consistent the goals of
the programs are with the agency's overall goal. This example illustrates three
key points about the character of a program goal:

— First, a program goal simplifies the reason for the program to exist and
provides direction for its workers.
— Second, program goals of different but related programs within the same
agency may differ, but they must all be linked to the agency's overall
goal. They must all reflect both their individual purpose and the purpose
of the agency of which they are a part.

— Third, program goals are not *measurable*. Consider the individual goals of the three group homes in Figure 2.6; none of them is measurable in its present form.

Concepts such as happiness, security, self-sufficiency, and full potential mean different things to different people and cannot be measured until they have been clearly defined. Many social work goals are phrased in this way, putting forth more of an elusive intent than a definite, definable, measurable purpose. Nor is this a flaw; it is simply what a goal *is*: a statement of an intended result that must be clarified before it can be measured. As we will see next, program goals are clarified by the objectives they formulate.

TYPES OF PROGRAM OBJECTIVES

A program's objectives are derived from its goal. Program objectives are nothing more than measurable indicators of the goal; they articulate the specific outcomes that the program wishes to achieve; stated clearly and exactly, they make it possible to tell to what degree the program's results have been achieved. All program objectives must be client-centered— they must be formulated to help a client in relation to the social problem articulated by the program goal. Social service programs often are designed to change either clients': (1) knowledge, (2) affects, or (3) behaviors.

Knowledge-Based

Knowledge-based program objectives are commonly found within educational programs, where the aim is to increase the client's knowledge in some specific area. The words "to increase knowledge" are key here: They imply that the recipient of the education will have learned something. For example, "to increase teenage mother's knowledge about the stages of child development between birth and two years." The hoped-for increase in knowledge can then be measured by testing her knowledge levels before and after the program. The program objective is achieved when it can be demonstrated (via measurement) that learning has occurred.

Affective-Based

Affective-based program objectives focus on changing either feelings about oneself or feelings about another person or thing. For example, a common affective-based program objective in social work is to raise a client's self-esteem, and attempts are often made to decrease feelings of isolation, increase marital or sexual satisfaction, and decrease depression. As well, feelings toward other people or things are important in a variety of situations. To give just a few examples, many educational programs try to change public attitudes toward minority groups, homosexuality, or gender roles.

"Affects" here includes attitudes, because attitudes are rarely based on knowledge but more often spring from learned feelings about types of people or things. "Affects" also encompasses belief systems because a belief, by definition, is not knowledge, but is rather a conviction or feeling that something is true. For example, the mother of a child who has been sexually abused might believe that the child is lying and the abuse did not actually occur.

Behaviorally Based

Very often, a program objective is established to change the behavior of a person or group: to reduce drug abuse among adolescents, to increase the use of community resources by seniors, or to reduce the number of fights a married couple has in a month. Sometimes, knowledge or affective objectives are used as a means to this end. The social worker might assume that adolescents who know more about the effects of drugs will use or abuse them less; that seniors who know more about available community resources will use them more often; or that married couples who have more positive feelings toward each other will fight less frequently. Sometimes these assumptions are valid; sometimes they are not. In any case, a responsible worker will verify that the desired behavior change has actually occurred.

QUALITIES OF PROGRAM OBJECTIVES

Whether program objectives target knowledge, affect, or behavior, they ought to possess four qualities. They must be: (1) meaningful, (2) specific, (3) measurable, and (4) directional.

Meaningful

A program objective is *meaningful* when it bears a sensible relationship to the longer-term result to be achieved—the program goal. If a program's goal is to promote self-sufficiency of teenage street people, for example, improving their ability to balance a monthly budget is a meaningful program objective; increasing their ability to recite the dates of the reigns of English monarchs is not, because it bears no relation to the program's goal of self-sufficiency. The point here—and a point that will be stressed over and over in this text—is that an effective social service organization must demonstrate meaningful *linkages* among an agency's overall goal (the reason for being) and its objective (the programs it creates), its programs' goals, and its programs' objectives.

As mentioned before, the overall goal of an agency must be linked to the needs of the people it intends to serve. If these meaningful linkages do not exist—and, furthermore, cannot be *seen* to exist—then the program has failed to establish its program logic model and cannot be evaluated.

Ideally, program objectives are derived from an existing knowledge base—existing research studies, prior evaluations, or theoretical models. Below are three meaningful program objectives that were derived from the goal of a family preservation program.

— Program Goal: To preserve family units where children are at-risk for out-of-home placements due to problems with physical abuse. The program aims to strengthen interpersonal functioning of family members through intensive home-based services.

    ✓Program Objective 1: To increase parents' repertoire of noncorporal child discipline strategies (Knowledge).

    ✓Program Objective 2: To increase parents' positive feelings toward their children (Affective).

    ✓Program Objective 3:To increase problem-solving skills for family members (Behavioral).

In the above example, it should be noted that the program objectives are logically linked, in a meaningful way, to the program's goal. We have left out the time frames in which each objective is to be achieved in an effort not to confuse the reader with too much detail at this time. In addition, all program objectives should be formulated, or derived, from the existing literature.

Or to put it another way, the existing literature should provide enough information to support the creation of a program's objectives. It has been our past experience, however, that many social service organizations have program objectives that are not theoretically linked to their program goals via the literature. In addition, it is also unfortunate that many agencies have programs that are not linked to their overall goal, thus decreasing their creditability. If evaluation of social service programs is to contribute to our profession's knowledge base, then it makes sense that program logic models are founded on what is known about the target population and problem.

Specific

In addition to being meaningful and logically linked to the program's goal, program objectives must also be *specific*. They must be complete and clear in their wording. A simple way to write a specific program objective is to use the following model:

Model:
To (verb) (specific program objective) (time frame).

Example:
To increase (verb) marital satisfaction of the couple (specific program objective) after six sessions (time frame).

Three useful verbs for writing client-centered program objectives are: to increase, to decrease, and to maintain. It must be noted that all three examples of program objectives that were used above began with the words *to increase*. These objectives would ideally have specific time frames contained within them, although many times the time frame is implied by the program scope (e.g., duration of the program).

Measurable

The third quality required of a program objective is *measurability*. The purpose of measurement is to gather data. A measure is usually thought of as a number: an amount of money in dollars, the length of a depression episode, or scores on simple self-administered standardized measuring instruments.

The purpose of setting a program objective is to effect change, which, if obtained, will contribute to the obtainment of the program's goal. One of the main purposes of making a measurement is to define a perceived change, in terms of either numbers or clear words. A measurement might show, for example, that the assertiveness of a woman who has been previously abused has increased by five points on a standardized measuring instrument (a program objective), or that a woman's sexual satisfaction has increased by 45 points (another program objective). If the hoped-for change cannot be measured there is really no point in setting it as a program objective. In the following chapters we will present ways of measuring program objectives, but, for the time being, we will turn to the fourth important quality of an objective—directionality.

Directional

The final requirement for a program objective is that it must have a *direction*. All social work interventions are intended to effect some kind of change. That is, interventions are undertaken so that clients will come to have more or less of something than they had before: The level of parenting skills, aggression, racist beliefs, or whatever is to be changed, will have gone up or down. The very idea of change involves direction: Without movement in the direction of less or more, better or worse, higher or lower, no change can occur.

PROGRAM AND PRACTICE OBJECTIVES

Practice objectives are not program objectives. Practice objectives refer to the personal objectives of an individual client, whether that client is a community, couple, group, individual, or institution. Practice objectives are also commonly referred to as *treatment objectives, individual objectives, therapeutic objectives, client objectives, client goals,* and *client target problems*.

All practice objectives formulated by the social worker and the client must be logically related to the program's objectives, which are linked to the program's goal. In other words, all practice objectives for all clients must be delineated in such a way that they are logically linked to one or more of the program's objectives. If not, then it is likely that the client's needs will not be met by the program.

If a social worker formulates a practice objective with a client that does not logically link to one or more of the program's objectives, the social worker may be doing some good for the client but without program sanction or support. In fact, why would a program hire a social worker to do something the worker was not employed to do? At the risk of sounding redundant, a social service program is always evaluated on its program objectives. Thus, we must fully understand that it is these objectives that we must strive to attain: All of our efforts must be linked to them.

Let us put the concept of a practice objective into concrete terms. By glancing at Figure 2.6 for a moment, imagine that Bob, a resident of Group Home *X,* is expected to become self-sufficient in order to meet the program's goal, and to achieve his full potential in order to meet the agency's overall goal. But what are Bob's practice objectives? What social, personal, practical, and academic skills does Bob need to acquire in order to achieve self-sufficiency? Three plausible practice objectives in this case might be: to increase Bob's social contacts outside the home, to increase Bob's money management skills, and to increase Bob's language skills.

These three interrelated practice objectives for Bob demonstrate a definite link with the program's objective, which in turn is linked to the program's goal, which in turn in linked to the agency's goal. However, no one can tell, for example, whether Bob has made "more social contacts outside the home" until a "social contact" has been defined more precisely. Does saying "hello" to a fellow worker count as a social contact? It may that Bob is habitually silent at work. For a different individual, a social contact may involve going on an outing with fellow workers, or attending a recreational program at a community center.

It should be evident by now that defining a practice objective is a matter of stating what is to be changed. This provides an indication of the client's current state, or where the client is. Unfortunately, knowing this is not the same thing as knowing where one wants to go. Sometimes the destination is apparent, but in other cases it may be much less clear.

Suppose that Jane, for example, has presented job dissatisfaction as a general problem area. Enquiry has elicited that her dissatisfaction has nothing to do with the work itself, nor with the people at work, nor with such job-related factors as advancement, pay, benefits, and vacations. Instead, her dissatisfaction springs from the fact that she is spending too much time at work and too little time with her children.

Various practice objectives are possible here. Perhaps Jane should try to find a different, less demanding, full-time job; or maybe she should improve her budgeting skills so that her family can manage if she works only part-time. Perhaps she should make different arrangements for her children's care, so that she feels more comfortable about their welfare. Or maybe the real problem is that she herself feels torn between pursuing a career and being a full-time mother. It may be that what she really wants is to stay home with her children, provided that she can do so without guilt, with her partner's support, and without undue financial stress.

It is apparent that Jane's underlying problem has not yet been really defined. Often, an attempt to formulate a practice objective—to specify where Jane and the practitioner want to go—will reveal that Jane is not where she thought she was; that the problem so carefully elicited by the worker is not Jane's *real* problem after all. If this is the case, additional exploration is needed to redefine the problem before trying, once again, to set the practice objective.

When the real problem has been defined, the next task is to establish a related practice objective. If possible, it should be couched in positive terms, that is, in terms of what the client should do or feel rather than in terms of what she should not. For example, if the problem is Antoinette's immaturity, and "immaturity" is operationalized to mean getting out of her seat at school without permission, then one natural practice objective is "to decrease the number of times Antoinette gets out of her seat without permission." But it may be written just as usefully, "to increase the length of time Antoinette stays in her seat during class." Many practice objectives that are aimed at decreasing a negative quality can be reformulated to increase a positive quality while still achieving the desired change.

Finally, practice objectives must be comprehensive and precise. Each one must stipulate what is to be achieved, under what conditions, to what extent, and by whom.

PROGRAM ACTIVITIES

So far we have focused on the kinds of goals and objectives that social workers hope to achieve as a result of their work. The question now arises: What is that work? What do social workers *do* in order to help clients achieve higher knowledge levels, feelings, or behaviors? The answer, of course, is that they do many different things. They show films, facilitate group discussions, hold therapy sessions, teach classes, and conduct individual interviews. They attend staff meetings, do paperwork, consult with colleagues, and advocate for clients.

The important point about all such activities is that they are undertaken to move clients forward on one or more of the program's objectives. A social worker who teaches a class on nutrition hopes that class participants will learn certain specific facts about nutrition. If this learning is to take place, the facts

FAMILY PRESERVATION PROGRAM

Program Goal and Philosophy

To preserve family units where children are at-risk for out-of-home placement due to problems with physical abuse (goal). The program aims to strengthen interpersonal functioning of family members through intensive home-based services (philosophy).

Program Objectives

1. To increase positive social support for parents.
   — *Literary Support:* A lack of positive social support has been repeatedly linked to higher risk for child abuse. Studies indicate that parents with greater social support and less stress report more pleasure in their parenting roles.
   — *Sample of Activities:* Refer to support groups; evaluate criteria for positive support; introduce to community services; reconnect clients with friends and family.
   — *Measuring Instruments:* Client log; *Provision of Social Relations* (Turner, Frankel, & Levin, 1987).

2. To increase problem-solving skills for family members.
   — *Literary Support:* Problem solving is a tool for breaking difficult dilemmas into manageable pieces. Enhancing individuals' skills in systematically addressing problems increases the likelihood that they will successfully tackle new problems as they arise. Increasing problem-solving skills for parents and children equips family members to handle current problems, anticipate and prevent future ones, and advance their social functioning.
   — *Sample of Activities:* Teach steps to problem solving; role-play problem-solving scenarios; supportive counseling.
   — *Measuring Instrument: The Problem-Solving Inventory* (Heppner, 1987).

3. To increase parent's use of noncorporal child management strategies.
   — *Literary Support:* Research studies suggest that deficiency in parenting skills is associated with higher recurrence of abuse. Many parents who abuse their children have a limited repertoire of ways to discipline their children.
   — *Sample of Activities:* Teach noncorporal discipline strategies; inform parents about the criminal implications of child abuse; assess parenting strengths; provide reading material about behavior management.
   — *Measuring Instruments:* Goal Attainment Scaling; Checklist of Discipline Strategies.

FIGURE 2.7   Program-Level Service Conceptualization

to be learned must be included in the material presented. In other words, our activities must be directly related to our objectives.

It is critically important that social workers engage in activities that have the best chance to create positive client change. Over the years we have seen numerous instances in which social workers say they are trying to raise their clients' self-esteem, for example. When asked what specific activities they are doing to achieve this notable objective, they reply, "nothing specific, just supporting them when they need it." Defining program activities is an essential ingredient to understanding what interventions work.

Generating program activities serves as a smorgasbord of interventions for program workers to choose from. The list of activities is dynamic in that workers can add, drop, and modify activities to suit the needs of individual clients. Reviewing a list of a program's activities, however, gives stakeholders an idea of the nature of client service delivery offered by the program.

PROGRAM LOGIC MODEL: AN EXAMPLE

Figure 2.7 displays a concise example of a completed program logic model for a family preservation program. Included in the model is the program goal, three program objectives (with theoretical or empirical support), program activities, and strategies for measurement (to be discussed in future chapters). Organized in this way, the family preservation program is primed for any kind of evaluation.

SUMMING UP AND LOOKING AHEAD

This chapter discussed what is meant by an agency, a program, a program goal, a program objective, a practice objective, a measurement, and an activity. Most importantly, we discussed the linkages that must exist among these elements through the development of program logic models. When a program has a simple logic model such as the one displayed in Figure 2.7, it can then be evaluated by various types of evaluations—the topic of the following chapter.

KEY TERMS

Activities: What practitioners do with their clients to achieve their practice and facilitative objectives.

Affective Program Objective: An objective that focuses on changing an individual's emotional reaction to himself or herself or to another person or thing.

Agency Goal: Broad unmeasurable outcomes the agency wishes to achieve; they are based on values and are guided by the agency's mission statement.

Agency Objective: A program established to help in the achievement of the agency's goal.

Behavioral Program Objective: An objective that aims to change the conduct or actions of clients.

Conceptualization: The process of defining a social service program by a goal, objectives, measurements, and activities.

Maintenance Program Objective: An objective formulated in an effort to keep a program financially viable; constructed for the program's benefit.

Mission Statement: A unique written philosophical perspective of what an agency is all about; states a common vision for the organization by providing a point of reference for all major planning decisions.

Practice Objective: A statement of expected change identifying an intended therapeutic result tailored to the unique circumstances and needs of each client; logically linked to a program objective. Practice objectives, like program objectives, can be grouped into knowledge, affects, and behaviors.

Program Goal: A statement defining the intent of a program that cannot be directly evaluated. It can, however, be evaluated indirectly by the program's objectives, which are derived from the goal. Not to be confused with program objectives.

Program Objective: A statement that clearly and exactly specifies the expected change, or intended result, for individuals receiving program services. Qualities of well-chosen objectives are meaningfulness, specificity, measurability, and directionality. Program objectives, like practice objectives can be grouped into knowledge, affects, and behaviors. Not to be confused with program goal.

Program Structure: Fixed elements of a program that are designed to support social service workers in carrying out client service delivery. Examples include: staff-worker ratio, supervision protocols, support staff, training, and salaries

STUDY QUESTIONS

1. What is a social service agency? Provide an example of one that you are familiar with. Name as many social service agencies in your local community as you can. What target populations does each one serve? Why?

2. What are agency mission statements? How are they used within agencies? Do you believe they are necessary? If so, why? If not, why not?

3. What are agency goals? Do you believe they are necessary? If so, why? If not, why not?

4. What are the requirements for an agency's goal? Provide an example using all of the requirements.

5. What are agency objectives? Do you believe they are necessary? If so, why? If not, why not?

6. What are social service programs? How are they similar and different from social service agencies? Provide an example in your discussion.

7. Discuss the main differences between an agency and a program.

8. Discuss the usefulness of program logic models. How are they used to formulate social work programs? Do you believe they are necessary? If so, why? If not, why not?

9. What are program objectives? Do you believe they are necessary? If so, why? If not, why not?

10. What are unintended program results? Provide an example that you know of in your discussion.

11. Discuss the differences and similarities between an agency goal and a program goal. Use one common example throughout your discussion.

12. Discuss the different types of program objectives. Provide an example of each one in your discussion.

13. Discuss the qualitites of program objectives. Provide an example of each one in your discussion.

14. Discuss the differences and similarities between program objectives and practice objectives. Provide an example of each one in your discussion.

15. What are program activities? Provide as many examples as you can and distinguish each one from a program objective.

16. Create a hypothetical social service program based on the model contained in Figure 2.7. What are its strengths and weaknesses?

REFERENCES AND FURTHER READINGS

Beckman, D. (Ed.). (1987). *Using program theory in evaluation.* San Francisco: Jossey-Bass.

Blase, K., Fixsen, D., & Phillips, E. (1984). Residential treatment for troubled children: Developing service delivery systems. In S.C. Paine, G.T. Bellamy, & B. Wilcox (Eds.), *Human services that work: From innovation to standard practice.* Baltimore: Paul H. Brookes.

Hudson, J., & Grinnell, R.M., Jr. (1989). Program evaluation. In B. Compton & B. Galaway (Eds.), *Social work processes* (4th ed., pp. 691–711). Belmont, CA: Wadsworth.

Unrau, Y.A. (1993). A program logic model approach to conceptualizing social service programs. *The Canadian Journal of Program Evaluation, 8,* 33–42.

3

Chapter Outline

Types of Evaluations

A S PRESENTED IN THE PREVIOUS TWO CHAPTERS, there are many facets to evaluation. In Chapter 1 we learned that there are many reasons why evaluation is important to social work practice; some people fear evaluation; the scope of evaluation is broad; evaluation can be performed using a project or monitoring approach; and evaluation is essential to organizational growth and development. Chapter 2 described a strategy to conceptualize and organize social service programs. We learned that clearly and concisely conceptualizing programs is a first step to conducting any type of evaluation. Armed with the knowledge of the previous two chapters, this chapter is a logical continuation as it examines the types of program-level evaluations that can be done within programs. The five different types of program-level evaluations and their respective purposes are:

— **Needs Assessment:** Determines the nature, scope, and locale of a social problem (if one exists) *and* proposes feasible, useful, and relevant solution(s) to the problem(s).

— **Evaluability Assessment:** Determines a program's "readiness" for evaluation.

— **Process Evaluation:** Describes the nature (e.g., type, frequency, duration) of *actual* program operations and client service activities.

— **Outcome Evaluation:** Determines the amount and direction of change experienced by clients during or after a program's services.

— Cost-Benefit Evaluation: Demonstrates fiscal accountability and raises awareness of costs associated with studying and providing services to specific populations.

We present each type of evaluation in what we consider to be the ideal order for starting a new social service program. First, a needs assessment verifies that a need exists and offers possible program solutions. Second, evaluability assessment assesses the conceptual and operational logic of the program, which in turn is monitored through a process evaluation. After establishing that the program is being implemented as designed, we then assess its impact on client change using an outcome evaluation. Efficiency of client change, or the cost of outcomes, is then assessed using cost-benefit evaluation.

Each type of evaluation is presented separately in this chapter; however, most real-life evaluations mix-and-match strategies from many types of evaluation, thus using a multimodal evaluation plan. Moreover, as will be presented in later chapters, the various forms of evaluation use similar tools such as sampling and data collection methods (Chapter 5), measurement techniques (Chapter 6), and evaluation designs (Chapters 7 & 8).

NEEDS ASSESSMENT

The evaluation of need, more commonly called "needs assessment," is a type of evaluation that aims to establish the degree to which a social need (e.g., day care facilities) actually exists (Do we really need day care facilities?), as well as corresponding solutions (e.g., programs and policies). Thus, and under ideal conditions, a needs assessment should take place *before* a program (or a new program component) is conceptualized, funded, staffed, and implemented.

Needs assessments are born out of gaps in (or absence of) existing social services. Community leaders in response to public unrest, landmark cases, fluctuations in political and economic conditions, and changes in basic demographic trends often request needs assessments. A director of a family social service agency, for example, may notice low attendance at parent support groups and may request a needs assessment to determine if the agency's group intervention is outdated or, perhaps, targeting the wrong needs. Or, a child is abducted from a public school ground during the lunch hour and an inquiry is undertaken to explore the general safety of children and supervision practices at all public schools. A third scenario could be that the number of street panhandlers is observed to be growing, so a municipal task force is formed to learn more about "the problem" and to decide what action, if any, the city should take.

When conducting needs assessments, it is not enough to establish that social problems exist (e.g., child prostitution, drug abuse, discrimination), it is also extremely important to identify possible strategies in order to address them.

Visibility of Social Problems

Some social problems present a visible threat to how society is organized and to what people believe is necessary for a basic level of well-being. Domestic violence, juvenile crime, child abuse, unemployment, racism, poverty, and suicide are examples of problems that threaten social stability in local and national communities, and as such generally have been given a great deal of attention in popular media. These visible problems have been the traditional focus of our profession since its inception. They are the social problems for which our society has drawn a minimum line of acceptability. Once the line is crossed—a child is physically abused, a teenager is caught selling drugs—there is some societal action that takes place to "solve" the problem. Generally, the more visible the social problem, the more aware people are of it, and the more response it gets.

Other less-visible problems are regularly addressed by social workers but are not as prominent for the general public. These problems do not have a definite "bottom-line" to indicate when and what action ought to take place. Children with behavior problems, individuals with low self-esteem, marital dissatisfaction, and unfair employment policies are only a few examples of problems that might be considered part and parcel of daily life. Further, these problems are less likely to receive the attention of public money unless they are paired with one or more visible needs, as described above. In short, needs assessments are extremely useful in that they help us to learn more about seen and unseen problems in our society.

Wants, Demands, and Needs

In developing a definition of need, it is helpful to distinguish among the terms *wants, demands*, and *needs*. A want is something people are willing to pay for and a demand is something people are willing to march for. These two definitions differentiate wants and demands by people's actions—that is, what people are willing to do for a particular situation or cause. These two definitions help define a "need," which is a basic requirement necessary to sustain the human condition, to which people have a right.

Clearly, how one defines wants, demands, or needs is open to considerable debate and is dependent on personal views and beliefs. Prison inmates, for example, may protest the removal of televisions from their cells, thereby *demanding* that televisions are a necessary part of their recreational outlets. The public, on the other hand, may not see a *need* for televisions in prison and feel that inmates' basic recreational outlets are met through educational magazines and radio programming.

Perceived and Expressed Needs

When considering any social problem we must differentiate between perceived needs and expressed (or felt) needs. Perceived needs are the opinions and views of people who are not directly experiencing the problem of interest. Perceived needs are typically shaped by consulting experts in the field, research or published reports, or people who are experiencing the problem. Perceived needs are commonly held by politicians, funders, agency directors, and helping professionals.

Expressed needs (or felt needs), on the other hand, are made known when the people experiencing them talk about how the problem impacts them personally and, perhaps, what they feel should be done about it. In short, the users of social services have expressed needs. For example, inner-city parents that have teenage runaways have expressed needs, as do the teenagers who are running away. Unless the city's mayor also has a teenager on the run, the mayor has only perceived needs about this problem. Because one individual can have two perspectives, we must be clear about which perspective we are interested in.

Identifying who is defining a need helps us to become aware of what perspective is being represented. It is always preferable, if possible, to include both perspectives (perceived and expressed) in a single needs assessment. If the two different perspectives agree, then we obviously have stronger support for the social needs that we determine to exist. On the other hand, when perceived needs and expressed needs differ to some extent, it is usually necessary to include an educational component as part of our proposed solution. The educational intervention may target people with perceived needs, people with expressed needs, or both.

Social workers at an AIDS clinic, for example, may have concerns about an increasing number of sexually active youth who are not practicing "safe sex" (perceived need). While adolescents may admit to being sexually active, they may not express any concerns about sexually transmitted diseases, pregnancy, or AIDS (expressed need). A reasonable solution to this mismatch of perceptions is to educate the youths in the community about the risks of unprotected sex and how to practice "safe sex."

So how do we come up with a definition of need? The most important thing to remember when answering this question is to include input from the various people who have a stake in the social problem being investigated. We might solicit the views of professionals, researchers, clients, and so on. It is a big mistake to develop a definition of need in isolation from other people. Because a needs assessment is usually conducted within a specific community (geographic or population), we must include as many divergent perspectives as possible.

Needs Assessment Questions

Questions asked in needs assessments are usually exploratory in nature. Open-ended questions are used to produce a wide array of possible answers. At the core of needs assessment questions is an effort to better understand a social need. In addition, they also seek innovative strategies to respond to the problems identified. Of course, it is always possible for needs assessments to reveal that a particular need or problem does not exist, or does not exist in the way that we had thought. A simple mail survey to local residents of a particular community, for example, can easily obtain useful needs assessment data. Figure 3.1 presents such a survey.

How we frame needs assessment questions influences the kinds of data (answers) we receive. Consider the following two questions.

— What are the most pressing social problem(s) (or issues) affecting residents of your nearest inner-city neighborhood (e.g., Figure 3.1)?

— What additional social services do residents of your nearest inner-city neighborhood need?

The first question directs us to better understand the current state-of-affairs for inner-city residents and poises us to learn more their *needs*. In turn, we can

The purpose of this part of the survey is to learn more about your perceptions of these problems in the community. Listed below are a number of problems some residents of Northside have reported having.

Please place a number from 1 to 3 on the line to the right of the question that represents how much of a problem they have been to you within the last year:

1. No problem (or not applicable to you)
2. Moderate problem
3. Severe problem

Questions	Responses		
1. Finding the product I need	1	2	3
2. Impolite salespeople	1	2	3
3. Finding clean stores	1	2	3
4. Prices that are too high	1	2	3
5. Not enough Spanish-speaking salespeople	1	2	3
6. Public transportation	1	2	3
7. Getting credit	1	2	3
8. Lack of certain types of stores	1	2	3
9. Lack of an employment assistance program	1	2	3
10. Finding a city park that is secure	1	2	3
11. Finding a good house	1	2	3

FIGURE 3.1   Example of a Needs Assessment Questionnaire

then devise new solutions or modify existing services based on our understanding of residents' most salient needs. In contrast, the second question steers us away from efforts to further understand current problems in our inner-city neighborhood and directs us toward adding *solutions*. If the latter question alone were the main focus of our needs assessment, we would risk recommending more of the same social services without considering other problems or solutions for the community.

Suppose, for example, that the adolescent runaway shelters in our inner-city report that they are filled to capacity and are turning *away* teen runaways daily. It is tempting and easy to conclude that more shelter space is needed to accommodate teens that are being turned away. Is the problem fixed? Not necessarily. Foisting a "space" solution on the community without any data to help us better understand the current state of the problem at best only provides a Band-Aid solution to a difficult problem. As social workers, we want to develop and implement effective and lasting solutions, which means that we must fully assess problems before intervening. For example, we could ask the following questions to learn more about the inner-city teen runaway problem:

— Who are the teens using the shelter?
— What reasons are given to explain why the teens are running away?
— Where are the teens running away from?

The answers to these questions may lead us to arrive at a different solution than proposing more shelter space. A crisis-counseling program could be added to the shelter, for example, to help teens negotiate with their parents or caregivers to return home, or to stay with friends or relatives. It may also be that a large percentage of teens using the shelters are actually homeless, in which case we might propose a different program altogether.

There are many examples of how needs assessments can help us in our professional practice (see Box 3.1). The questions they can answer can be classified under five general categories:

— **Demographics:** What is the demographic profile of the community, or the people experiencing the need? For example, what is the average age, socioeconomic level, family constellation, and so on?
— **Timeliness:** Are existing services outdated? If so, in what ways? What are the *current* needs of the community? What are the most pressing needs within the community?
— **History:** Have needs changed over time? What conditions have changed in the community in the past five years? What types of solutions have worked in the past?
— **Demand:** Are existing program services meeting the needs of the people being served? What are the gaps in existing services? Are there specific groups asking for services but not receiving any?
— **Strengths:** What are the positives in the community? What are the signs of resiliency in the community?

BOX 3.1_____

PUBLISHED EXAMPLES OF NEEDS ASSESSMENTS
(Substantive Areas in **Bold**)

Berkman, B., Chauncey, S., Holmes, W., Daniels, A., Bonander, E., Sampson, S., & Robinson, M. (1999). Standardized screening of **elderly patients'** needs for social work assessment in primary care. *Health and Social Work, 24,* 9–16.

Chen, H., & Marks, M. (1998). Assessing the needs of **inner city youth**: beyond needs identification and prioritization. *Children and Youth Services Review, 20,* 819–838.

Davidson, B. (1997). Service needs of **relative caregivers**: A qualitative analysis. *Families in Society, 78,* 502–510.

Ford, W.E. (1997). Perspective on the integration of **substance user** needs assessment and treatment planning. *Substance Use and Misuse, 32,* 343–349.

Gillman, R.R., & Newman, B.S. (1996). Psychosocial concerns and strengths of **women with HIV infection**: An empirical study. *Families in Society, 77,* 131–141.

Hall, M., Amodeo, M., Shaffer, H., Bilt, J. (2000). **Social workers** employed in substance abuse treatment agencies: A training needs assessment. *Social Work, 45,* 141–154.

Herdt, G., Beeler, J., & Rawls, T. (1997). Life course diversity among **older lesbians and gay men**: A study in Chicago. *Journal of Gay, Lesbian, and Bisexual Identity, 2,* 231–246.

Palmeri, D., Auld, G., Taylor, T., Kendall, P., & Anderson, A. (1998). Multiple perspectives on nutrition education needs of **low-income Hispanics**. *Journal of Community Health, 23,* 301–316.

Pisarski, A., & Gallois, C. (1996). A needs analysis of Brisbane **lesbians**: Implications for the lesbian community. *Journal of Homosexuality, 30,* 79–95.

Safyer, A.W., Litchfield, L.C., & Leahy, B.H. (1996). **Employees with teens**: The role of EAP needs assessments. *Employee Assistance Quarterly, 11,* 47–66.

Shields, G., & Adams, J. (1996). **HIV/AIDS** among youth: A community needs assessment study. *Child and Adolescent Social Work Journal, 12,* 361–380.

Weaver, H.N. (1997). The challenges of research in **Native American communities:** incorporating principles of cultural competence. *Journal of Social Service Research, 23,* 1–15.

Weiner, A. (1996). Understanding the social needs of **streetwalking prostitutes.** *Social Work, 41,* 97–105.

Zahnd, E., Klein, D., & Needell, B. (1997). **Substance use** and issues of violence among **low-income, pregnant women**: The California perinatal needs assessment. *Journal of Drug Issues, 27,* 563–584.

EVALUABILITY ASSESSMENT

Evaluability assessment is simply assessing a program's readiness for evalua-tion. Ideally, it occurs *after* a needs assessment and *before* a process, an outcome, or a cost-benefit evaluation. How do we get a program ready for an evaluation? By creating program models—a program plan or design that describes a program's approach to resolving the social problem being targeted for an identified population (as discussed in Chapter 2).

Strange as it may seem, many social service programs do not have a clearly documented program model or an accepted client service delivery system. In these cases, evaluability assessment can expose areas of the program's conceptualization and/or organization that interfere both with the delivery of its services and with the program evaluation effort itself.

Indeed, many social service programs are not "evaluatable" in their current states. Many do not have a program goal or program objectives written. These programs are not necessary ineffective or inefficient. They just have a great degree of difficulty proving otherwise.

Program Development

Social service programs are dynamic organizations that exist in a context of political, economic, and social flux. Whether new or old, programs must be responsive to their surroundings and be continually evolving into more efficient and effective service delivery systems. In short, social service programs are in a constant state of program development, and evaluability assessment gives direction and structure to this growth.

In Chapter 2, we introduced the program logic model with three major components: a single program goal, one or more program objectives, and scores of program activities. When starting a new program, evaluability assessment involves creating these essential program components, as well as ensuring logical consistency among them. Beginning anew generally creates an invigorating and innovative climate for conducting evaluability assessments because program staff are not rooted in traditions or loyal to existing structures.

Evaluability assessment, however, usually takes place after programs have been established and in operation for some time. The excitement of building a program logic model is somewhat dampened in existing programs because old practices come under close scrutiny and change is inevitable. Moreover, many social service programs drift from their original mandate over time.

Evaluability assessment can assist the workers and staff in regaining focus and taking charge of program development.

A ten-year-old after-school program for children from urban low-income families, for example, was originally established with a program objective to increase children's involvement in positive recreational activities during after-school hours. Program activities included: organized sports, crafts, one-to-one coaching, positive reinforcement for group participation, sticker charts for displaying friendship skills, and so on. A favorite activity of program staff and children alike was an annual ski trip—an opportunity that children could access only through the program because their parents could not afford such extravagant recreational outlets. For most children, the program ski trip was the one and only time that they would experience skiing.

In the early years of the program, the ski trip was just that—one activity of many that was popular with the children. Without the benefit of a program logic model, however, program staff focused on this one activity and over time began adjusting program activities accordingly. In short, the program began to drift. For example, rather than playing organized sports after school, children were instead engaging in fund-raising activities that were necessary to fund the ski trip.

As part of an evaluability assessment, program staff examined the ski trip in light of the program's original objective—*to increase children's involvement in positive recreational activities during after-school hours.* The result was the realization that the "ski trip" had taken program resources and staff attention away from the program's original objective. In particular, planning for the ski trip meant that other positive and more accessible recreational activities (e.g., sports, reading storybooks, and crafts) were done away with.

By developing a program logic model for the after school program, staff were able to revisit their program goal, objectives, and activities giving a renewed direction for planning program development. The ski trip was re-conceptualized as only one of many positive recreational activities, and staff turned their program development energy to efforts at coming up with various other activities to increase children's involvement in positive recreational activities during after-school hours.

Teamwork

Development of a program logic model is best accomplished through teamwork. Ideally, a "team" involves representatives from different stakeholder groups such as funders, administrators, practitioners, and clients. It is more typical, however, for program administrators and practitioners to assume major responsibility for this task, particularly since monitoring a program model is an ongoing effort.

The importance of teamwork is that all levels of program staff participate in the creating, implementing, and evaluating the program model. With participation comes a professionalism that promotes an atmosphere of quality service and change for the better. The benefits of working as a team toward a common purpose (i.e., goal) is that staff morale is higher, turnover is less, service delivery is superior, and knowledge generated by the program has more meaning.

Evaluabilty Assessment Questions

Evaluability assessment questions are subject to the same political and personal influences as needs assessment questions. The natures of evaluability assessment questions, however, are different and fall into four categories.

— **Program Design:** Is the program model logically organized? Does it easily communicate the program's intent to stakeholders? Is the program goal clear and concise, identifying the target population, social problem, direction of change, and means of achieving the desired change?
— **Coverage:** Do program objectives appropriately target knowledge-based, affective-based, and behaviorally based change?
— **Feasibility:** Given the scope (e.g., size, duration, and innovativeness) of the program, can its objectives be reasonably accomplished? Are program objectives meaningful, specific, measurable, and directional?
— **Integrity:** Do program staff accept the program model as a desirable approach to practice? How much involvement do staff have in modifying the program? Were research and theory considered in the development of the program model?

PROCESS EVALUATION

A process evaluation focuses on the program's approach to client service delivery, as well as on how the program manages its day-to-day operations. It is not interested in the end result of a program. In short, a process evaluation examines how a program's services are delivered to clients and what administrative mechanisms exist within the program to support these services.

Ideally, a process evaluation occurs before, or at the same time, as an outcome evaluation. It clearly makes sense to check whether a program is implemented in the way it was intended before evaluating its outcomes. This is particularly the case since it is our assumption (or hope) that the program's services will produce the desired client change as articulated by the program's objectives.

In the language of our program logic model, program processes refer specifically to the activities and characteristics that describe how a program operates. In general, there are two major categories of processes—the client service delivery system within the program and the program's administrative support systems that sustain client service delivery. Client service delivery is composed of what workers do (e.g., interventions, activities) and what clients bring to the program (e.g., client characteristics). On the other hand, administrative support systems comprise the organizational activities that exist to support the program's client service delivery system (e.g., supervision, support staff, emergency petty cash funds, evaluation activities).

Process evaluation, therefore, involves monitoring and measuring things such as communication flow, decision-making protocols, staff workload, client record-keeping, program supports, staff training, and worker-client activities. Indeed, the entire sequence of activities that a program undertakes to achieve its objectives or outcomes is open to evaluation.

An evaluation of process might include the sequence of events throughout the entire program or it might focus on a particular program component such as assessment, treatment, or follow-up. A careful examination of *how* something is done may help us to understand *why* or *how* it is more or less effective or efficient. Ultimately, we undertake process evaluations to improve services for clients. Thus, even when evaluating internal mechanisms of a program such as staff communication between departments, we want to do so not just for the results of increasing staff morale but because we believe that higher-quality staff communication will lead to better services for clients.

Formative and Summative Evaluations

A process evaluation is sometimes referred to as a *formative evaluation:* the gathering of relevant data for the continuous ongoing feedback and improvement of the client-related services a program offers. While formative evaluations generally include measures of client outcome, their purpose is to fine-tune services that the programs deliver to their clients. In this spirit, a process evaluation is a critical component of delivering quality social services. By monitoring their interventions and activities, workers can assess whether they are helping their clients in the best way possible. Similarly, administrators are responsible for maintaining a healthy, supportive, and progressive work environment.

The opposite of formative evaluations are *summative evaluations*. Summative evaluations gather relevant data for the conclusive determination of a program's success or failure in affecting their target population. As such, they necessarily pair program processes with program outcomes. Summative evaluations are most likely to be carried out using a project approach to evaluation, while formative evaluations utilize a monitoring approach (see Chapter 1).

Given that process evaluations play a critical role in shaping how a program develops over time, we recommend that they begin by focusing on improving client service delivery systems. After a well-conceptualized program is established (a procedure that can take up to two years), a process evaluation can shift its emphasis to the program's administrative operations. The reason for beginning with direct client service delivery is that all worker supervision, training, and other administrative support ultimately exists to support direct services that workers provide to their clients. Unless we are clear about what the nature of the program's client service delivery approach, is our beginning attempts to design and implement supporting systems to help workers may be misdirected.

Client Flow Charts

A useful tool for describing client service delivery systems within a program is a *client path flow chart*. An example of one is contained in Figure 3.2, which illustrates how adolescent clients move through the Adolescent Program (AP). The chart displays the general sequence of events that clients will experience from first contact with the program to termination. Additionally, the chart shows critical decision-making points where agreements to provide AP services to clients are either made (e.g., referral and assessment) or renewed (e.g., contracting and reassessment).

By mapping out program processes, we gain a better understanding of what types of interventions (and associated activities) lead to what type of client

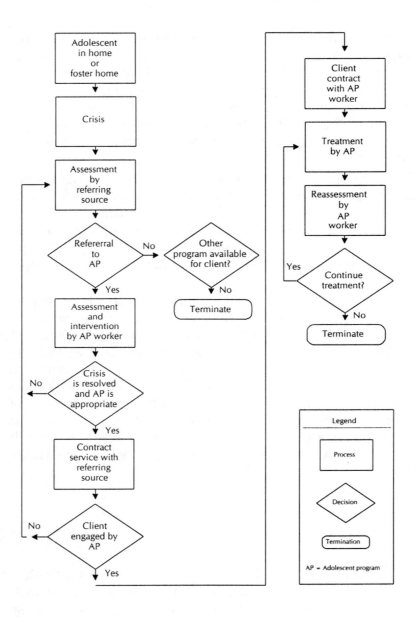

FIGURE 3.2   Example of a Client Path Flow

outcomes (positive and negative). These data are a first step to uncovering the mystery of the "black box" of intervention that, as we will see, is ignored in outcome evaluations.

Process Evaluation Questions

There are many examples of how process evaluations can help us in our professional practice (see Box 3.2). The questions they can answer can be classified under six general categories:

— **Program Structures:** What is the program's organizational structure? What is the flow of communication? How are decisions made? What are the minimum qualifications for staff hiring?

— **Program Supports:** What program supports exist to help workers do their jobs? How much and what type of staff training and supervision is available?

— **Client Service Delivery:** What is the nature of worker activity? What do workers do? How often? At what level?

— **Decision Making:** How are practice decisions made? How are worker activities and decision making documented?

— **Program Integrity:** Is the program being implemented in the way that it was designed? If not, how does the program deviate from the original program "blueprint?"

— **Compliance:** Is the program meeting standards set by funders, accrediting bodies, or governmental agencies?

OUTCOME EVALUATION

The fourth type of evaluation focuses on program outcomes. Outcome evaluation aims to demonstrate the degree and nature of change, if any, for clients after they have received program services—that is, after they have left the program. Outcome evaluation is the most popular of the five evaluation types that we discuss.

The essence of an outcome evaluation is captured by the familiar phrase "begin with the end in mind." Outcome evaluations serve as a conceptual program map because they tell us where program staff and clients are headed as they work together. This focus helps to keep program administrators and workers in sync with the program's mandate (which is reflected in the program's goal).

Outcome evaluations primarily stem from an interest in knowing whether social programs benefit the clients they serve. Funders and policymakers are

BOX 3.2_____

PUBLISHED EXAMPLES OF PROCESS EVALUATIONS
(Substantive Areas in **Bold**)

Allen, J., Philliber, S., & Hoggson, N. (1990). School-based prevention of **teen-age pregnancy and school dropout**: Process evaluation of the National Replication of the Teen Outreach Program. *American Journal of Community Psychology, 18,* 505–524.

Andersson, L. (1984). Intervention against loneliness in a group of **elderly women:** A process evaluation. *Human Relations, 37,* 295–310.

Bazemore, G., & Cruise, P. (1993). Resident adaptations in an Alcoholics Anonymous based residential program for the **urban homeless**. *Social Service Review, 67,* 599–616.

Bentelspacher, C., DeSilva, E, Goh, T., & LaRowe, K. (1996). A process evaluation of the cultural compatibility of psycho-educational family group treatment with **ethnic Asian** clients. *Social Work with Groups, 19,* 41–55.

Berkowitz, G., Halfon, N., &; Klee, L. (1992). Improving access to health care: Case management for **vulnerable children**. *Social Work in Health Care, 17,* 101–123.

Blaze Temple, D, & Honig, F. (1997). Process evaluation of an Australian EAP. *Employee Assistance Quarterly, 12,* 15–35.

Deacon, S., & Piercy, F. (2000). Qualitative evaluation of **family therapy** programs: A participatory approach. *Journal of Marital and Family Therapy, 26,* 39– 45.

Dehar, M., Casswell, S., & Duignan, P. (1993). Formative and process evaluation of health promotion and disease prevention programs. *Evaluation Review, 17,* 204–220.

Devaney, B., & Rossi, P. (1997). Thinking through evaluation design options. *Children and Youth Services Review, 19,* 587–606.

Jackson, J. (1991). The use of psycho-educational evaluations in the clinical process: **Therapists** as sympathetic advocates. *Child and Adolescent Social Work Journal, 8,* 473–487.

Jones, L., & Strandness, D. (1991). Integrating research activities, practice changes, and monitoring and evaluation: A model for academic health centers. *Quality Review Bulletin, 17,* 229–235.

Miller, T., Veltkamp, L., & Janson, D. (1988). Projective measures in the clinical evaluation of **sexually abused children.** *Child Psychiatry and Human Development. 18,* 47–57.

Pithers, W. (1994). Process evaluation of a group therapy component designed to enhance sex offenders' empathy for **sexual abuse survivors**. *Behavior Research and Therapy, 32,* 565–570.

Pithers, W. (1999). Empathy definition, enhancement, and relevance to the treatment of **sexual abusers**. *Journal of Interpersonal Violence, 14,* 257–284.

Sieppert, J.D., Hudson, J., & Unrau, Y.A. (2000). **Family group conferencing** in child welfare: Lessons from a demonstration project. *Families in Society, 81,* 382–391.

Smith, M., Knickman, J., & Oppenheimer, L. (1992). Connecting the disconnected adult day care for **people with AIDS** in New York City. *Health and Social Work, 17,* 273–281.

the major stakeholder groups that apply external pressure on programs to produce outcome data. Enforcing accreditation standards, legislating record-keeping protocols, and setting guidelines for annual program reports apply such pressures. Administrators, in turn, are charged with the responsibility of ensuring that outcome evaluations occur in their programs. Finally, practitioners are given the task of collecting outcome data from clients. This task can provide practitioners with meaningful data and insight into how program services are impacting clients—a result that is of interest to all stakeholder groups, as presented in Chapter 1.

Outcome evaluations are always designed for a specific social service program. Their results tell us about specific program objectives and not general social indicators. For example, a four-week unemployment program showing that 75 percent of its clients found employment after being taught how to search for jobs cannot make any claims about impacting the general unemployment rate. The results are *specific* to one *specific* group of clients, experiencing the *specific* conditions of one *specific* program over a *specific* time frame at a *specific* time.

Outcome evaluations tell us *whether* programs are working, but they are silent about *why* programs are working (or failing to work). For this reason they are often dubbed the "black box" evaluation. Nor is there any mention of the costs associated with of client success. After all, if a program achieves what it is supposed to achieve, via the attainment of its program objectives, what does it matter how it achieves it? If the program is to be replicated or even improved, it does matter; nevertheless, client outcome alone is the focus of many evaluations.

Outcomes and Outputs

Outcomes are sometimes confused with outputs. Outputs are completed products or amount of work done resulting from internal program activities. For example, the number of clients served, the total hours of counseling services provided, and the number of crisis calls received. The pressure to collect data on program outputs typically comes from program funders. While *outputs* focus on the results of program operations, *outcomes* focus on the results of client change. As we discussed in Chapter 2, programs declare their targeted outcomes by articulating and documenting program objectives.

The distinction between outcomes and outputs is important to understand because high outputs are not always associated with positive outcomes, and vice versa. For example, a program that aims to reduce the number of high school dropouts among Native American youth may report high outputs (e.g., an average of 10 counseling hours per week to all 12 Native American youth in a school for the three-month period of the program) but poor outcomes (e.g., half of the 12 youth drop out of high school by the end of the three-month period).

When outcomes are defined in terms of counting events or occurrences, they can be measured with little effort. It is relatively easy to tally the number of kids that stay in school, or how many welfare recipients find full-time work, or the number of completed adoptions in a given year. Outcome evaluations of social service programs, however, are not simple counting exercises because the targeted events or occurrences are often beyond the scope of the programs. For example, a school year is 10 months long but the drop-out prevention program only lasts for three months. Additionally, outcomes sometimes identify difficult-to-measure concepts—such as family functioning and acceptance of diversity.

As we discussed in Chapter 1, social service programs are often faced with limited resources (e.g., not enough staff, time, money), as well as a limited knowledge base. In the face of these limitations, social workers define program objectives or outcomes in terms of smaller client changes that, if accomplished, will eventually lead to positive outcomes. The program to prevent Native American youth from dropping out of high school may pare down its objectives to increase youths' self-esteem or to improve students' literacy skills, for example. These program objectives are targeted because workers believe that increased self-esteem and improved literacy skills will keep Native American youth in school.

Benchmarking

A challenge of selecting outcomes (or objectives) for a specific social service program is setting sites for desired change high enough to produce a meaningful amount of client change but not so high that the program will never successfully achieve its objectives. We have already addressed this challenge to some degree by paying attention to how we phrase program objectives. Instead of claiming to eradicate domestic violence, for example, program objectives are more likely to claim "reducing" domestic violence. Rather than expunge social problems, programs aim to restore positive conditions or diminish negative ones.

How much change programs can reasonably expect to achieve can be thought out through benchmarking, which is a strategy that flags expected rates of change. Examples of benchmarking program outcomes include: 95 percent of clients will secure full-time employment within six months of completing the program, 70 percent of adolescents will show a minimum increase of 10 self-esteem points (as measured on a self-esteem scale) by the end of the program. In short, benchmarking concretizes the program's objectives by setting numerical markers of change. Of course, benchmarking can also be applied to program outputs.

How does one decide a benchmark value? Is it likely that 95 percent of clients will secure full-time employment within six months of a program, or is 55 percent a more realistic figure? Most social service programs address chronic social problems that are unlikely to disappear with one dose of a single program. One way to establish benchmark values is to examine outcome rates of other similar programs. Evaluation and research studies of family preservation programs, for example, typically report that 80 percent or more families are preserved (i.e., a child that was at-risk for out-of-home placement remained in the home) after about three months of intensive in-home intervention. New family preservation programs, therefore, can safely choose to benchmark their preservation rate at 80 percent, or perhaps 70 percent to give leniency to program start-up pains.

When programs address social problems where repeat offenses are high (e.g., perpetrators of child sexual abuse and drug addictions) or problems are chronic (e.g., developmental disabilities or mental illness), the benchmark value for change may be low, say 10 percent improvement. To set a program's sites unrealistically high is to set up false hopes and unrealistic expectations for program workers and clients alike.

The most important feature of benchmarking is selecting a known value. If a benchmark value cannot be discerned from existing research or evaluation reports, then programs can determine their own rates by establishing a baseline measure. This is simply achieved by avoiding benchmarks altogether for the first year of the program. At the year's end, the program can calculate the average amount of change by clients using data collected to measure program objectives. This figure then can be used or adjusted (higher or lower) as the benchmark for the following year.

Consumer Satisfaction

Consumer satisfaction is an elusive concept for social service programs. As social workers, we want our clients to feel content with their experiences in our programs. Yet, for many social service clients a move to positive change involves periods of considerable personal discomfort and distress. A battered woman must often be confronted with the realities of risk to her (and her children's) physical safety, for example, before she will choose to leave an abusive partner. Moreover, many clients do not end up reaching the expected outcomes pledged by the programs they receive services from. Nevertheless, measuring satisfaction of social service program is a concern of all stakeholder groups.

Satisfaction measures can yield fertile data for programs that serve hard-to-reach or diverse client groups. Program services must be marketed, offered, implemented, and evaluated in diversity-sensitive ways. When serving diverse populations (e.g., gay and lesbian, racial and ethnic minorities, women, elderly), satisfaction measures can gauge whether the program is neglecting or offending important values of particular groups.

Policymakers, administrators, funders, and practitioners want reassurance that clients and the general public are satisfied with the services they receive from social programs. Since clients are direct users of the social services, it is they who are most often asked about their satisfaction with program services, as well as any results they experienced.

In a nutshell, satisfaction, as an outcome, measures clients' contentment or approval with a program. As it is, most clients who respond to satisfaction surveys do so favorably; that is, programs can expect that the majority of their clients will report being reasonably satisfied with program services. Programs with less than 75 percent of clients expressing satisfaction are atypical. As such, most programs that choose to benchmark client satisfaction can safely aim for 75 percent satisfaction from their clients.

Staff in programs with less than 75 percent of clients expressing satisfaction with services may well want to reflect on their program operations and client service delivery system in light of the complaints received. Client satisfaction is almost never the central focus of outcome evaluation because such measures show little variation. Additionally, satisfaction is rarely the only measurement in an outcome evaluation.

Outcome Questions

There are many examples of how outcome evaluations can help us in our professional practice (See Box 3.3). The questions they can answer can be classified under five general categories:

- **Program Integrity:** Is the program achieving the desired client change? To what degree is the program accomplishing its program objectives? Is the program achieving predetermined minimum standards of achievement (benchmarks)?

- **Program Effects:** Are people who have been through the program better for it? Are they better off than others who went through similar programs? How long do client improvements last?

- **Differential Effects:** Given the demographics of clients served, are there subgroups of clients who experience more success than others?

- **Causality:** Is there any evidence that the program can claim responsibility for positive changes in clients?

- **Satisfaction:** Are stakeholders satisfied with program services?

COST-BENEFIT EVALUATION

Administrators of social service programs are concerned with the costs associated in producing their programs' objectives, which leads us to a fifth type of evaluation, cost-benefit evaluation. While improving human lives and social conditions is a priority of all social service programs, we are expected to accomplish a program's objectives in an efficient and cost-effective manner. A program is considered cost-efficient when it is able to achieve its program objectives at lower cost, compared to another program striving for the same program objectives.

A "probation program," for example, costs less than a "jail program" simply because the probation program is not required to have 24-hour supervision, an institutional facility, and so on. If the probation program is successful in preventing future criminal behavior, the savings are even greater. Costs associated with prevention, however, are difficult to estimate because we cannot know for certain whether the absence of the problem was a result of the program.

Cost-benefit evaluations alone provide us with data and information associated with program expenses. When combined with process and outcome evaluation, data from cost-benefit evaluations can give us valuable insight as to how program resources are best allocated. Because cost-benefit evaluations produce dollar figures for program processes and outcomes, they have utility only when we know precisely what the program is doing (process evaluation) and precisely how much client change is produced (outcome evaluation).

BOX 3.3————————————————————————

PUBLISHED EXAMPLES OF OUTCOME EVALUATIONS
(Substantive Areas in **Bold**)

Auslander, W., Haire-Joshu, D. Houston, C., Williams, J.H., & Krebill, H. (2000). The short-term impact of a health promotion program for **low-income African American women**. *Research on Social Work Practice, 10,* 78–97.

Bacha, T., Pomeroy, E.C., Gilbert, D. (1999). A psychoeducational group intervention for **HIV-positive children**: A pilot study. *Health and Social Work, 24,* 303–306.

Bagley, C., & Young, L. (1998). Long-term evaluation of group counseling of **women with a history of child sexual abuse**: Focus on depression, self-esteem, suicidal behaviors, and social support. *Social Work with Groups, 21,* 63–73.

Barber, J., & Gilbertson, R. (1998). Evaluation of a self-help manual for the **female partners of heavy drinkers**. *Research on Social Work Practice, 8,* 141–151.

Barker, S.B., Knisely, J.S., & Dawson, K. (1999). The evaluation of a consultation service for delivery of **substance abuse services** in a hospital setting. *Journal of Addictive Diseases, 18,* 73–82.

Burry, C.L. (1999). Evaluation of a training program for **foster parents** of infants with prenatal substance effects. *Child Welfare, 78,* 197–214.

Collins, M.E., Mowbray, C.T., & Bybee, D. (1999). Measuring coping strategies in an educational intervention for **individuals with psychiatric disabilities**. *Health and Social Work, 24,* 279–290.

Comer, E., & Fraser, M. (1998). Evaluation of six **family-support programs**: Are they effective? *Families in Society, 79,* 134–148.

Conboy, A., Auerbach, C., Schnall, D., & LaPorte, H. (2000). **MSW student** satisfaction with using single-system design computer software to evaluate social work practice. *Research on Social Work Practice, 10,* 127–138.

Deacon, S.A., & Piercy, F.P. (2000). Qualitative evaluation of **family** therapy programs: A participatory approach. *Journal of Marital and Family Therapy, 26,* 39–45.

de Anda, D. (1999). Project Peace: The evaluation of a skill-based violence prevention program for **high school adolescents**. *Social Work in Education. 21,* 137–149.

Deschenes, E., & Greenwood, P. (1998). Alternative placements for **juvenile offenders**: Results from the evaluation of the Nokomis challenge program. *Journal of Research in Crime and Delinquency, 35,* 267–294.

Ford, C.A., & Okojie, F.A. (1999). A multidimensional approach to evaluating **family preservation programs**. *Family Preservation Journal, 4,* 31–62.

Harrison, R.S., Boyle, S.W., Farley, W. (1999). Evaluating the outcomes of family-based intervention for **troubled children**: A pretest-posttest study. *Research on Social Work Practice, 9,* 640–655.

Hughes, R.H., & Kirby, J. (2000). Strengthening evaluation strategies for **divorcing family support services**: Perspectives of parent educators, mediators, attorneys, and judges. *Family Relations, 49,* 53–61.

Jenson, J.M., Jacobson, M., Unrau, Y.A., & Robinson, R.L. (1996). Intervention for victims of child sexual abuse: An evaluation of the children's advocacy model. *Child and Adolescent Social Work Journal, 13,* 139–156.

BOX 3.3 CONTINUED_____

Jinich, S., & Litrownik, A. (1999). Coping with **sexual abuse**: Development and evaluation of a videotape intervention for nonoffending parents. *Child Abuse and Neglect, 23,* 175–190.

Myers, L., Rittner, B. (1999). Family functioning and satisfaction of **former residents of a non-therapeutic residential care facility:** An exploratory study. *Journal of Family Social Work, 3,* 54–68.

Nicholson, B.C., Brenner, V., & Fox, R.A. (1999). A community-based parenting program with **low-income mothers of young children**. *Families in Society, 80,* 247–253.

Prior, V., Lynch, M.A., & Glaser, D. (1999). Responding to **child sexual abuse:** an evaluation of social work by children and their carers. *Child and Family Social Work, 4,* 131–143.

Raschick, M., & Critchley, R. (1998). Guidelines for conducting site-based evaluations of intensive **family preservation programs**. *Child Welfare, 77,* 643–660.

Salzer, M.S., Rappaport, J., & Segre, L (1999). Professional appraisal of professionally led and **self-help groups**. *American Journal of Orthopsychiatry, 69,* 530–540.

Scriven, M . (1999). The fine line between evaluation and explanation. *Research on Social Work Practice, 9,* 521–524.

Secret, M., Jordan, A., & Ford, J. (1999). Empowerment evaluation as a social work strategy. *Health and Social Work, 24,* 120–127.

Shifflett, K, & Cummings, E.M. (1999). A program for educating parents about the effects **of divorce and conflict on children:** An initial evaluation. *Family Relations, 48,* 79–89.

Short, J.L (1998). Evaluation of a substance abuse prevention and mental health promotion program for **children of divorce**. *Journal of Divorce and Remarriage, 28,* 139–155.

Smith, L., Riley, E., Beilenson., P., Vlahov, D., & Junge, B. (1998). A focus group evaluation of drop boxes for safe **syringe disposal**. *Journal of Drug Issues, 28,* 905–920.

Stone, G., McKenry, P., & Clark, K. (1999). Fathers' participation in a **divorce education program:** A qualitative evaluation. *Journal of Divorce and Remarriage, 30,* 99–113.

Welsh, W., Jenkins, P., & Harris, P. (1999). Reducing **minority** over-representation in juvenile justice: Results of community-based delinquency prevention in Harrisburg. *Journal of Research in Crime and Delinquency, 36,* 87–110.

Figuring Costs

A simple way to calculate general costs of a program is to first determine the total amount of monies spent on program operations. These expenditures include costs associated with personnel (e.g., salaries, benefits, training), facilities (e.g., office space, computers, telephone, photocopying), clients (e.g., petty cash, special services, food), and other needs of the program. Once the overall costs have been determined, we can divide this amount by the total number of clients served for that fiscal period. The result will be an "outside estimate" of how much the program spent per client. For more detailed information on program effectiveness, we need to pay attention to program structure and process, something we do through process evaluation. The figures at the end of our calculations fluctuate depending on what we have included in program costs and how we have counted clients.

Neither of these tasks is as straightforward as it may seem. Do we include overtime, secretarial support, and advertising in our program costs, for example? In the case of counting clients, do we include repeat clients, or clients who drop out of the program after the first day? Do we factor in clients who call the program for information but never actually participate? The way a social service program is conceptualized has a considerable influence on the way data are collected and analyzed, as well as how costs are calculated.

Valuing Human Experiences

Cost-benefit evaluations in social services are necessary for fiscal accountability but are not sufficient for understanding the nature of human conditions or how social programs endeavor to improve them. It is difficult, if not impossible, to place a dollar amount on people's experience with social problems. How much does it cost to stop child abuse, for example? How much should society spend to bring discrimination of the elderly to an end? Such questions cannot be addressed in program-level evaluations.

Cost-benefit evaluations are particularly difficult to carry out in social work because so many of our client outcomes cannot be realistically (socially and professionally) measured in terms of dollars. In fact, it would be unthinkable to measure some client outcomes in terms of efficiency—such as counseling terminally ill cancer patients. Efficiency in terms of what?

The benefits of a job-training program that removes its clients from welfare rolls can be more easily quantified in terms of efficiency (cost savings) than a program that is designed to reduce the feeling of hopelessness in terminal cancer patients. Nevertheless, there is only so much money available for social service programs, and decisions regarding which ones to fund, no matter how difficult, have to be made—especially if funding decisions are made on efficiency criteria. We do not need to put a price on program results in order to use costs in decision making, but it is necessary to be able to describe in detail what results have been achieved via the expenditure of what resources.

BOX 3.4_____

PUBLISHED EXAMPLES OF
COST-BENEFIT EVALUATIONS
(Substantive Areas in **Bold**)

Beshai, N.N., (1991). Providing cost efficient detoxification services to **alcoholic patients**. *Public Health Reports, 105,* 475–481.

Egger, G.M., Friedman, B., & Zimmer, J.G. (1990). Models of **intensive case management**. *Journal of Gerontological Social Work, 15,* 75–101.

Ell, K. (1996). Social work and **health care practice** and policy: A psychosocial research agenda. *Social Work, 41,* 583–592.

Essock, S.M., Frisman, L.K., & Kontos, N.J. (1998). Cost-effectiveness of assertive **community treatment teams**. *American Journal of Orthopsychiatry, 68,* 179–190.

Fahs, M.C., & Wade, K. (1996). An economic analysis of two models of hospital care for **AIDS patients**: Implications for hospital discharge planning. *Social Work in Health Care, 22,* 21–34.

Greene, V.L., Lovely, M.E., & Ondrich, J.I. (1993). The cost-effectiveness of community services in a **frail elderly population**. *The Gerontologist, 33,* 177–89.

Holosko, M.J., Dobrowolsky, J. Feit, M.D. (1990). A proposed cost effectiveness method for use in policy formulation in **human service organizations**. *Journal of Health and Social Policy, 1,* 55–71.

Holtgrave, D.R, & Kelly, J.A. (1998). Cost-effectiveness of an **HIV/AIDS prevention intervention for gay men**. *AIDS, and Behavior, 1,* 173–180.

Hughes, W.C. (1999). Managed care meets community support: Ten reasons to include **direct support services** in every behavioral health plan. *Health and Social Work, 4,* 103–111.

Jackson, N., Olsen, L, & Schafer, C. (1986). Evaluating the treatment of **emotionally disturbed adolescents**. *Social Work, 31,* 182–185.

Keigher, S.M. (1997). What role for social work in the new **health care practice** paradigm? *Health and Social Work, 22,* 149–55.

Knapp, M. (1988). Searching for efficiency in long-term care: De-Institutional- isation and privatisation. *The British Journal of Social Work, 18,* 149–171.

Levy, R.L., & Bavendam, T.G. (1995). Promoting **women's urologic self-care**: Five single-case replications. *Research on Social Work Practice, 5,* 430–441.

Pike, C.L., & Piercy, F.P. (1991). Cost effectiveness research in **family therapy**. *Journal of Marital and Family Therapy, 16,* 375–388.

Pinkerton, S.D, & Holtgrave, D.R. (1998). A method for evaluating the economic efficiency of **HIV behavioral risk reduction interventions**. *AIDS, and Behavior, 2,* 189–201.

Prentky, R., & Burgess, A.W. (1990). Rehabilitation of **child molesters**: A cost-benefit analysis. *American Journal of Orthopsychiatry, 60,* 108–117.

Robertson, E., & Knapp, M. (1988). Promoting **intermediate treatment**: A problem of excess demand or excess supply? *The British Journal of Social Work, 8,* 131–147.

The role of cost-benefit evaluation for social service programs is not to attempt placing a value on human lives or experiences. Rather, it provides social workers a means to demonstrate responsible use of public funds. In so doing, we report not only the outputs and outcomes accomplished with support of program funds but also significant developments in our program's processes. Highlighting program developments along with program outcomes can show how we, as a profession, contribute to the understanding the complexities of the populations and problems targeted.

Another role of cost-benefit evaluation is to bring to light the real costs associated with studying and resolving social problems in society. Moreover, such evaluations can provide data that not only support future program funding requests but also allocate money to pay for associated evaluation efforts.

Cost-Benefit Questions

There are many examples of how cost-benefit evaluations can help us in our professional practice (see Box 3.4). The questions they can answer can be classified under three general categories:

— Unit Costs: What is the average cost per client? What is the average cost per unit of service (e.g., intake, assessment, intervention, follow-up)?
— Cost Distribution: What percentage of costs go to direct client services, administrative activities, and program development? What services were not provided due to lack of funds?
— Cost Reduction/Recovery: Is there any way in which cost could be reduced without loss of effectiveness, perhaps by offering group therapy instead of individual therapy? Are strategies for cost recovery possible?

SUMMING UP AND LOOKING AHEAD

This chapter briefly presented five types of evaluations. It stressed that each one has its separate purpose and each one answers a different type of evaluation question. The following chapter builds upon this one as it illustrates how we can plan and focus an evaluation.

KEY TERMS

Client Satisfaction: A program variable that measures the degree to which clients are content with various aspects of the program services that they received.

Cost-Effective: Describes a social service program that is able to achieve its program objectives in relation to its costs.

Cost-Efficient: Describes a social service program that is able to achieve its program objectives at less cost, compared to another program striving for the same objectives.

Demands: In needs assessment, something that is so desired by people that they are willing to "march" for it; to be differentiated from *needs* and *wants*.

Efficiency Assessment: An evaluation to determine the ratio of effectiveness or outcome to cost; does not contain data that may explain why the program is or is not efficient.

Evaluability Assessment: An appraisal of a program's components and operations intended to determine whether a program can, in fact, be evaluated for outcome, efficiency, or process; mainly used to construct meaningful and measurable program objectives that are derived from the program's goal.

Expressed Needs: In needs assessment, the opinions and views of people who are directly experiencing a problem; also known as *felt needs*.

Flow Chart: A diagram of client service delivery in which symbols are used to depict client movement throughout the service delivery system.

Formative Evaluation: See *process evaluation*.

Needs: In needs assessment, something that is considered a basic requirement necessary to sustain the human condition; to be differentiated from *demands* and *wants*.

Needs Assessment: An evaluation that aims to assess the need for a human service by verifying that a social problem exists within a specific client population to an extent that warrants services.

Outcome Assessment: See *outcome evaluation*.

Outcome Evaluation: A program evaluation that is designed to measure the nature of change, if any, for clients after they have received services from a social service program; specifically measures change on a program's objectives; also known as *summative evaluation* and *outcome assessment*.

Perceived Needs: In needs assessment, the opinions and views of people who are not directly experiencing a problem themselves.

Process Analysis: See *process evaluation*.

Process Evaluation: A type of evaluation that aims to monitor a social service program to describe and assess (1) the services provided to clients and (2) how satisfied key stakeholders are with the services provided. Data are used to provide ongoing feedback in order to refine and improve program service delivery; also known as *formative evaluation*.

Summative Evaluation: See *outcome evaluation*.

Wants: In needs assessment, something that is so desired by people that they are willing to "pay" for it; to be differentiated from *demands* and *needs*.

STUDY QUESTIONS

1. List the types of evaluation and discuss how each one can be used within a social service program that focuses upon "homelessness." What are their commonalities? What are their differences? Which one of the five do you believe is most needed in our profession? Justify your answer. Which one do you feel is the least useful in our profession? Once again, justify your answer.

2. How do needs assessments and evaluability assessments differ in purpose? How do the results of each affect client service delivery? Provide a concrete social work example throughout your discussion.

3. The social work program you are enrolled in is a social service program. Discuss how each one of the five evaluations could be utilized to evaluate it. Be very specific. Who are its stakeholders (Chapter 1)? Why?

4. What are *wants, demands,* and *needs*? How are they similar? How are they different?

5. What are perceived needs? Provide an example. What are expressed needs? Provide an example. Discuss the similarities and differences between the two, using one common social work example in your discussion.

6. After reading the first three chapters in this book, discuss in detail why it is important for a program to be well-conceptualized before it can be evaluated. Provide a concrete social work example throughout your discussion.

7. What are the similarities and differences between formative and summative evaluations. Provide a concrete social work example throughout your discussion.

8. How can client flow charts be useful for programs? Provide a concrete social work example throughout your discussion.

9. What are the similarities and differences between outcomes and outputs? Provide a concrete social work example throughout your discussion.

10. What is benchmarking? How can it be useful for program evaluations? Provide a concrete social work example throughout your discussion.

11. List and discuss the common characteristics of all evaluations as presented in this chapter. Provide a concrete social work example throughout your discussion.

REFERENCES AND FURTHER READINGS

Baugher, D. (1981). *Measuring effectiveness.* San Francisco: Jossey- Bass.

Bell, A. (1983). *Assessing health and human service needs.* New York: Human Sciences Press.

Booth, A., & Higgins, D. (1984). *Human service planning and evaluation for hard times.* Springfield, IL: Charles C. Thomas.

Borus, M.E., Tash, W.R., & Buntz, C.G. (1982). *Evaluating the impact of health programs.* Cambridge, MA: MIT Press.

Bryk, A.S. (1983). *Stakeholder-based evaluation*. San Francisco: Jossey-Bass.

Buros, O.K. (Ed.). (1978). *The eighth mental measurements yearbook* (2 vols.). Highland Park, NJ: Gryphon Press.

Chelimsky, E., & Shadish, W.R. (1997). *Evaluation for the 21st Century: A resource book*. Thousand Oaks, CA: Sage.

Ciarlo, J.A. (Ed.). (1981). *Utilizing evaluation: Concepts and management techniques*. Thousand Oaks, CA: Sage.

Guba, E.G., & Lincoln, Y.S. (1981). *Effective evaluation*. San Francisco: Jossey-Bass.

Ihilevich, D., & Gleser, G.C. (1982). *Evaluating mental health programs*. Lexington, MA: Lexington Books.

Isaac, S., & Michael, W.B. (1980). *Handbook in research and evaluation*. San Diego, CA: EDITS.

Kettner, P.M., Moroney, R.M., & Martin, L.L. (1990). *Designing and managing programs: An effectiveness-based approach*. Thousand Oaks, CA: Sage.

Levin, H.M. (1983). *Cost-effectiveness: A primer*. Thousand Oaks, CA: Sage.

Lidz, C.S. (Ed.). (1987). *Dynamic assessment*. New York: Guilford Press.

Lincoln, Y., & Guba, E. (1985). *Naturalistic inquiry*. Thousand Oaks, CA: Sage.

Love, A.J. (1991). *Internal evaluation: Building organizations from within*. Thousand Oaks, CA: Sage.

Madaus, G.F., Scriven, M., & Stufflebeam, D. (Eds.). (1983). *Evaluation models*. Boston: Kluwer-Nijhoff.

Mohr. L.B. (1995). *Impact analysis for program evaluation* (2nd ed.). Thousand Oaks, CA: Sage.

Murray, J.G. (1980). *Needs assessment in adult education*. Ottawa, Ontario, Canada: National Library of Canada.

Nowakowski, J. (Ed.). (1987). *The client perspective on evaluation*. San Francisco: Jossey-Bass.

Pecora, P.J., Fraser, M.W., Nelson, K.E., McCroskey, J., & Meezan, W. (1995). *Evaluating family-based services*. New York: Aldine.

Price, R.H., & Politser, P.E. (1980). *Evaluation and action in the social environment*. New York: Academic Press.

Reviere, R., Berkowitz, S., & Graves Ferguson, C. (Eds.). (1996). *Needs assessment: A creative and practical guide for social scientists*. Bristol, PA: Taylor & Francis.

Rossi, P.H. (1982). *Standards for evaluation practice*. San Francisco: Jossey-Bass.

Rossi, P.H., & Freeman, H.E. (1993). *Evaluation: A systematic approach* (5th ed.). Thousand Oaks, CA: Sage.

Rush, B., & Ogborne, A. (1991). Program logic models: Expanding their role and structure for program planning and evaluation. *The Canadian Journal of Program Evaluation, 6,* 95–106.

Rutman, L. (1980). *Planning useful evaluations*. Thousand Oaks, CA: Sage.

Scriven, M. (1991). *Evaluation thesaurus* (4th ed.). Thousand Oaks, CA: Sage.

Silkman, R.H. (Ed.). (1986). *Measuring efficiency*. San Francisco, CA: Jossey-Bass.

Thompson, M.S. (1980). *Benefit-cost analysis for program evaluation*. Thousand Oaks, CA: Sage.

Trochim, W.M. (1984). *Research design for program evaluation: The regression-discontinuity approach*. Thousand Oaks, CA: Sage.

Unrau, Y.A. (1997). Implementing evaluations. In R.M. Grinnell, Jr. (Ed.), *Social work research and evaluation: Quantitative and qualitative approaches* (5th ed., pp. 588–604). Itasca, IL: F.E. Peacock Publishers.

Washington, R.O. (1980). *Program evaluation in the human services*. Lanham, MD: University Press of America.

Weiss, C.H. (1972). *Evaluation research: Methods of assessing program effectiveness*. Englewood Cliffs, NJ: Prentice-Hall.

4

Chapter Outline

Planning and Focusing
an Evaluation

AN IMPORTANT PART of evaluation is planning—an exercise that involves clearly identifying what specific evaluation questions are to be answered and what decisions are to be made from evaluation results. The critical importance of planning and focusing an evaluation before its implementation is understood if we think about an event such as a family vacation. Rarely does a family embark upon their annual vacation without prior thinking and planning. To do so would risk ending up with a very expensive and unsatisfactory experience. To increase the likelihood that a vacation will stay within budget and meet the wishes of all family members requires up-front research of vacation possibilities, discussion with family members, and consideration of the family's resources—especially the family budget.

Planning evaluations are similar to planning a family vacation in that we want to research evaluation possibilities, have discussions with program stakeholders, and end up with a satisfactory experience. Of course, evaluations must stay within the limits of existing program resources as they aim to address specific questions or objectives. In addition, we need to know what specific data will be required to answer these questions, which in turn will help in the decision-making process. This is also the time to identify any other pressures of evaluation, such as accountability reports to funders.

By focusing an evaluation around clearly defined questions and issues, evaluation activities can be kept manageable, economical, and efficient. All too often stakeholders identify more interests than the evaluation can reasonably manage. Thus, the planning stage of an evaluation is a time to identify priority areas of interest and to identify data that can provide information about them. Evaluations that are not sufficiently focused generally result in large data collection efforts. Unfortunately, the large quantity of data collected usually compromises the quality of data collected, with much having poor reliability and validity.

On the other hand, a tightly focused evaluation makes it much easier to maintain the integrity of the data collection process and produce credible results. Thus, in general, it is preferable to carefully focus evaluation efforts on fewer areas of interest than to cast a broad net, looking at many things in the hope that marginal topics will benefit the program in some obtuse way.

Focusing an evaluation does not imply that only one part or aspect of a program or service will be of interest. In fact, there are usually a number of different interests that can be accommodated within a single evaluation. As we shall see in this chapter, an evaluation can focus on interests in areas of program need, process, and outcomes. Focusing an evaluation means that these interests are first identified and the evaluation activities are organized around them. Thus, there can be multiple points of focus within an evaluation, but it is important that these be clearly identified and planned from the beginning.

The focal points selected need not remain static. Focal points may be added or deleted as circumstances and experience dictate. This is particularly true in the monitoring approach to quality improvement, where the evaluation system is active over a longer period of time. However, developing an initial focus for an evaluation provides an organizing framework for carrying out the evaluation activities. Such a framework provides a common language for stakeholders as they discuss evaluation efforts over time, and provides an anchor for assessing change as the evaluation evolves.

Because programs and services are much more complex and multifaceted than the provision of direct services, our discussion of planning and focusing evaluations assumes a program-level evaluation (Chapter 8). However, planning is required at the case level as well (Chapter 7).

EVALUATION AS REPRESENTATION

In 1963, when President Kennedy was assassinated in Dallas, several photographers were on the scene and captured various perspectives on the unfortunate event. Abraham Zapruder, an amateur photographer, took a home movie that shows the entire ordeal. Two other people also took home movies that show part of the incident, and as many as six still photographers took at least one picture while shots were being fired. In addition, several other photographers took pictures before or after the assassination.

If we think carefully about it, it is obvious that none of the photographers or movie makers captured the incident itself, but each captured a *representation* of it. Some of these representations were more complete and more accurate than others. But in the end, each was only a representation. Mr. Zapruder's home movie is considered the most complete record. However it is shot from a great distance and is relatively grainy—at least by today's standards. In addition, it did not, as was true of home movies of the day, record sound. Thus, even this most complete record of the assassination captured only one element of it. In general, the representations created by the various photographers varied in their completeness and detail, as well as in what was actually captured on film.

The reader can relate to this by leafing through a family wedding album that captures key moments of that important day. Again, an album of a wedding is only a representation of it. Different representations are possible. Pictures could be taken from different perspectives at different times and the subjects within the photos may be composed in a different way. The accuracy of the representations depends on the photographer's equipment, location, timing, luck, and skill.

Evaluations are also representations. Any program is composed of hundreds of structures, processes, activities, and results. Although stakeholders sometimes hold beliefs to the contrary, no evaluation will capture all of these facets of a program. Of course, there are good and poor representations; a good evaluation will result in a representation in which stakeholders and decision makers can recognize key facets of the program.

Because an evaluation is a representation, an initial step in the evaluation process is to decide on the elements or facets of the program to be included in that representation. This is similar to the wedding photographer's deciding upon a picture format, a position from which to shoot the picture, the composition of the picture, the depth of field, and other technical elements that will constitute the album.

As you well know by now, social service programs are complex entities that contain numerous interlinking systems. A parent-teen mediation program, for example, will have specific procedures for intake, assessment, intervention, termination, and follow-up. An educational program, on the other hand, may deliver its services in the form of workshops, seminars, and presentations in addition to operating a library. These and other programs will be targeted toward specific population groups. The parent-teen mediation program, for example, may be designed to meet the needs of junior high school students and their caregivers in a specific geographical area.

The considerations just discussed are all client related, but there are also administrative systems supporting these services such as the activities of professional workers, volunteers, continuing education, and community relations. And we could enumerate a list of other processes, such as service activities and client outcomes, that could be of potential interest in an evaluation process.

COMMON CHARACTERISTICS OF ALL EVALUATIONS

As we know from the previous chapter, each of the five types of evaluation has a distinct purpose. Nevertheless, they all have much in common when it comes to planning and implementation. Common considerations to evaluation planning and implementation are introduced here, but they are discussed in more detail in other chapters of this book.

Program Models

As we have discussed in Chapter 2, if evaluations are to enhance quality improvement in programs, they must begin with a program blueprint or model. Indeed, program models provide the platform or stage for displaying "snapshots" or representations of the program.

The program logic model framework presented in Chapter 2, however, does not account for all operations of a program. In this text, *program objectives* are understood as being client related. Of course, a program has non–client-related objectives (such as to provide 5,000 hours of counseling, to admit 432 more clients by the end of the year, to enroll 35 adolescents in a certain program by a certain time), which are necessary in order for that program to survive, but they are hardly criteria by which to evaluate whether the program is making a quality impact on the lives of its clientele. These other non–client-related objectives are best understood as measuring *outputs* rather than *outcomes*.

Program survival necessarily means that program outputs must be monitored as part of evaluation. As such, an evaluation plan may include *maintenance or intermediate objectives* to this end, often for the exclusive purpose of satisfying funders or accreditation bodies. Such objectives are formulated in an effort to keep the program financially viable and involve efforts such as "to increase private donations by 25 percent in the next fiscal year," "to recruit 25 volunteers in the next six months," "to have three individuals complete the internship program by the end of the school year," and "to recruit and utilize four volunteers in covering the telephone lines."

Objectives that deal with training staff, recruiting clients, reaching a service quota, acquiring improved equipment, or restructuring the organization all serve a program maintenance function. In theory, a program that operates smoothly will yield more client success. Thus, while maintenance objectives are constructed for the program's benefit, they ought to indirectly link to improving client outcomes. Maintenance objectives, although necessary to the program's continued existence, are not the reason that the program is being funded. That is, programs are not funded merely to exist and perpetuate themselves; they are funded to produce positive social change, as would be reflected in their goal statements. Maintenance objectives are to programs what food is to human beings: We need to eat, we may even get great pleasure from eating, but in the final analysis we do not live to eat—we eat to live.

Resource Constraints

All evaluation types are subject to the same kinds of resource constraints—not enough time, staff, money, or evaluation know-how within a program. Additionally, many social service programs lack technological equipment such as computers and data base systems that can facilitate evaluation efforts. Nevertheless, evaluations can be conducted on a small or large scale and with or without the aid of technological advances.

The only thing worse than pressing forward with an evaluation in a program that does not have enough staff or money is pushing on within an unreasonably short time frame. Table 4.1 provides an evaluation time line that moves through each type of evaluation. Depending on the scope of the program, time lines can vary. However, note that a program that moves one cycle of each evaluation type in sequential order can expect to take 25 to 44 months to complete its efforts, between two and three and a half years.

TABLE 4.1   Implementation Time
                   for Evaluations

Types of Evaluations	Time Range
— Needs Assessment	3 to 6 months
— Evaluability Assessment	3 to 6 months
— Process Evaluation	12 to 18 months
— Outcome Evaluation	6 to 12 months
— Cost-Benefit Evaluation	1 to 2 months
Total	25 to 44 months

Evaluation Tools

No matter which evaluation type (i.e., needs, evaluability, process, outcome, cost-benefit) is used to carry out a program evaluation, evaluators draw from the same evaluation "toolbox." *Who* (or *what*) is chosen to provide evaluation data is a sampling issue, and *how* data are actually gathered is guided by data collection methods; both topics are covered in Chapter 5. The credibility of data collection instruments used in an evaluation is assessed by considering principles of measurement, which are discussed in Chapter 6. *When* data are collected is partly a design issue. Case-level designs are presented in Chapter 7, while program-level designs are covered in Chapter 8.

Politics and Ethics

It should be no surprise to hear that all evaluations are value-based—influenced by the beliefs and ideals of various stakeholder groups. Chapter 9 discusses the role of politics, ethics, and professionalism in conducting evaluations.

Cultural Considerations

The importance of cultural competence for evaluation is no less than it is for social work practice. The very nature of social work brings us in contact with diverse client groups. Race, ethnicity, gender, sexual orientation, disabilities, and age are all important features in understanding culture. Chapter 10 discusses issues for conducting culturally appropriate evaluations.

Presentation of Evaluation Findings

No matter what type of evaluation, we must establish evaluation procedures and protocols to ensure that they generate high-quality data. Chapter 11 presents strategies for monitoring evaluation activities.

It goes without saying that the conclusions reached in any type of evaluation must be useful for decision making. Useful evaluation results guide decisions concerning program policies, procedures, and practices. Therefore, before beginning any kind of evaluation it is worthwhile to project into the future the kinds of decisions we hope the evaluation results will address. Chapter 12 presents methods of translating evaluation data into information and how they can be useful for the quality improvement process.

FOCUSING AN EVALUATION

The experience of focusing evaluation is a bit like building a bridge across a great divide. The path leading up to the bridge is one filled with overcoming fears of evaluation, understanding the scope and types of evaluation, as well as rooting the program in a logic model (topics in earlier chapters of this book). The path ahead involves implementing evaluation through the use of trusted age-old social science procedures that are customized to suit individual program evaluation needs (topics of later chapters in this book). Thus, this chapter—focusing an evaluation—is about bridging the thinking and doing of evaluation by laying down our bricks and mortar—our evaluation plans—and thus making a commitment regarding how to proceed.

The most important thing to remember in this chapter is that any evaluation must have a specific, well-defined, meaningful focus. Even relatively small social service programs have virtually unlimited processes, activities, relationships, results, and outcomes—each of which could be of interest in an evaluative effort. This is true whether an evaluation is a one-shot project type evaluation or a monitoring type of evaluation in which data are continuously collected to obtain continuing feedback. When an evaluation is not sufficiently focused, it becomes diffuse, and more often than not it will fail to provide reliable and valid data to adequately answer the evaluation questions. As well, such evaluations may impose a major burden on the data collection and analysis phase. In short, poorly focused evaluations can become very disruptive to a program's ongoing provision of client service.

Focusing an evaluation is a science and an art form at the same time. It is not a task for the evaluator alone and must be undertaken in consultation with key stakeholders. Before stakeholders can make informed decisions about what should be included in an evaluation, however, it is important for them to understand what can be reasonably accomplished in a single evaluation. The achievements of any evaluation, of course, depend on many things such as the scope of the program, the number of stakeholders, the program's previous experience with evaluation, and the political support for evaluation. It is the role of the planner to communicate what is possible and not possible given the program's circumstances. One evaluation cannot do it all.

In our work with stakeholders there is often an initial confusion about what evaluations are and what products they can produce. Many mistakenly believe that an evaluation is actually an alternate version of the program and will capture every possible facet or nuance. Thus, stakeholders often press to include an unrealistic number of questions for the evaluation to address. The irony here is that many stakeholders, particularly line-level practitioners, initially oppose the idea of an evaluation altogether. Once they become involved in its planning, however, they push for including many evaluation questions and multiple interests, many of which may be relevant only to specific or unusual situations.

Unfortunately, more does not translate into better, and too many questions can lead to a fuzzy representative picture of the program. Thus, an evaluator's role in planning the evaluation is often one of helping stakeholders to focus on the key elements, or questions, that are to be included in the evaluative picture. Key elements are those that contribute most to the program's representation, which in turn will lead to a solid understanding of essential program processes and outcomes, which in turn will provide useful, relevant, reliable, and valid data for decision-making purposes.

PLANNING WITH STAKEHOLDERS

Stakeholders have a major interest in the effective operations and outcomes of a social service program. The types of stakeholders as presented in Chapter 1 include policymakers, administrators, practitioners, funders, general public, and clients. Each of these groups will undoubtedly have a variety of questions about a program's operations and outcomes. In some cases, these questions will overlap, and in others they will be unique to the specific type of stakeholder. In addition, one of these groups will usually have initiated the evaluation and may provide the funds to carry it out. Clearly, an evaluation will need to respond to the interests of the funding sponsor in addition to providing data useful to other stakeholder groups as well.

The process of focusing an evaluation involves identifying the questions and interests of the relevant stakeholder groups and prioritizing among these as necessary. During this phase the evaluator works collaboratively with the stakeholder groups, separately or in combinations.

An obvious place to begin this process is to clearly identify the logic model of the program and concentrate on its objectives and activities. Although these are often documented to some extent, there is seldom a comprehensive list of objectives and activities that are clearly understood by the various stakeholder groups. Thus, working with stakeholders to generate a full listing of objectives and activities both helps to make these explicit and furthers stakeholders' understanding of the program and the services it offers.

In addition to creating questions related to a program's objectives and activities, stakeholders can be encouraged to generate other relevant questions. Finally, stakeholders can also be assisted in examining the key decisions they need to make and in identifying the type of data that would be helpful in making these decisions.

Planning with stakeholders should end with clear statements about the program's objectives (client and maintenance), as well as a comprehensive listing of program activities, evaluation questions, and other information needs related to decision making—from the perspective of each stakeholder group. There will undoubtedly be some overlap among the lists generated by each stakeholder group and it is also likely that the list of items generated will be far greater than can be reasonably addressed in a project type evaluation or tracked in a monitoring situation.

The evaluator then needs to facilitate a process—involving the stakeholder groups individually or in groups—to identify high-priority items. As well, attention needs to be paid to what can be reasonably accommodated within the framework of the evaluation, taking into account the resources and time available, the effort required to collect the data, and what data are likely to be utilized to make specific recommendations.

As mentioned, stakeholders tend to generate too many questions for an evaluation rather than not enough. Not all questions, however, carry the same weight in an evaluation effort. For example, a politician may press for data that display the race of clients served by a program, while a line-level practitioner may question the effectiveness of group counseling interventions on client success. The politician's interest is "less weighty" and is easily addressed by collecting data on client race as part of regular intake procedures. The practitioner's question is "more weighty" because it has implications for overall program service delivery and evaluation design. First of all, the practitioner's question must be solidly rooted in the program's logic model in order to be considered as a part of the evaluation plan. Additionally, the question is one of cause-and-effect (i.e., Does group counseling lead to improved client outcomes?), and as such has direct implications for what evaluation design ought to be used.

The evaluator brings the technical evaluation expertise, and the stakeholders bring information about the program and their interests to the planning process. This requires effective communications, relationship skills, and negotiations between and among these people. It is important that the evaluator is able to help each group give voice to its requirements and to help reconcile multiple and often conflicting demands in a way that they can be accommodated within the finite scope of an evaluation project.

IDENTIFYING DATA NEEDS

Focusing an evaluation begins with identifying the data that are needed in order to make useful decisions. Generally these needs can be summarized into two broad categories:

1. Data that will help to make decisions (i.e., decisions about client need, program logic modeling, program processes, client outcomes, and cost-benefit; see Chapter 3)
2. Data that are required for other purposes such as accountability (i.e., coverage, service delivery, stakeholder, fiscal, legal, and professional; see Chapter 1)

Discussions and negotiations in the planning phase of an evaluation will lead to prioritizing the various (and sometimes competing) data needs of different groups of stakeholders. Consideration will then move to how and when the required data will be collected. It is always desirable to collect data in the most economical and nondisruptive manner possible. If practical, the best strategy is to integrate the data collection process of an evaluation with the data collection processes normally undertaken within the program itself. Collecting data is costly. Thus, it is important that the cost of including any variable in the evaluation plan will be justified by the benefit of the information derived from the data.

Integrating data collection into regular paperwork or documentation procedures of a program is easy to imagine but difficult to do. Adding client race to an intake form, for example, can be accomplished by including various categories of race that represent the local population served by a program. Common categories are: African American, Asian, Caucasian, Latino, and Native American. If the local population includes a large proportion of one racial group, then more specific categories may be warranted. Asian subgroups may include Chinese, East Indian, Korean, and Japanese, for example. The difficulty of integrating data collection items is especially apparent when trying to get many stakeholders to agree on priorities.

Adding race as one variable is simple enough, but what if there are 20 or more other variables of interest addressing areas such as client demographics, social service history, referral problems, and so on? The limit of how many questions to ask is set by the amount of time the program allots for intake procedures or similar data collection activities. Ultimately, some items will have to be deleted from data collection forms, so as not to compromise other aspects of client service delivery and not to overwhelm the client. The burden of deciding which data collection items to retain or reject can be lessened by evaluating each item with the priority evaluation questions decided by stakeholder groups. Items that are integral to answering questions are retained, while items that are distant or unrelated to the questions posed are rejected.

As previously discussed, evaluations are only representations, or snapshots if you will, of a social service program. They are not meant to reflect every aspect of it. However, effective evaluations provide data about a reasonable sampling of the most relevant processes, activities, and outcomes of a social service program. This is particularly the case where an evaluation takes the form of a monitoring system that provides periodic feedback about key aspects of the program's operations and outcomes. Carefully selecting what specific elements of a program's process and outcomes to track is a very important task.

SELECTING WHAT TO MONITOR

This section is based on work conducted with a family service program that has put into place a monitoring evaluation system and serves as an example of how to focus an evaluation. The primary purpose was to obtain timely feedback about key program processes and outcomes for the purpose of program development. A secondary purpose was to obtain useful information, via the collection of data, that would meet the accountability requests of funders and other outside stakeholders.

After considerable discussion with both the program's administrators and line-level social workers, it was decided that the program would track data in five areas: (1) client demographics, (2) service statistics, (3) quality standards, (4) feedback, and (5) client outcomes. As such, the evaluation would incorporate elements of needs assessment, evaluability assessment, process evaluation, and outcome evaluation.

Client Demographics

It is always desirable to have reliable and valid data about the clientele actually being served by the program, not only to ensure compliance with funding contracts, but also to identify any changes or trends in client profile. Client demographic data are useful in all types of evaluations. Table 4.2 provides a simple illustration of the types of variables that can be tracked in the client demographic area (left side) as well as methods of measuring these variables (right side). As can be seen, the client demographics to be measured are stated in the form of simple straightforward benchmarks. The target values of each benchmark were derived from the program's funding contract as well as from the program's goal, which reflects what kind of clientele is targeted by the program. By specifying client demographics as benchmarks, the program has clear targets toward which to work. Criteria are also explicitly established against which evaluation results can be eventually assessed.

Alternatively, it is also possible to phrase benchmarks in the format of objectives. Recall that qualities of clear objectives are that they are meaningful, specific, measurable, and directional (as described in Chapter 2). These qualities apply to both client-centered objectives and to maintenance or instrumental objectives. Objectives differ from benchmarks in that they do not specify a target value, as is the case in Table 4.2. It may be, for example, that instead of setting a benchmark to serve 200 individuals per month, a program

TABLE 4.2   Client Demographics

Benchmarks	Measures
— Serve 200 individuals overall, per month	— Count of Client Intake Forms
— 60% of clients will be single-parent families	— Item on Client Intake Form
— Less than 10% of clients will be clients who have been previously served	— Item on Client Intake Form

aims only to maintain the overall number of clients served from the previous year. Using objectives is preferable to using benchmarks when a specific target value is uncertain or cannot be reasonably estimated. Some people would also argue that using benchmarks alone tends to create a climate of "bean counting" more so than is the case with objectives.

In general, client demographics measure the number of clients served and their corresponding characteristics that are considered relevant to program services and outcomes. The variables in Table 4.2 can be easily tracked by data gleaned from a client intake form. Data about whether a client is new to the program, for example, can be readily captured by including one extra item (perhaps a checklist) on the program's intake form. Of course, it is important in the planning and focusing phase of an evaluation to determine that it is of interest to know if a client is, or is not, new to the program. If the data collection system is designed to capture these data in advance, it will be a simple matter to track this issue. If not, it may be inconvenient, confusing, and costly, to revise data collection or, if it is possible, to reconstruct the data at a later date. Using our example, the following simple item could be added to an intake form without much hassle:

Is this the first time you have received services from this program?

___ Yes

___ No

Client demographic data are important to funders, program administrators, and practitioners. By tracking these variables, program administrators can provide data to funders to verify that their programs' services are indeed being provided to the groups they intended. Funders, in turn, will welcome assurances that their funding is being used in the manner they have targeted.

Data about client demographic variables are useful for a number of reasons. If benchmarks are being met, for example, program administrators will be reassured to continue the services that have been provided. On the other hand, unmet benchmarks will alert administrators and practitioners alike to explore the reasons behind the shortfall. Perhaps program practices can be adjusted to ensure that intended clients are informed of the services offered and are welcomed to the program.

Alternatively, it is possible that the social needs within the community have changed over time and earlier targets are no longer realistic, as would be the case in a transient community where population demographics change regularly. Immigrants who had once lived downtown, for example, may now be moving into the suburbs and young professionals are perhaps moving in to replace them. In such a case, the program will have an early indication that its services should be adjusted to meet current needs.

Service Statistics

Service statistics provide a second focal point for our evaluation example. Service statistics are similar to client demographic data. However, the focus is on the services provided by the program (i.e., program processes) rather than on the program's clientele. Service, or process, data are of interest for accountability purposes in addition to program feedback and development.

Again, program administrators and funders will take interest in these data to ensure that the quantity of the program services corresponds to initial funding expectations, as well as to expectations as set out in the program's logic model. In addition, service statistics can also add to a solid understanding of program service delivery and operations. By tracking changes in various components of service delivery, for example, program administrators are in a better position to make informed decisions about reallocating their scarce resources. In short, with relevant data they will be able to manage resources more effectively and efficiently. For example, data about the volume of services provided during evening hours may lead to the reduction (or increase) of those hours.

Table 4.3 provides a simple example of benchmarks related to service statistics. The value set for the volume of services (in our case, 500 counseling sessions per month) corresponds to levels set in the funding agreement. The second service benchmark (in our case, 20 percent of services will be provided out of the center) reflects the program's intention to be more responsive to client needs by moving services out of the office and into the community.

TABLE 4.3   Service Statistics

Benchmarks	Measures
— 500 counseling sessions per month	— From Contact Information Form
— 20% of counseling sessions will take place out of center	— Item on Contact Information Form

Tracking service statistics related to the location where the services were delivered provides feedback about whether the current practices are in line with this objective.

As indicated in Table 4.3, data about a program's services can generally be captured through data entered on a program's contact form, or an equivalent document for recording case notes. As long as the type of service is recorded along with the amount of services provided, the volume of each type of service can be easily tracked. To determine the location and the time of service, specific items may need to be added to the contact form, or collected in a systematic way. To minimize paperwork, these items can be designed as check boxes.

Quality Standards

Quality standards are about practices that the program believes will lead to positive client outcome. These practices may be described by relevant standard setting through the professional literature or by official accrediting agencies such as the Council on Accreditation. Quality standards are usually a focal point for process evaluations, as they relate to practices that are expected to lead to certain client outcomes. The assumption is that "good" social work practices lead to "good" client outcomes.

Most social service programs hold strong beliefs about practices thought to best serve clients, but very few actually monitor the implementation of them. Of course, many social work practices, or interventions, are relatively complex and difficult to capture within a single evaluation effort. Nevertheless, some quality standards, as shown in Table 4.4, can be addressed within an evaluative framework.

The benchmarks specified in Table 4.4 relate to program beliefs that the most effective services are those provided to larger client systems, other than

TABLE 4.4   Quality Standards

Benchmarks	Measures
— Less than 25% of services will be provided only to single individuals	— Item on Contact Information Form
— A minimum of one community resource suggestion per family will be made during service provision	— Item on Contact Information Form

an individual—for example, to a parent-child dyad or to an entire family. The benchmark speaks to this by specifying that over 75 percent of "client contacts" will involve more than one person. Similarly, the program believes in the impact and helpfulness of community resources in strengthening and supporting families. Thus, another target is that at least one community resource suggestion per family will be made during the course of service provision.

The data needed to monitor these benchmarks can be collected through the creation of appropriate items on the contact form, or any other client log. Again, through strategic design, a check-box format will easily allow the capture of the data needed to track these two simple objectives.

Data relating to the achievement of quality standard objectives are helpful in the program planning and development process of an evaluation. Through collecting such data over time, the program can ensure that its beliefs about effective practices are translated into actual practice. Results falling short of the benchmark could result in revising the set values included in the benchmark or revising the program operations in some way to increase the likelihood of achieving the original value.

Alternatively, it may be determined that the gap is the result of unmet training need or attitudes held by staff members. In such a case, further staff development might be planned. On the other hand, if the benchmarks are met, as evidenced via credible data, existing practices and procedures could be examined in greater detail. For example, program practices could be monitored to determine what approaches are most effective in getting individual clients to accept help as part of a larger group (e.g., parent-child dyad, family). Additionally, benchmarks might be modified so that they align better with the professed quality standards.

In short, tracking quality standards provides data about the actual practices of a program and reveals when practices are not consistent with beliefs. Such data would lead to an examination of those practices with a view to further developing them.

Feedback

Feedback received from relevant stakeholders is another area to focus on in our evaluation example. Relevant groups may include clients, volunteers, referring agencies, or other stakeholder groups. More often than not, relevant feedback usually centers on client satisfaction of some kind. While such feedback does not clearly fit in any of the traditional types of evaluations, it is typically collected as an outcome but reflects client perceptions about program processes. High client satisfaction, or an otherwise high opinion of a program, does not necessarily correspond with successful client outcomes. In other words, clients may like a program but not experience any positive change as a result of it. Nevertheless, it is desirable that a program draws favorable opinions and comments from its stakeholders. If not, administrators and staff alike should be aware that satisfaction with the program is not high.

Table 4.5 provides a simple example of benchmarks relating to feedback—in this case, client feedback. The data to track this objective are collected by asking clients to fill out a simple client satisfaction survey at the time of the completion of services. In this case, there were five items on the survey, designed specifically for this program. The items deal with such matters as the helpfulness of services, the supportiveness of staff, and overall satisfaction with the program's services. Each item is in the form of a rating scale with four possible response categories. For example, helpfulness was measured by the item:

The services were helpful (check one):
___ Strongly Disagree
___ Disagree
___ Agree
___ Strongly Agree

TABLE 4.5   Feedback (Client)

Benchmarks	Measures
— 70% of clients rate item *helpfulness* as "Agree" or "Strongly Agree"	— Satisfaction Survey Item 1
— 75% of clients rate item *satisfaction* "High" or "Very High"	— Satisfaction Survey Item 5

As Table 4.5 shows, the program set a benchmark that a minimum of 70 percent of service recipients will rate this item as "Agree" or "Strongly Agree." To measure overall satisfaction, an item was included that read:

My overall satisfaction with these services is:

___ Very Low

___ Low

___ Moderate

___ High

___ Very High

The benchmark set was that 75 percent of the clients should rate this item as "High" or "Very High." This would in turn indicate a minimum expected level of overall satisfaction with the services offered by the program.

Client Outcomes

An evaluation system is seldom complete without some attention to client outcomes, or client results, which is the reason that the social service organization exists in the first place. Thus, client outcomes always lie outside of the program, with the clients; they reflect changes in clients. Client outcomes are always directly tied to program objectives as stated in the program logic model.

Table 4.6 provides examples of benchmarks used to monitor program objectives, or client outcomes. As can be seen, one benchmark is expressed in terms of a minimum mean score of 3.4 on five items of a rating scale, designed

TABLE 4.6   Client Outcomes

Benchmarks	Measures
— Grand mean of 3.4 on first 5 items of Educational Outcomes Form	— Educational Outcomes Feedback Form designed specifically for the program
— Average self-esteem score less than 30 on exit from program	— Hudson's Index of Self-Esteem
— Average improvement of 15 points in peer relations on exit from program	— Hudson's Index of Peer Relations

specifically for the program. Of course, the value 3.4 has meaning only if we know the possible range of the rating scale. If scores can range from 1 to 5 (and 5 is high), we would interpret the data more positively than if scores ranged from 1 to 10 (and 10 is high). Chapter 6 discusses rating scales as methods of measurement; they can easily be constructed in such a way that they can directly and meaningfully monitor program objectives.

The two other benchmarks included in Table 4.6 are expressed as an average minimum score and an average gain score on two separate standardized measuring instruments, Hudson's Index of Self-Esteem (Figure 6.1) and Hudson's Index of Peer Relations. As we will see in the Chapter 6, standardized instruments are always preferable to use in outcome measurements because their reliability and validity have been previously determined and demonstrated. Thus, such measures generally have more credibility than locally constructed instruments.

It should be noted that the last two outcome benchmarks imply different research designs. Specifying a score of less than 30 on the exit from the program on the Index of Self-Esteem implies a one-group posttest only design. As we will see in Chapter 8, such a design allows a description of the level at which clients leave at the end of the service, but the design does not make it possible to determine the amount of change, if any, that has taken place. However, because the Index of Self-Esteem is known to have a clinical cutting score of 30 (i.e., scores higher than 30 indicate a clinical problem), the meaning of the objective can be interpreted more clearly.

The objective specifying an average improvement of 15 on the Index of Peer Relations (this would actually be a reduction of 15 points because this instrument uses higher numbers to indicate greater problems) implies a one-group pretest-posttest design. That design not only provides a description of the group at the end of the service, but also provides a description of the group at the time of entry and therefore allows a determination of what change has taken place. Of course, because the design involves only clients who have received program services, it cannot be concluded that the program caused the change. A control group (a parallel group of clients who did not receive program services) is needed to conclude such causality.

Outcome measurement is an increasingly important topic among social service programs. Evaluation data relating to outcomes serve the needs of multiple stakeholders. Funders and administrators can use it to assure themselves of the effectiveness of the program and thereby demonstrate accountability. To ensure that the program is operating in the most effective manner possible, administrators and staff can examine outcome results and make program adjustments as necessary. For professionals providing direct services, outcome measures provide a framework for case-level evaluations and facilitate accurate and honest communications with clients.

SUMMING UP AND LOOKING AHEAD

This chapter looked at the planning of an evaluation from a broad perspective by demonstrating how an overall plan for an evaluation can be developed and provides an example of what one program chose to monitor. In next chapters, we will look at how the overall plan is operationalized by the tasks of sampling, data collection, design, data management, and information reporting.

KEY TERMS

Client Demographics: Client variables that are usually obtained from Client Intake Forms.

Client Outcomes: Data on how well clients are doing upon completion of the program (and follow-up as well).

Feedback: Data generated by various stakeholder groups that shed light on how the program is meeting its objectives.

Program Model: A clear understanding of how a social service program is organized to achieve successful client outcomes.

Quality Standards: Standards that the program believes will lead to positive client outcomes.

Resource Constraints: Various types of physical and monitory constraints that are placed upon a social service program and hinder the program from achieving successful client outcomes.

Service Statistics: These data are used primarily for funding purposes and feedback on how the program is doing. They are usually generated from Client Contact Forms.

STUDY QUESTIONS

1. Discuss why planning an evaluation is a very important aspect of its total success. Provide a social work example throughout your discussion.

2. Discuss why an evaluation is only a representation of the "total picture."

3. Discuss the common characteristics of all evaluations and present a common social work example throughout your discussion.

4. Discuss in detail why we should use program models in social service agencies.

5. List and discuss the various resource constraints that need to be taken into account before doing a program evaluation.

6. What are evaluation tools?

7. Discuss why it is important to include as many stakeholders as possible in the initial development of an evaluation.

8. List and discuss the various concepts a social service program could monitor that could be used in an evaluation.

9. This chapter stresses the importance of planning and focusing an evaluation before carrying it out. List the difficulties an evaluator would likely encounter if he or she did not develop an evaluation plan *before* beginning evaluation activity.

10. As part of a program evaluation, an executive director of a social service program wants to know how satisfied are all of her stakeholders with program services. What does the executive director need to consider if she wants to ensure that the evaluation findings will provide broad representation of *all* stakeholder groups?

11. Identify the common characteristics that impact planning and focusing activities for all types of evaluation. How do these common features help an evaluator in putting together an evaluation plan?

12. A major strategy for focusing an evaluation is developing clearly articulated evaluation questions. Explain how such questions can be used to guide evaluations once they are underway.

13. A common problem of getting input from multiple stakeholders is developing too many evaluation questions, which in turn produces too much data. Discuss how too much data can be problematic for a social service program.

14. What are client demographics? Why are they important data to collect in a program evaluation?

15. It is possible to plan an evaluation of a social service program around multiple focal points such as client demographics, service statistics, quality standards, stakeholder feedback, and client outcomes. Think of a social service program that you are familiar with and develop two questions that might be asked of each focal point.

16. Think about the grade you are striving to achieve for this class. Imagine that you are going to evaluate your class performance to monitor your learning. You decide on three key focal points for your evaluation: class attendance, reading class material, and class participation. Develop a benchmark for each focal point that you believe is necessary to achieve in order to assist you with earning the grade that you desire.

17. This chapter presented an example of a program that picked five focal points for monitoring an evaluation: client demographics, service statistics, quality standards, stakeholder feedback, and client outcomes. Rank these focal points in order of most to least important. Provide a rationale for your rankings.

18. What is the difference between quality standards and service statistics? Give examples of data that might be collected for each.

19. An executive director is under pressure to produce an evaluation of his program in a short period of time. As a consequence, he does not want to include all stakeholder groups in planning the evaluation. Imagine that you are hired as the evaluator. What guidance would you provide the executive director around his decision to exclude some stakeholder groups from the planning phase of the evaluation?

REFERENCES AND FURTHER READINGS

Council on Social Work Education. (2000). Baccalaureate and masters curriculum policy statements. Alexandria, VA: Author.

Gabor, P.A., & Grinnell, R.M., Jr. (1994). *Evaluation and quality improvement in the human services.* Boston: Allyn & Bacon.

Gabor, P.A., Unrau, Y.A., & Grinnell, R.M., Jr. (1997). *Evaluation and quality improvement in the human services* (2nd ed.). Boston: Allyn & Bacon.

Gabor, P.A., Unrau, YA., & Grinnell, R.M., Jr. (2001). Program-level evaluation. In R.M. Grinnell, Jr. (Ed.), *Social work research and evaluation: Quantitative and qualitative approaches* (6th ed., pp. 481–509). Itasca, IL: F.E. Peacock Publishers.

Grinnell, R.M., Jr. (2001). Introduction to research. In R.M. Grinnell, Jr. (Ed.), *Social work research and evaluation: Quantitative and qualitative approaches* (6th ed., pp. 1–19). Itasca, IL: F.E. Peacock Publishers.

Grinnell, R.M., Jr., & Siegel, D.H. (1988). The place of research in social work. In R.M. Grinnell, Jr. (Ed.), *Social work research and evaluation* (3rd ed., pp. 9–24). Itasca, IL: F.E. Peacock Publishers.

Hornick, J.P., & Burrows, B. (1988). Program evaluation. In R.M. Grinnell, Jr. (Ed.), *Social work research and evaluation* (3rd ed., pp. 400–420). Itasca, IL: F.E. Peacock Publishers.

National Association of Social Workers (1999). *Code of ethics.* Washington, DC: Author.

Raymond, F.B. (1985). Program evaluation. In R.M. Grinnell, Jr. (Ed.), *Social work research and evaluation* (2nd ed., pp. 432–442). Itasca, IL: F.E. Peacock Publishers.

Rubin, A., & Babbie, E. (1997). Program-level evaluation. In R.M. Grinnell, Jr. (Ed.), *Social work research and evaluation: Quantitative and qualitative approaches* (5th ed., pp. 560–587). Itasca, IL: F.E. Peacock Publishers.

Unrau, Y.A., & Gabor, P.A. (2001). Evaluation in action. In R.M. Grinnell, Jr. (Ed.), *Social work research and evaluation: Quantitative and qualitative approaches* (6th ed., pp. 510–526). Itasca, IL: F.E. Peacock Publishers.

Weinbach, R.W. (2001). Research contexts. In R.M. Grinnell, Jr. (Ed.), *Social work research and evaluation* (6th ed., pp. 41–54). Itasca, IL: F.E. Peacock Publishers.

P a r t   II

Tools of Evaluation

111

5

Chapter Outline

Data Sources, Sampling, and Data Collection

THIS CHAPTER PRESENTS the basic tools for the evaluation enterprise. These tools are borrowed from quantitative and qualitative research methods that are common in social science research. As is the case in any line of work, evaluators who master the proficient use of their tools produce better-quality products than those who do not. The evaluation toolbox is filled with strategies to create, maintain, and repair evaluation plans. This chapter covers the tools that assist us in determining where our evaluation data will come from and how to obtain these data.

Using the image of an evaluation toolbox helps us to understand that there is little use in rummaging through our tools without having a project or purpose in mind. It is fruitless, for example, to debate strategies for measuring client outcomes when program objectives have not yet been formulated (see Chapter 2). It is also unproductive to deliberate who ought to supply evaluation data in the absence of clearly articulated evaluation questions (see Chapters 3 and 4). When program structure and logic models are ambiguous and/or reasons for conducting an evaluation are vague, there is not much in the evaluation toolbox that will help us produce a meaningful evaluation.

In this chapter we present well-known strategies to select data sources and methods to collect data that will address our evaluation questions. These two tool sets are more commonly known as sampling and data collection. Thus, our discussion ought to bring back fond memories of basic research principles and concepts learned in previous research courses.

DATA SOURCES

Data sources furnish either new or existing data that are used in an evaluation. *New data sources* are original data provided specifically for the purposes of responding to current evaluation questions. Who are these providers? They are any number of individuals that represent our stakeholder groups (Chapter 1). For example, federal and state personnel such as politicians, government officials, and staff from professional organizations can be data sources. Among program workers there are therapists, caseworkers, case aides, as well as many collateral professionals such as teachers, psychologists, and workers from other programs, to supply data. Clients, as a stakeholder group, are a common data source. A client can refer to an individual, a family, a group, a community, or an organization depending on how a program defines it.

Existing data sources are previously recorded documents or artifacts that contain data relevant to current evaluation questions. Generally speaking, existing data were originally collected for some purpose other than our current evaluation. Most likely, stakeholders supplied the original data some time ago but data can be found in documents or databases in one of three areas:

— Client data and information (e.g., client records, social histories, genograms, service plans, case notes, clinical assessments, progress reports)
— Program data and information (e.g., program logic models, previous evaluation reports, program contracts or funding applications, meeting minutes, employee time and activity logs, employee resumes, quality assurance records, accounting records)
— Public data and information (e.g., census data, government documents, published literature)

How do we decide whether to use new or existing data sources? It depends on the specific focus of our evaluation. In particular, the final questions developed for an evaluation guide us to who, or what, is our best data source for our inquiry. For example, a needs assessment aimed at increasing understanding about the adolescents involved in crime in their community may phrase its evaluation questions to emphasize different data sources:

— Do adolescents who commit crimes see themselves as having a future in their community?

— To what degree do parents feel responsible for their children's criminal behavior in the community?
— What are the legal consequences for adolescents who commit crimes in the community?

Clearly, the first question targets adolescents as an essential data source, while the latter questions give priority to parents of adolescents and legal professionals or documents, respectively. Each question, of course, can be answered by any number of data sources. No doubt, parents have opinions about their children's futures and, certainly, the legal community has a perspective on adolescent crime. Each data source, however, can only speculate about questions that ask what others are thinking or feeling.

The *best* data sources are those that have firsthand or direct knowledge regarding the experience that is the subject of evaluation. Adolescents, for example, have firsthand data relating to their perceptions about their future. In contrast, data sources that have indirect knowledge about an experience can provide only secondhand data. Adolescents, for example, can offer secondhand data about their parents' feelings either through speculation or by sharing observations about their parents' behaviors. In needs assessments, firsthand data are referred to as expressed needs, while secondhand data are called perceived needs.

Given that firsthand data sources are not always available or easily accessible for evaluation purposes, we often look to secondhand data to inform us. Client records, for example, are filled with data that describe client problems and strengths, as well as their patterns of change. Practitioners and not the clients themselves, however, typically provide these data. As such, evaluation findings that are based solely on client records as a data source are weaker than those that use firsthand data sources or multiple data sources.

This discussion of firsthand and secondhand data sources raises questions as to which can provide the most accurate and truthful data. Who is in a better position to say which interventions most effectively help clients? Is it the clients themselves, the practitioners who work with them, or the funders who shell out the money to pay for services? Do practitioner notes truly reflect practitioner perceptions about their cases or is it necessary to interview them firsthand? These types of questions have no easy answers. As a result, it is desirable to include a variety of data sources in any evaluation so that multiple perspectives are considered.

Our bias is to give priority to data sources that have directly experienced the social need, the program process, or the program outcome that is being evaluated. As mentioned earlier, firsthand data sources generally convey their experiences with more candor and accuracy than anyone who has only indirect involvement. A pregnant teenager, for example, can more aptly speak to her fears of motherhood than anyone else, including her own mother. Likewise, a worker can more succinctly describe the details of an interaction with a client than a supervisor or a professional colleague. Generally speaking, the further removed a data source is from the experience or event in question, the greater the possibility for misrepresentation of the actual experience, or the more vague the data will be.

SAMPLING

After selecting data sources for an evaluation, our next step is to develop a comprehensive list of every single person, document, or artifact that could possibly provide the data for our evaluation. This list is called a *sampling frame* and identifies all units (i.e., people, objects, events) of a population from which a sample is drawn. A needs assessment, for example, may target *people*—every community member, regardless of what stakeholder group they represent. A process evaluation, on the other hand, may target *objects*—all client records opened in the last fiscal year. Or an outcome evaluation may target events— every client discharge after a minimum of two weeks of program services. Of course, each evaluation type can sample people, objects, or events, depending on its focus.

If our sampling frame includes only a small number of units, then it is feasible to include each one as a data source. A social service program employing 12 practitioners can easily collect data from all of its workers. On the other hand, the 12 practitioners, each with caseloads of 40, together serve 480 clients at one time, which amounts to oodles of data collection activity— perhaps more than the program can manage. Having more data source units than we can handle is a problem that our sampling tools can help fix.

After a sampling frame is defined, we then want to develop a plan that tells us how many units to pick and which specific units to choose. Do we want every member of a community to provide data or only a select number? Do we review every client record opened in the last fiscal year, or just a portion of them? A sampling plan gives us explicit criteria so that there is no question as to which units will provide data for our evaluation and which units will not.

There are two sampling approaches for to consider for any evaluation: probability and nonprobability sampling. A *probability* sampling approach is one that ensures that each unit in a sampling frame has an equal chance of being picked for an evaluation. Units are selected randomly and without bias.

BOX 5.1_____

TYPES OF PROBABILITY SAMPLING STRATEGIES

Simple Random Sampling

• Each unit included in the sample is selected using a chance procedure (e.g., rolling dice, random numbers, flipping a coin).

Systematic Random Sampling

1. Determine the total number of units in a population (e.g., $N = 400$ client sessions)
2. Determine the desired sample size for the evaluation (e.g., $N = 100$ client sessions).
3. Calculate the interval to select units; that is, divide the total number of units by the desired sample size (e.g., 400/100 = 4, every 4th session will be selected).
4. Randomly select the starting point using chance procedures (e.g., rolling dice) to pick a number between 1 and 4 (e.g., 3).
5. Begin with session 3, and pick every 4th one thereafter (e.g., 003, 007, 011 to session 399)

Stratified Random Sampling

1. Variables or strata relevant to evaluation are identified (e.g., African American, Caucasian, Latino community members).
2. The percentage of each variable category in the population is determined (e.g., African American, 28%, Caucasian, 60%, and Latino, 12%).
3. The total sample size is determined (e.g., $N = 100$).
4. Strata totals are calculated (e.g., 28% of 100 = 28 African American, 60% of 100 = 60 Caucasian, 12% of 100 = 12 Latino).
5. Use simple random sampling procedures to select units for each strata until all totals are filled.

Cluster Sampling

1. Determine sample size (e.g., $N = 250$).
2. Identify naturally occurring clusters of units within a population (e.g., $N = 200$ residential blocks within a community).
3. Use simple random sampling to select a portion of clusters (e.g., 40 residential blocks).
4. Calculate the number of units within the selected clusters (e.g., 10 homes per block = 400 units)
5. Use random sampling procedures to selected 250 homes from 400.

Those that are chosen will provide data for the evaluation, while units that are not picked will not. Four common probability sampling strategies are summarized in Box 5.1.

The major benefit of probability sampling approaches is that they produce samples that are considered to be representative of the larger sampling frame from which they were drawn. As such, data collected from the sample can be generalized, or applied, to the sampling frame as a whole. Suppose that we randomly pick 100 out of a possible 821 members of the community that is the focus of a needs assessment evaluation. If the 100 people in our sample were picked using probability sampling approaches, then we can be confident that the data they provide will give the same information as if we had collected data from all 831 members. Probability sampling, therefore, saves time and money by using a randomly selected subset to provide information about a larger group.

In contrast, *nonprobability* sampling methods do not give each unit in a sampling frame an equal chance of being picked for an evaluation study. In other words, individual people, objects, or events do not have an equal opportunity to supply data to an evaluation. Four types of nonprobability sampling strategies are summarized in Box 5.2.

Nonprobability sampling methods are used in situations where it is desirable to limit our pick of data sources based on some unique characteristic. It may be that we want to collect data only from clients who drop out of treatment before completion. Or, we may want only data related to cross-cultural worker-client interactions. When it is possible to decisively identify conditions or characteristics that define a subset of data sources, it is not necessary to sample beyond it. In other words, it is not necessary to sample from all units when the data of interest are possessed by only a select few.

Nonprobability sampling strategies aim to produce quality firsthand data from sources that share something in common. They are often used when evaluation questions seek to more fully understand the dynamics of particular experiences or conditions rather than questions that aim to generalize the characteristics of a sample to the larger sampling frame from which it was drawn. This latter aim is achieved by using probability sampling methods.

When is it necessary to use sampling strategies in an evaluation plan? Sampling strategies or tools can effectively address the following problems that are commonplace in all types of evaluations:

— The sampling frame is so large that data cannot realistically be collected from every unit (e.g., needs assessment of a community of 10,000 people, a process evaluation of daily worker-client interactions in an institutional setting).

— Previous efforts to include all units in a sampling frame have failed (e.g., client response rate to satisfaction surveys is low, client records are voluminous and not systematically organized).

BOX 5.2 _____

TYPES OF NONPROBABILITY SAMPLING STRATEGIES

Convenience or Availability Sampling

- *grp of C's assess to*
- Includes nearest or most available units.
- *seeking volunteers out of prg.*

Purposive Sampling

- Includes units known or judged to be good data sources based on some theoretical criteria.

  target people who are best informants

Quota Sampling

1. Variables relevant to evaluation are identified (e.g., gender, age)
2. Variables are combined into discrete categories (e.g., younger female, younger male, older female, older male).
3. The percentage of each category in the population is determined (e.g., 35% younger female, 25% younger male, 30% older female, 10% older male).
4. The total sample size is determined (e.g., $N = 200$).

5. Quotas are calculated (e.g., 35% of 200 = 70 younger females, 25% of 200 = 50 younger males, 30% of 200 = 60 older females, 10% of 200 = 20 older males).
6. The first available data sources possessing the required characteristics are selected until each quota is filled.

Snowball Sampling *Use for hard to reach clients*

1. A small number of data sources are located in the population of interest.
2. At the same time that data are collected from these sources, they are also asked to identify others in the population.
3. The newly identified data sources are contacted, data are obtained, and requests for additional data sources are made.
4. Continue until the desired sample size is obtained.

— Only data sources with unique characteristics are desired (e.g., practitioners who balance their workload well, clients that successfully complete treatment, client reports that influence courtroom decisions).

— Program resources are limited and can support data collection from only a portion of the sampling frame (e.g., program costs for evaluation are limited, program only employs one or two practitioners who are responsible for data collection).

— Multiple data sources are desired (e.g., data are collected from clients, workers, records).

DATA COLLECTION

While data sources supply data, *data collection methods* are concerned with the manner in which data are obtained. Data collection methods consist of detailed plans of procedures that aim to gather data for a specific purpose—that is, to answer our evaluation questions. No matter what data collection method is used, we want to develop protocols that will yield credible data. That is, we want our data to be judged as accurate and trustworthy by any reviewer.

It should be clear by now that how an evaluation question is stated guides the selection of the data collection method(s). As discussed earlier, we do not want to subscribe to a data collection method before we know our evaluation questions. To do so risks collecting a flurry of data that in the end are worthless. Put simply, the combination of data sources and data collection methods chosen can influence the nature and type of data collected. Having well-thought-out and meaningful evaluation questions before we reach for our data collection tools helps to steer clear of disaster that comes when evaluation plans drift apart from an evaluation's purpose.

How we go about collecting data to answer evaluation questions depends on many practical considerations—such as how much time, money, and political support is available at the time of the study. Political factors affecting an evaluation study are discussed in Chapter 9. For now, it is enough to say that given the resource limitations affecting most programs and the importance of a program's developmental history, it is worthwhile to explore existing data before making data collection plans.

In the vast majority of evaluations, existing data are not adequate to answer current evaluation questions, and new data must be collected. For comprehensive coverage, an evaluation ought to use multiple data sources and data collection methods—as many as are feasible for a given program.

There are various data collection methods available, and each one can be used with a variety of data sources, which are defined by who (or what) supplies the data. As discussed above, data collection methods are concerned with either existing or new data.

Obtaining Existing Data

Given that existing data are previously recorded, they can be used to address questions that have an historical slant. Existing data can be used to profile recent and past characteristics or patterns that describe communities, clients, workers, or program services. For example, we may be interested in knowing the past demographic characteristics of a community, or a synopsis of worker qualifications for recent employees, or the general service trends of a program since its beginning.

When existing data are used, the method of data collection is primarily concerned with detailing the steps taken to assemble relevant materials. In other words, what are the rules for including or excluding existing data? The challenge of gathering existing data is in recovering old documents or artifacts that may not be easily accessible. It may be, for example, that program start-up events were recorded but they are in the possession of a former employee, or that client records are sealed by court orders. It may also be that there are no existing data because none was ever recorded. Existing data can be found in documents and data sets.

Documents and Reports

Reviewing existing documents is a process whereby we examine data that have been previously analyzed and summarized. In other words, someone has already studied the raw, or original, data and presented his or her interpretations or conclusions. Examples of such materials include published research studies, government documents, news releases, social service agency directories, agency annual reports, client reports, and worker performance reviews.

The data available in existing documents and reports are typically presented in either narrative or statistical form. *Existing narrative data* are presented as words or symbols that offer insight into the topic being addressed. Reading the last 10 annual reports for a program, for example, can shed light on the program's evolution. Examining training materials for workers can reveal strengths and weaknesses of program services. Reviewing client files can give strong clues about underlying practice principles that drive client service delivery.

Existing statistical data involve numbers and figures that have been calculated from original raw data. These data provide us with information about specific client or program features in a summarized form. The most recent program annual report, for example, may state that client racial makeup is 35 percent African American, 40 percent Caucasian, 15 percent Hispanic or Latino, and 10 percent other. Or it may report that program clients, on average, received 10 more service hours compared to clients from the previous year. These reports rarely include the raw data used to formulate such summary statements, but they are informative. Box 5.3 illustrates how Fran, a clinical director of a private nonprofit agency, gathered existing statistics to inform her evaluation questions.

By looking at what others have already done, we can save valuable time and frustration—learning from mistakes made by others and avoiding unnecessarily reinventing the wheel. Data and information gleaned from existing published reports and articles provide us with a picture of how much attention our evaluation questions have previously received, if any. Additionally, we can find out if other similar evaluations or studies have taken place. If so, what did they find? What tools were used, either successfully or unsuccessfully? In short, existing reports provide a starting point from which to begin and refine current evaluation plans.

Data Sets

Data sets, also called databases, store existing raw or original data and organize them such that all data elements can be connected to the source that provided them. For example, a typical client database for a program stores demographic data (e.g., age, race, gender) for each client. Because data in existing data sets were collected for purposes other than answering our evaluation questions, they are called secondary data.

Before we get ahead of ourselves, it is important to note that data sets or databases can be manual or automated. Most social service programs use *manual* data sets, which amount to no more than a collection of papers and forms filed in a folder and then stored in a filing cabinet. In contrast, *automated* data sets store data electronically in computers. The format or setup of an automated database can mirror its manual predecessors but because of the power of computers, it is far more sophisticated and efficient.

Even though many social service programs are beginning to automate, old data sets will likely remain in manual form until the day comes when an ambitious evaluator determines that the old data are needed to inform current evaluation questions. Whether manual or automated, databases can accommodate secondary data in both narrative and statistical form. Two common data sets that evaluators can tap into are census and client and/or program data sets.

BOX 5.3_____

USING GOVERNMENTAL AND PRIVATE-AGENCY STATISTICS

Fran is clinical director of a private, nonprofit agency that provides foster care, group-home care, and residential treatment for children in a small city in Arizona. She has noticed that there is a higher number of ethnic minority children in her agency's caseload than would be expected based on the proportion of ethnic minority children in the general population. She decides to do a study of this issue using existing statistics already gathered by various sources as her data collection method.

Fran first talks with the information specialist at the local library, asking for help to conduct a computer search through the library's existing data bases. The search reveals a series of reports, titled *Characteristics of Children in Substitute and Adoptive Care,* that were sponsored by the American Public Welfare Association and that provide several years of data reported by states on their populations of children in various kinds of foster and adoptive care.

She also locates an annual publication produced by the Children's Defense Fund, and this provides a variety of background data on the well-being of children in the United States. Next, Fran checks in the library's government documents section. She locates recent census data on the distribution of persons under the age of 18 across different ethnic groups in her county.

Fran now quickly turns to state-level resources, where a quick check of government listings in the telephone book reveals two agencies that appear likely to have relevant data. One is the Foster Care Review Board, which is comprised of citizen volunteers who assist juvenile courts by reviewing the progress of children in foster care statewide.

A call to the Board reveals that they produce an annual report that lists a variety of statistics. These include the number of foster children in the state, where they are placed, and how long they have been in care, and descriptive data.

Fran also learns that the Board's annual reports from previous years contain similar data, thus a visit to the Board's office provides her with the historical data needed to identify trends in the statistics she is using. Finally, she discovers that two years earlier the Board produced a special issue of its annual report that was dedicated to the topic of ethnic minority children in foster care, and this issue offers additional statistics not normally recorded in most annual reports.

Another state agency is the Administration for Children, Youth, and Families, a division of the state's social services department. A call to the division connects her with a staff member who informs her that a special review of foster children was conducted by the agency only a few months before.

Data from this review confirm her perception that minority children are overrepresented in foster care in the state, and it provides a range of other data that may be helpful in determining the causes of this problem.

From these sources Fran now has the data she needs to paint a detailed picture of minority foster children at the national and state levels. She also has the ability to examine the problem in terms of both point-in-time circumstances and longitudinal trends, and the latter suggest that the problem of overrepresentation has grown worse. There is also evidence to indicate that the problem is more severe in her state than nationally.

Finally, corollary data on related variables, together with the more intensive work done in the special studies by the Foster Care Review Board and the Administration for Children, Youth, and Families, give Fran a basis for beginning to understand the causes of the problem and the type of research study that must be done to investigate solutions.

Census Data

Census data are periodic summaries of selected demographic characteristics, or variables, that describe a population. Census takers obtain data about variables such as, age, gender, marital status, and race. To obtain data in specific topic areas, census takers sometimes obtain data for such variables as income level, education level, employment status, and presence of disabilities. Census data are extremely useful for evaluations in that they aim to compare a program sample to the larger population. For example, is the racial or gender makeup of a program's clientele similar to that of the community at large?

Census data also are useful for providing a general picture of a specific population at a certain point in time. The more data obtained during a census taking, the more detailed the description of the population. The disadvantage of census data is that they can become outdated quickly. Census surveys occur every ten years and take considerable time to compile, analyze, and distribute. In addition they give only a general picture of a population. The census, for example, provides data only on the average age of residents in a community, or the percentage of childless couples living in a certain area. While these data are useful for developing an average community profile, they do not provide us with a clear idea of individual differences or how the members of the community describe themselves.

Client and Program Data

More and more social service programs rely on client and program data to produce reports that describe the services they provide. They most likely utilize data taken from client and program records. Client data sets consist of data elements that are collected as part of normal paperwork protocols. Intake forms, assessments, progress reports, and critical incident reports all produce a wealth of client data that range from client demographics to rates of treatment progress.

Program data sets encompass various administrative forms that are part and parcel of program operations. They include such things as time sheets; employee resumes and performance evaluations; audit sheets; accreditation documents; training and supervision schedules; and minutes of meetings. Program data sets also yield rich data, including variables such as number of clients served, worker demographics and qualifications, type of service provided, amount of supervision and training, and client outcomes.

There are two problems associated with client and program data sets. First, the data are often incomplete or inconsistently recorded. Because data collection occurred previously, it is usually not possible to fill in missing data or correct errors. Second, the data apply to a specific point in time. If program conditions are known to change rapidly, then past data may no longer be relevant to present evaluation questions. For example, social service programs that rely on workers to collect client and program data and who suffer from high staff turnover rates are faced with the problem that data collected by past workers may not be pertinent to present situations.

Obtaining New Data

Existing data provide us with general impressions and insights about a program but rarely can they address all questions of a current evaluation. As such, the activities of an evaluation almost always involve the process of collecting new or original data. Four basic strategies for collecting new data are: (1) face-to-face individual interviews, (2) surveys, (3) group interviews, and (4) observation.

Face-to-Face Individual Interviews

Individual interviews with data sources can produce new, or original, data about social needs, program processes, or program outcomes. Interviewing is a data collection method that requires us to identify, approach, and interview specific people who are considered knowledgeable about our questions. Interviewees are sometimes referred to as key informants and can include various people: professionals, public officials, agency directors, program clients, and select citizens, minorities, to name a few.

Interviews can be formal, and use a structured interview schedule such as the one presented for a needs assessment in Box 5.4. Overall, face-to-face interviews with individuals are generally used to ask questions that permit open-ended responses. To obtain more detailed data, we simply develop additional questions to provide more structure and help to probe for answers with more depth. Question 4 in Box 5.4, for example, could be expanded so that key informants are asked to consider past or present services, or gaps in services. Structured interview schedules are used when we have some prior knowledge of the topic being investigated and we want to guide data sources

BOX 5.4_____

NEEDS ASSESSMENT QUESTIONS

1. With what social problems or issues are area residents confronted?

2. What perceptions do residents have regarding their community?

3. What types of services are viewed by residents as being important?

4. Which services are needed most?

5. To what extent are residents satisfied with the present level of social services in Airdrie?

6. Is there a transportation problem for residents who use services that are available in Calgary?

---

to provide us with particular kinds of information. On the other hand, when very little is known about our problem area, we can use informal unstructured interviews to permit more of a free-flowing discussion. Informal interviews involve more dialogue, which produces not only rich and detailed data but also more questions.

Suppose, for example, we want to learn more from a group of community residents who stay away from using our social service program (needs assessment). We might begin each interview by asking a general question, What keeps you from using our social service program? Depending on the responses given, subsequent questions may focus on better understanding the needs of our interviewees, or how existing services might be changed to become more accessible. Both structured and unstructured interviews rely on interviewer-interviewee interaction to produce meaningful data.

Surveys

The main goal of surveys is to gather opinions from numerous people in order to describe them as a group. Such data can be collected using in-person or telephone interviews, or via mailed surveys. Surveys differ from the structured and unstructured interview schedules used in face-to-face data collection. Specifically, survey questions are more narrow and yield shorter responses. Additionally, they do not rely on interviewer skills to generate a response.

Creating survey questions that yield valid and reliable responses is a prickly problem because it is a task that appears simple but is not. Consider the likely reactions of students if a teacher were to include a vague or confusing question on a class test. Generally speaking, people do not like or do not respond to questions that do not make sense or are presented ambiguously. This is an important issue and one that we discuss in detail in the next chapter.

Whether surveys are conducted in-person, by telephone, or by mail depends upon several factors. The advantages and disadvantages of each are presented in Figure 5.1. Given that one of the major disadvantages of mail surveys is a low response rate, we present the following strategies to increase the number of respondents.

— A cover letter stating the purpose of the evaluation is sent with each mailed survey. The letter confirms that all responses are confidential and is most effective when signed by a high-ranking official (e.g., program executive director, minister, school principal, politician).

— Use extremely clear and simple instructions.

— Include a stamped, self-addressed return envelope with the survey.

— Include free incentives to potential respondents (e.g., movie passes, fast-food coupons, pencil with agency logo).

— Send a follow-up letter to all respondents as a prompt to complete the survey.

— Offer respondents the opportunity to request the results of the evaluation.

Group Interviews

Conducting group interviews is a data collection method that permits us to gather the perspectives of several individuals at one time. They are more complex than individual interviews because they involve interaction between and among data sources. Three strategies for group interviews—presented from least to most structure—are open forums, focus groups, and nominal groups. The procedures for carrying out each group interview are summarized in Box 5.5

Open Forums   Open forums have the least structure of the three group interview strategies. They are generally used to address general evaluation questions. Holding an open forum involves inviting stakeholders to discuss matters of interest to our evaluation. Open forums include such things as town

Technique	Advantages	Disadvantages
Face-to-face Interview	◦ Highest response rate ◦ Subjects tend to provide more thoughtful answers ◦ Allows for longer, more open-ended responses ◦ Allows recording of nonverbal information ◦ Can reach disabled or illiterate respondents ◦ Interviewer can clarify questions for respondent ◦ Subjects more willing to answer sensitive questions	◦ Highest cost ◦ Highest chance for introduction of experimenter bias ◦ Respondent may react to personality of interviewer rather than content of the interview ◦ Interviewer may mis-record response
Mail Survey	◦ Lowest cost ◦ Subjects can read and respond to questions at their own pace ◦ Visual arrangement of items on written instrument can facilitate comprehension ◦ Provides greatest sense of anonymity/ confidentiality ◦ Lowest chance of introduction of experimenter bias	◦ Lowest response rate ◦ Feasible only with subjects having relatively good reading skills ◦ No opportunity to clarify confusing items ◦ Difficult to get in-depth or open-ended responses ◦ Cannot ensure that intended respondents are the actual respondents
Telephone Survey	◦ Relatively low cost ◦ Can be completed quickly ◦ Interviewer can clarify questions for respondent ◦ Can reach respondents with poor reading/writing skills ◦ Allows direct computer data entry	◦ Not useful for low-income respondents who do not have a telephone ◦ High initial vocal inter-action, misses nonverbal responses ◦ Requires simple questions, unless a copy of the survey instrument is mailed in advance

FIGURE 5.1   Advantages and Disadvantages to Three Principal Approaches to Data Collection in Survey Research

BOX 5.5

GROUP INTERVIEWING STRATEGIES AND PROCEDURES

Open Forums

- Identify the event or problem to be addressed.
- Allow individuals to spontaneously share responses and reactions.
- Record responses as given, without editing or discussion.

Focus Groups

- Develop open-ended questions.
- Give orientation or introduction to topic of focus.
- Allow time for participants to read or review material if necessary (maximum 30 minutes).
- Determine how data are going to be recorded (e.g., audiotape, videotape, observation, notetaking).
- Facilitator begins with first open-ended questions and facilitates discussion.
  Four major facilitation tasks:
  - Keep one person or small group from dominating discussion.
  - Encourage quiet ones to participate.
  - Obtain responses from the entire group to ensure fullest possible coverage.
  - Balance between role of moderator (managing group dynamics) and interviewer.
- When responses are exhausted, move to next question.
- Analyze data from group.

Nominal/Delphi Method

- Develop open-ended questions.
- Put 6-9 people in a comfortable seating arrangement, preferably a circle.
- Procedures are to give overview of the group task, give each member a sheet with questions on it (and room to record answers), instruct members NOT to talk to each other, allow time for individuals to record responses privately.
- Use round-robin approach to list all answers from step 3. No discussion.
- Discussion focuses on clarifying what responses mean to ensure that everyone has a common understanding of each response.
- Individually rank top 5 responses.
- Round-robin to list rankings.
- Brief discussion for clarification if necessary.

hall meetings or phone-in radio talk shows. They simply provide a place and an opportunity for people to assemble and air their thoughts and opinions about a specific topic.

Open forums are generally most useful in gaining reactions or responses to a specific event or problem. An executive director, for example, might hold an open forum for all program stakeholders to announce plans to conduct a program evaluation. The forum would provide stakeholders the opportunity to respond to the idea, as well as give input. The advantage of public forums is that they offer widespread involvement. Their main disadvantage is that they tend to draw a deliberate and select group of people who have strong opinions (one way or another) that are not necessarily shared by all.

Focus Groups   Focus groups aim to gather data for the purposes of exploring or testing ideas. They consist of individuals who are reasonably familiar with the topic slated for discussion but not necessarily familiar with each other. Focus groups involve an interactive discussion that is designed to gather perceptions about a predefined topic of interest from a group of select people in an accepting and nonthreatening setting.

Conducting focus groups requires the skills of a group facilitator who sets the ground rules for the group and helps to guide discussion. The facilitator, as a group leader, provides guidelines for group process and aids the dialogue for group members. Questions prepared in advance help to set the parameters for discussion. Indeed, the questions presented earlier in Box 5.4 could be used to guide a focus group for a needs assessment.

The main task of focus group facilitators is to balance group discussion such that group members stay centered on the questions being asked but also stimulate one another to produce more in-depth and comprehensive data. The results of a focus group may show similar and divergent perceptions of participants.

Nominal Groups   The nominal group technique is a useful data gathering tool for evaluation because it provides for an easy way to collect data from individuals in a group situation. The composition of a nominal group is similar to that of a focus group in that it includes individuals who can answer a particular question of interest but may or may not know each other. A nominal group, however, is far more structured than a focus group, and group interaction is limited. The nominal group process involves members working in the presence of others but with little interaction. Refer again to Box 5.5 for a summary of the steps for conducting a nominal group.

The most obvious advantage of a nominal group is collecting data from numerous sources in an efficient manner. Nominal group process typically takes two to four hours, depending on the size of the group and the number of questions asked. Because of the gamelike nature of the technique, participants can find the experience fun. When a cross section of group participants is recruited, the process can yield a comprehensive response to evaluation questions.

Observation

Observation as a data collection method is different from interviewing and surveying in that the data source watches a person, event, or object of interest and then records what was seen. A major tenet of observation as a data collection method is that it produces objective data based on observable facts. Two types are structured observation and participant observation.

Structured Observation   Structured observations occur under controlled conditions and aim to collect precise, valid, and reliable data about complex interactions. An impartial observer is trained to fix his or her eyes on particular persons or events and to look for specifics. The observation can take place in natural or artificial settings, but the conditions and timing of them are always predetermined. The data recorded reflect the trained observers' perceptions of what they see; and the observers are not directly involved with the people or the event being observed.

For example, a program may want to set up observations of parent-adolescent dyads to better understand how families learn to problem-solve together. The dimensions of problem solving are predefined such that the observer knows precisely what to look for. It may be that the observer watches for each time the parent or child verbally expresses frustration with the other as they work through a problem. Another dimension of problem solving to watch for may be the degree of confidence parents convey to their children at the beginning, middle, and end of the problem-solving exercise. To obtain objective data, the observer cannot be directly or indirectly involved with the case being observed. In other words, workers and their supervisors are not eligible to observe families on their caseload.

Another evaluation effort may seek to describe exemplary cross-cultural supervision practices. In this scenario, the observer follows a protocol to tease out supervisory behaviors that demonstrate cultural competence. Once again, the rules for observation and recording data are set out ahead of time and the observer adheres to these fixed guidelines. In this case, the observer records only observations related to cultural competence and not general competence, for example.

Because structured observations rely on observer interpretation, it is useful to capture the observation episode on videotape to allow for multiple viewing and multiple viewers. Also, training observers to a level of unmistakable clarity about what to watch for and what to document is essential. The more precise the protocols for structured observation, the more consistent the data.

Participant Observation   Participant observation differs from structured observation on two main features: The observer is not impartial and the rules for observation are far more flexible. As participant to the event under scrutiny, the observer has a vested interest in what is taking place. An executive director could be a participant observer in a sobriety support group offered by her program, for example, given that she has influence in how the group is run and has a stake in the group's success.

The challenge of participant observers is to balance their dual roles so that data are based on fact and not personal impressions. The benefit of participant observation is that members of group are in a better position to pick up subtle or cultural nuances that may be obscure to an impartial viewer. Consider the scenario of the parent-adolescent dyad working toward improving their problem-solving skills. Choosing to use a participant observer such as the assigned worker or another family member may well influence data collection. Specifically, an observer that is personally known to the parent and adolescent can better detect verbal expressions of frustration or parent behaviors displaying confidence than can a stranger.

Unlike structured observers, participant observers interact with the people they are watching. In other words, the participant observer is free to dialogue with his or her research subjects to verify observations and to check out interpretations. Participant observer interviews are unique in their tone and how they are carried out. Figure 5.2 compares the features of a participant observer interview with a typical in-person survey interview.

FITTING DATA COLLECTION TO THE PROGRAM

Program workers conduct most data collection for program evaluation. As a result, it is necessary to choose data collection tools that fit well within the normal range of paperwork duties for workers. Feasible data collection methods possess three qualities. They are: (1) easy to use, (2) they fit within the flow of program operations, and (3) they are designed with user input.

Ease of Use

Data collection methods should help workers to do their jobs better—not tie up their time with extensive paperwork. Data collection tools that are easy to use also minimize the amount of writing that workers are expected to do and the

Survey Interview	Participant Observation Interview
1. It has a clear beginning and conclusion.	1. The beginning and end are not clearly defined. The interview can be picked up later.
2. The same standard questions are asked of all research participants in the same order.	2. The questions and the order in which they are asked are tailored to certain people and situations.
3. The interviewer remains neutral at all times.	3. The interviewer shows interest in responses, encourages elaboration.
4. The interviewer asks questions, and the interviewee answers.	4. It is like a friendly conversational exchange, but with more interview-like questions.
5. It is almost always with a single research participant.	5. It can occur in group setting or with others in area, but varies.
6. There is a professional tone and businesslike focus. Diversions are ignored.	6. It is interspersed with jokes, asides, stories, diversions, and anecdotes, which are recorded.
7. Closed-ended questions are common, with rare probes.	7. Open-ended questions are common, and probes are frequent.
8. The interviewer alone controls the speed and direction of the interview.	8. The interviewer and insider jointly influence the pace and direction of the interview.
9. The social context in which the interview takes place is not considered and is assumed to make little difference.	9. The social context of the interview is noted and seen as essential for interpreting the meaning of responses.
10. The interviewer attempts to shape the communication pattern into a standard framework.	10. The interviewer adjusts to the insider's norms and language usage, following his or her lead.

FIGURE 5.2   Survey Research Interviews Versus Participant Observation Interviews

amount of time it takes to complete them. Data collection instruments that are easy to use develop through a process of trial and error. Often other programs have already created such instruments.

The National Center of Family Based Services, for example, has developed an intervention and activity checklist for use by home-based family service programs. The checklist contains various interventions and activities in which workers are instructed to check appropriate columns that identify which family members (e.g., children, primary caretakers, other adults) were involved in specific intervention activities (e.g., supportive counseling, problem-solving skills, home budgeting).

When data collection instruments have not yet been created, then program staff are faced with developing their own. Suppose, for example, that we asked workers employed at a youth drug and alcohol counseling program to record their daily intervention activities with clients by listing them out on a piece of paper. After reviewing their written annotations, we note that the following activities were recorded: gave positive feedback, rewarded youth for reduced alcohol consumption, discussed positive aspects of the youth's life, cheered youth on, and celebrated youth's new job. These descriptors all serve a common function—praise. Thus, for this group of workers, we might create a single checklist item called praise.

Clearly, the checklist approach loses important detail that was captured by workers in their handwritten notes, but a frequency of checklist items does give a picture as to what type of activities are being used by workers. The point here is that it is much easier for workers to check items off of a list than it is to record details of every interaction with a client.

Appropriateness to the Flow of Program Operations

Data collection tools should be designed to fit within the context of the social service program, to facilitate the program's day-to-day operations, and to provide data that will ultimately be helpful in improving program operations and client service delivery. Data that are routinely collected from clients ought to have both case- and program-level utility. For instance, if client intake forms have workers identify client referral problems, then these data ought to have utility for client assessment and intervention, as well as value for describing typical referral problems of program clientele. Data that are not used (i.e., not summarized or reviewed) should not be collected in the first place.

Ideal data collection instruments serve multiple program functions. First, they offer a record of case-level intervention that can be used to review individual client progress. Second, components of the data collection instruments can be aggregated to produce a program summary. Third, the instruments can be used as a principal component of supervisory meetings. Finally, they can also inform case review discussion as they can convey the major client problems, treatment interventions, and worker activities in a concise manner. Overall, data collection tools that are well integrated with program operations function to capture resourcefulness and innovativeness among workers; they do not thwart creativity by burying workers in unreasonable paperwork expectations.

Design with User Input

It should be clear by now that the major users of data collection instruments are line-level workers. Workers often are responsible for gathering the necessary data from clients and others. Therefore, their involvement in the development and testing of the data collection instruments is critical. Workers can provide valuable input in many areas. They can provide suggestions for formatting, procedures, and use. Workers who see the relevance of recording data will likely record more accurate data than workers who do not. Regardless of what data collection methods are used, training is inevitable if data collection is to produce consistent data.

DEVELOPING A DATA COLLECTION MONITORING SYSTEM

The monitoring system for data collection is closely linked to administration and supervision practices within a program. This is because program data are integral to delivering client services. Data about a program's background, client profile, and staff characteristics can, more or less, be collected at one time period. These data can be summarized and stored for easy access. Program changes such as staff turnover, hours of operation, or caseload size can be duly noted as they occur.

In contrast, data that are routinely collected ought to be monitored and checked for reliability and validity. Time and resources are a consideration for developing a monitoring system. When paperwork becomes excessively backlogged, it may be that there is simply too much data to collect, data collection instruments are cumbersome to use, or staff are not invested in the evaluation process.

Quality data collection requires several explicit procedures that need to be laid out and strictly followed. Minimal training is needed for consistent data collection. It is rather inefficient to train all social workers within a single program to collect data. Alternatively, it is advisable to assign data collection tasks to a small number of workers who are properly trained in the data collection effort. These individuals do not necessarily have to have any background in evaluation procedures; they simply need to have good interviewing skills and be able to following basic standardized instructions.

A monitoring system also functions as a feedback loop for data collected; that is, data collected are routinely shared with key stakeholders. Funders and policy makers receive feedback from annual reports or, perhaps, new proposals. Program data may also be disseminated more broadly, such as in an article in the local newspaper.

Developing a feedback system for internal stakeholders such as program administrators and workers is absolutely essential. Making data available on a regular basis helps to keep staff focused on the program's goal and objectives and allows them make incremental changes as needed. Discussing data can also stimulate important questions such as, What activities best explain client progress? Or regress? Are program services realistic? Are any client groups being ignored? When program personnel have an opportunity to respond to data they have collected, program development becomes more purposeful and focused.

SUMMING UP AND LOOKING AHEAD

This chapter covered some of the basic tools of evaluation—sampling and data collection. These tools are used only after programs have developed their logic models and articulated their evaluation questions. Evaluators can choose from numerous sampling and data collection methods. The pros and cons of each must be assessed in light of the unique context for each program. Ultimately, programs should strive to collect data from firsthand sources. Additionally, data collection methods ought to be easy for workers to use, fit within the flow of a program, and be designed with user input.

KEY TERMS

Census Data: A periodic governmental count of a population using demographic measurements.

Cluster Sampling: A multistage probability sampling procedure in which a population is divided into groups or clusters, and the clusters, rather than the individ- uals, are selected for inclusion in the sample.

Computerized Data Systems: An automated method of organizing single units of data to generate summarized or aggregate forms of data.

Contextual Data: Empirical or subjective data that reflect the circumstances of the problem and help to explain the outcome or score.

Data Collection Method: Procedures specifying techniques to be employed, measuring instruments to be utilized, and activities to be conducted in implementing a quantitative or qualitative research study.

Data Set: A collection of related data items, such as the answers given by respondents to all the questions in a survey.

Data Source: The provider of the data, whether it be primary—the original source, or secondary—an intermediary between the research participant and the researcher analyzing the data.

Direct Observation: An obtrusive data collection method in which the focus is entirely on the behaviors of a group, or persons, being observed.

Empirical Data: Isolated facts presented in numerical or descriptive form that have been derived from observation or testing, as opposed to data derived from inference or theory.

Focus Groups: A group of people brought together to talk about their lives and experiences in a free-flowing, open-ended discussion that typically focuses on a single topic; a semi-structured group interview.

Follow-Up Data: Collecting client data (as measured by a program's objectives) at specific points after clients have exited the program (e.g., three months, six months, one year).

Key Informants: Individuals who are considered knowledgeable about the social problem that is being investigated and who provide new or original data through interviews. Examples are professionals, public officials, agency directors, social service clients, and select citizens.

Multistage Probability Sampling: Probability sampling procedures used when a comprehensive list of a population does not exist and it is not possible to construct one.

Nominal Groups Technique: A group of people brought together to share their knowledge about a specific social problem. The process is structured using a round-robin approach and permits individuals to share their ideas within a group but with little interaction between group members; a structured group interview.

Nonsampling Errors: Errors in study results that are not due to sampling procedures.

Observer: One of four roles on a continuum of participation in participant observation research; the level of involvement of the observer participant is lower than the complete participant and higher than the participant observer.

Obtrusive Data Collection Methods: Direct data collection methods that can influence the variables under study or the responses of research participants; data collection methods that produce reactive effects.

One-Stage Probability Sampling: Probability sampling procedures in which the selection of a sample that is drawn from a specific population is completed in a single process.

Participant Observation: An obtrusive data collection method in which the researcher, or the observer, participates in the life of those being observed; both an obtrusive data collection method and a research approach, this method is characterized by the one doing the study undertaking roles that involve establishing and maintaining ongoing relationships with research participants who are often in the field settings, and observing and participating with the research participants over time.

Participant Observer: The participant observer is one of four roles on a continuum of participation in participant observation research; the level of involvement of the participant observer is higher than the complete observer and lower than the observer participant.

Probability Sampling: Sampling procedures in which every member of a designated population has a known chance of being selected for a sample.

Public Forum: A group of people invited to a public meeting to voice their views about a specific social problem; an unstructured group interview.

Purposive Sampling: A nonprobability sampling procedure in which individuals with particular characteristics are purposely selected for inclusion in the sample; also known as judgmental or theoretical sampling.

Qualitative Data: Data that measure quality or kind.

Quantitative Data: Data that measure quantity or amount in variables or constants.

Quota Sampling: A nonprobability sampling procedure in which the relevant characteristics of a sample are identified, the proportion of these characteristics in the population is determined, and participants are selected from each category until the predetermined proportion (quota) has been achieved.

Random Sampling: An unbiased selection process conducted so that all members of a population have an equal chance of being selected to participate in the evaluation study.

Sample: A subset of a population of individuals, objects, or events chosen to participate in or to be considered in a study; a group chosen by unbiased sample selection from which inferences about the entire population of people, objects, or events can be drawn.

Sampling Frame: A listing of units (people, objects, or events) in a population from which a sample is selected.

Sampling Theory: The logic of using methods to ensure that a sample and a population are similar in all relevant characteristics.

Secondary Analysis: An unobtrusive data collection method in which available data that predate the formulation of a research study are used to answer the research question or test the hypothesis.

Secondary Data: Data that predate the formulation of the research study and which are used to answer the research question or test the hypothesis.

Secondary Data Analysis: A data utilization method in which available data that predate the formulation of an evaluation study are used to answer the evaluation question or test the hypothesis.

Secondary Data Source: A data source that provides nonoriginal, secondhand, data.

Secondary Reference Source: A source related to a primary source or sources, such as a critique of a particular source item or a literature review, bibliography, or commentary on several items.

Simple Random Sampling: A one-stage probability sampling procedure in which members of a population are selected one at a time, without chance of being selected again, until the desired sample size is obtained.

Snowball Sampling: A nonprobability sampling procedure in which individuals selected for inclusion in a sample are asked to identify additional individuals who might be included from the population; can be used to locate people with similar points of view (or experiences).

Structured Observation: A data collection method in which people are observed in their natural environments using specified methods and measurement procedures. See Direct Observation.

Subjective Data: Isolated facts, presented in descriptive terms, that are based on impressions, experience, values, and intuition.

Survey: A method of collecting evaluation data in which individuals are asked to respond to questions that are designed to describe or study them as a group; can be conducted by mail or telephone.

Systematic Random Sampling: A one-stage probability sampling procedure in which every person at a designated interval in the population list is selected to be included in the study sample.

STUDY QUESTIONS

1. Imagine that you are asked to design an evaluation of your social work education program. List all data sources that you might include to inform the evaluation. What are the strengths and weaknesses of each? Identify the top three sources that you would recommend for use in the evaluation.

2. A social service program aims to collect satisfaction data from every client (over 200 per year) at termination of services using a mailed satisfaction questionnaire. Unfortunately, only 20 percent of clients ever return the questionnaire. How can random sampling be used to assist with this problem of low response rate? Given what you know about sampling, devise a strategy that might increase the program's response rate.

3. What are the advantages and disadvantages of using new data (and existing data) in an evaluation?

4. You are asked to develop an evaluation plan to address the following question: How do clients experience the intake process in a social service program. What data collection method would provide the "best" data for this evaluation? Explain your choice.

5. Surveys are one of the most common data collection methods used in program evaluation, however response rates are typically poor. Discuss strategies that an evaluator could use to increase the number of surveys that get returned.

6. What are the three different types of group interviews? Describe a program evaluation situation that would be ideal for use of each type.

7. Observation, as a data collection method, relies on the observer to interpret what he or she sees. What steps can observers take to minimize bias in their observations?

8. Discuss why it is important for data collection procedures to fit within the normal range of paperwork duties for workers in a social service program? What problems are likely to occur if evaluation data result in an excessive amount of paperwork?

9. What are three qualities of data collection methods that are considered *feasible*? Give an example of each.

10. Why is a data collection monitoring system important to an evaluation?

REFERENCES AND FURTHER READINGS_____

Gabor, P.A., & Ing, C. (2001). Sampling. In R.M. Grinnell, Jr. (Ed.), *Social work research and evaluation: Quantitative and qualitative approaches* (6th ed., pp. 207–223). Itasca, IL: F.E. Peacock.

Krysik, J.L. (2001). Secondary analysis. In R.M. Grinnell, Jr. (Ed.), *Social work research and evaluation: Quantitative and qualitative approaches* (6th ed., pp. 331–346). Itasca, IL: F.E. Peacock.

LeCroy, C.W., & Solomon, G. (2001). Content analysis. In R.M. Grinnell, Jr. (Ed.), *Social work research and evaluation: Quantitative and qualitative approaches* (6th ed., pp. 367–381). Itasca, IL: F.E. Peacock.

McMurtry, S.L. (2001). Survey research. In R.M. Grinnell, Jr. (Ed.), *Social work research and evaluation: Quantitative and qualitative approaches* (6th ed., pp. 297–330). Itasca, IL: F.E. Peacock.

Rogers, G., & Bouey, E. (2001). Participant observation. In R.M. Grinnell, Jr. (Ed.), *Social work research and evaluation: Quantitative and qualitative approaches* (6th ed., pp. 277–296). Itasca, IL: F.E. Peacock.

Sieppert, J., McMurtry, S.L., & McClelland, R. (2001). Utilizing existing statistics. In R.M. Grinnell, Jr. (Ed.), *Social work research and evaluation: Quantitative and qualitative approaches* (6th ed., pp. 347–366). Itasca, IL: F.E. Peacock.

Unrau, Y.A. (2001). Selecting a data collection method and data source. In R.M. Grinnell, Jr. (Ed.), *Social work research and evaluation: Quantitative and qualitative approaches* (6th ed., pp. 382–396). Itasca, IL: F.E. Peacock.

6

Chapter Outline

Measurement

A CONCEPT SUCH AS DEPRESSION can be defined in words and, if the words are sufficiently well chosen, the reader will have a clear idea of what depression is. When we apply the definition to a particular client, however, words may be not enough to guide us. The client may seem depressed according to the definition, but many questions may still remain. Is the client more or less depressed than the average person? If more depressed, how much more? Is the depression growing or declining? For how long has the client been depressed? Is the depression continuous or episodic? If episodic, what length of time usually elapses between depressive episodes? Is this length of time increasing or diminishing? How many episodes occur in a week? To what degree is the client depressed? Answers to questions such as these enable a professional worker to obtain greater insight into the client's depression—an insight essential for planning and evaluating a treatment intervention.

WHY MEASUREMENT IS NECESSARY

The word *measurement* is often used in two different senses. In the first sense, a measurement is the result of a measuring process: the number of times Bobby hits his brother in a day (a possible *frequency* practice objective); the length of time for which Jenny cries (a possible *duration* practice objective); the intensity of Ms. Smith's depression (a possible *magnitude* practice objective). In the

143

second sense, measurement refers to the measuring process itself; that is, it encompasses the event or attribute being measured, the person who does the measuring, the method employed, the measuring instrument used, and often also the result. Throughout this book, *measurement* will be taken to refer to the entire process, excluding only the results. The results of any measurement process will be referred to as *data*. In other words, measurement is undertaken in order to obtain data—objective and precise data, that is.

In any profession, from the human services to plumbing, an instrument is a tool designed to help the user perform a task. A tool need not be a physical object; it can just as easily be a perception, an idea, a new synthesis of known facts, or a new analysis of a known whole.

As we now know, an evaluation is an appraisal: an estimate of how effectively and efficiently objectives are being met in a practitioner's individual practice or in a human service program. In other words, an evaluation can compare the change that has actually taken place against the predicted, desired change.

Thus, an evaluation requires knowledge of both the initial condition and the present condition of the objective undergoing the proposed change. Therefore, it is necessary to have two *measurements,* one at the beginning of the change process and one at the end. In addition, it is always useful to take measurements of the objectives during the change process as well. Measurement, then, is not only necessary in the quality improvement process—it is the conceptual foundation without which the evaluative structure cannot exist.

A definition, no matter how complete, is useful only if it means the same thing in the hands of different people. For example, we could define a distance in terms of the number of days a person takes to walk it; or the number of strides needed to cross it, or the number of felled oak trees that would span it end to end. But since people, strides, and oak trees vary, none of these definitions is very exact. To be useful to a modern traveler, a distance must be given in miles or some other precisely defined unit.

Similarly, shared understanding and precision are very important in the human services. A worker who is assessing a woman's level of functioning needs to know that the results of the assessment are not being affected by her feelings toward the woman, her knowledge of the woman's situation, or any other biasing factor; that any other worker who assessed the same woman under the same conditions would come up with the same result.

Further, the practitioner needs to know that the results of the assessment will be understood by other professionals; that the results are rendered in words or symbols that are not open to misinterpretation. If the assessment is to provide the basis for decisions about the woman's future, via the treatment intervention chosen, objectivity and precision on the part of the human service professional are even more important.

Objectivity

Some practitioners believe that they are entirely objective; that they will not judge clients by skin color, ethnic origin, religious persuasion, sexual orientation, social class, income level, marital status, education, age, gender, verbal skill, or personal attractiveness. They may believe they are not influenced by other people's opinions about a client—statements that the client has severe emotional problems or a borderline personality will be disregarded until evidence is gathered. No judgments will be made on the basis of the worker's personal likes and dislikes, and stereotyping will be avoided at all costs.

Social workers who sincerely believe that their judgment will never be influenced by any of the above factors are deluding themselves. Everyone is prejudiced to some degree in some area or another; everyone has likes and dislikes, moral positions, and personal standards; everyone is capable of irrational feelings of aversion, sympathy, or outrage. Workers who deny this run the risk of showing bias without realizing it, and a worker's unconscious bias can have devastating effects on the life of a client.

A client may unwittingly fuel the bias by sensing what the practitioner expects and answering questions in a way that supports the worker's preconceptions. In extreme cases, clients can even become what they are expected to become, fulfilling the biased prophecy. The art of good judgment, then, lies in accepting the possibility of personal bias and trying to minimize its effects. What is needed is an unprejudiced method of assessment and an unbiased standard against which the client's knowledge, feelings, or behaviors can be gauged. In other words, we require a measurement method from which an impartial measure can be derived.

Precision

The other ingredient of the quality improvement process is precision, whose opposite is vagueness. A vague statement is one that uses general or indefinite terms; in other words, it leaves so many details to be filled in that it means different things to different people. There are four major sources of vagueness:

The first source of vagueness is terms such as *often, frequently, many, some, usually,* and *rarely,* which attempt to assign degrees to a client's feelings or behaviors without specifying a precise unit of measurement. A statement such as "John misses many appointments with his worker" is fuzzy; it tells us only that John's reliability *may* leave much to be desired. The statement "John missed 2 out of 10 appointments with his worker" is far more precise and does not impute evil tendencies to John.

The second source of vagueness is statements that, although they are intended to say something about a particular client, might apply to anyone; for example, "John often feels insecure, having experienced some rejection by his peers." Who has not experienced peer rejection? Nevertheless, the statement will be interpreted as identifying a quality specific to John. The human services abound with statements like this, which are as damaging to the client as they are meaningless.

A third source of vagueness is professional jargon, the meaning of which will rarely be clear to a client. Often professionals themselves do not agree on the meaning of such phrases as "expectations-role definition" or "reality pressures." In the worst case, they do not even know what they mean by their own jargon; they use it merely to sound impressive. Jargon is useful when it conveys precise statements to colleagues; when misused, it can confuse workers and alienate clients.

The last source of vagueness is tautology: a meaningless repetition disguised as a definition. For example: a delinquent is a person who engages in delinquent behaviors; "John is agoraphobic because he is afraid of open spaces;' "Betty is ambivalent because she cannot make up her mind," "Marie hits her brother because she is aggressive," "John rocks back and forth because he is autistic." Obviously, tautological statements tell us nothing and are to be avoided.

In summary, we need to attain objectivity and precision and avoid bias and vagueness. Both objectivity and precision are vital in the quality improvement process and are readily attainable through measurement.

TYPES OF MEASURING INSTRUMENTS

There are many types of measuring instruments. We will present only three types: (1) rating scales, (2) summated scales, and (3) goal attainment scaling.

Rating Scales

Rating scales use judgments by self or others to assign an individual (or program) a single score in relation to the program or practice objective being measured. What the various types of rating scales have in common is that they all rate clients on various traits or characteristics by locating them at some point on a continuum or in an ordered set of response categories, where numerical values are assigned to each category. Rating scales may be completed by the person being evaluated (self-rating) or by some significant other, such as a parent, supervisor, spouse, or practitioner. Sometimes a client and a significant other are asked to complete the same rating scale in order to provide the worker with two different views.

There are two types of rating scales that are useful for evaluative purposes: graphic rating scales and self-anchored rating scales.

Graphic Rating Scales

Graphic rating scales are structured with a program or practice objective described on a continuum from one extreme to the other, such as "low to high" or "most to least." The points of the continuum are ordered in equal intervals and are assigned numbers. Some or most points have descriptions to help people locate their positions on the scale. Below is one such scale, a "feeling thermometer," that asks children to rate their level of anxiety from "very anxious" to "very calm" (Kidder & Judd, 1986). The practice objective in this situation might be "to decrease a child's anxiety at home."

Check below how anxious you are:

___ 100 Very anxious
___ 90
___ 80
___ 70
___ 60
___ 50 Neither anxious nor calm
___ 40
___ 30

___ 20
___ 10
___ 0 Very calm

A second example of a graphic rating scale asks clients to rate their individual counseling sessions on a scale ranging from "not productive" to "very productive." The objective could be to increase a worker's understanding of how her clients view her effectiveness.

Please circle the number that comes closest to describing your feelings about the session you just completed.

1	2	3	4	5
Not productive		Moderately productive		Very productive

The major advantage of graphic rating scales is that they are easy to use, though one must take care to develop appropriate descriptive statements. For example, end statements so extreme that it is unlikely anyone would choose them, such as "extremely hot" or "extremely cold," should not be used.

Note that the first graphic rating scale above provides data about a client, whereas the second scale provides data about a service.

Self-Anchored Rating Scales

Self-anchored rating scales are similar to graphic rating scales in that clients are asked to rate themselves on a continuum, usually a 7- or 9-point scale from low to high. They differ in that *clients* define the specific referents, or *anchors*, for three points on the continuum on a self-anchored scale. An anchor point is the point on a scale where a concrete descriptor is given to define the condition represented by that point. This type of scale is often used to measure such attributes as intensity of feeling or pain. A self-anchored scale is an excellent source of data, because it is essentially developed by the person most familiar with the subtleties of the problem—the client.

For example, a client who has difficulty being honest in group sessions could complete the following question (the three anchor points are put in by the client), which is intended to measure his own perceptions of his honesty.

In the example below, the client writes in the three anchor points (i.e., can never be honest, can sometimes be honest, and can always be completely honest). A practice objective could be to increase his honesty within the group.

Indicate the extent to which you feel you can be honest in the group.

| 1 | 2 | 3 | 4 | 5 | 6 | 7 | 8 | 9 |

I Can never   I Can sometimes   I Can always be
be honest   be honest   completely honest

Suppose that a client is feeling trapped in her marriage and in her role as a homemaker. She might develop a 9-point scale such as the one shown below, ranging from "I feel completely trapped," through "I feel I have some options," to "I do not feel trapped at all." If she is not able to analyze her feelings well enough to identify three distinct emotional levels between 5 and 9 or 1 and 5, she may prefer to use a 5-point scale instead. She should certainly be told that the intervals are equal; the distance between 8 and 9 is the same as the distance between 7 and 8, and so forth.

| 1 | 2 | 3 | 4 | 5 | 6 | 7 | 8 | 9 |

I Do not feel   I Feel I have   I Feel completely
trapped at all   some options   trapped

If the problem is not the extent to which the woman feels trapped but the intensity of the trapped feelings, she might consider what sort of emotions she experiences when she feels most and least trapped. If being most trapped involves desperate or suicidal feelings, these feelings will define the high end of the scale.

From this example, we can deduce the two major advantages of self-anchored scales. First, they are specific to the client in a way that a scale developed by someone else cannot be. They measure emotions known only to the client, and may therefore yield the most complete and accurate portrayal of the situation. Second, they can measure the intensity of a feeling or attitude. Clients who suffer from feelings of anxiety or guilt or from physical ailments such as migraine headaches are often primarily concerned with intensity, and they may be more willing to fill out an instrument that reflects this concern.

There are also disadvantages to an instrument that is completed by the client. One major drawback is that clients may consciously or unconsciously distort their responses so as to appear more worthy or more deserving in the eyes of the worker. Analyzing an emotion thoroughly enough to rate it on a scale may result in changes to the emotion. This problem is known as "reactivity."

Self-anchored scales, then, are of particular value when the quality being measured is an emotion or thought pattern known only to the client, or when intensity is the primary concern. These scales can be used alone or in conjunction with other types of measuring instruments. They can also be used to supply data peripheral to the central problem: For example, a client whose practice objective is weight loss might use a self-anchored scale to measure changes in self-esteem associated with the weight loss.

Summated Scales

Where rating scales obtain data from one question about the program or practice objective, summated scales present multiple questions to which the client is asked to respond. Thus, summated scales combine responses to all of the questions on an instrument to form a single, overall score for the objective being measured. The responses are then totaled to obtain a composite score indicating the individual's position on the objective of interest.

Summated scales are widely used to assess individual or family problems, for needs assessment, and for other types of case-level and program-level evaluation efforts. The scale poses a number of questions and asks clients to indicate the degree of their agreement or disagreement with each. Response categories may include such statements as "strongly agree," "agree," "neutral," "disagree," and "strongly disagree." It is our opinion that summated scales provide more objectivity and precision in the concept that they are measuring than the two types of rating scales mentioned above. Figure 6.1 presents an excellent example of a summative scale. It measures one variable: self-esteem. Figure 6.2 is another example of a summative scale, only this measuring device has three scales in it, all combined in one measuring instrument. Finally, Figure 6.3 presents another measuring instrument that measures only variable (like Figure 6.1)—the degree of family support within a family.

A unidimensional summative measuring instrument only measures one variable, for example, self-esteem (Figures 6.1). On the other hand, a multidimensional one measures a number of variables at the same time (e.g., Figure 6.2). A multidimensional instrument is nothing more than a number of unidimensional instruments stuck together.

INDEX OF SELF-ESTEEM

Name: _____ Today's Date: _____

Context: _____

This questionnaire is designed to measure how you see yourself. It is not a test, so there are no right or wrong answers. Please answer each item as carefully and as accurately as you can by placing a number beside each one as follows:

1 = None of the time
2 = Very rarely
3 = A little of the time
4 = Some of the time
5 = A good part of the time
6 = Most of the time
7 = All of the time

_____

1. _____ I feel that people would not like me if they really knew me well.
2. _____ I feel that others get along much better than I do.
3. _____ I feel that I am a beautiful person.
4. _____ When I am with others I feel they are glad I am with them.
5. _____ I feel that people really like to talk with me.
6. _____ I feel that I am a very competent person.
7. _____ I think I make a good impression on others.
8. _____ I feel that I need more self-confidence.
9. _____ When I am with strangers I am very nervous.
10. _____ I think that I am a dull person.
11. _____ I feel ugly.
12. _____ I feel that others have more fun than I do.
13. _____ I feel that I bore people.
14. _____ I think my friends find me interesting.
15. _____ I think I have a good sense of humor.
16. _____ I feel very self-conscious when I am with strangers.
17. _____ I feel that if I could be more like other people I would have it made.
18. _____ I feel that people have a good time when they are with me.
19. _____ I feel like a wallflower when I go out.
20. _____ I feel I get pushed around more than others.
21. _____ I think I am a rather nice person.
22. _____ I feel that people really like me very much.
23. _____ I feel that I am a likeable person.
24. _____ I am afraid I will appear foolish to others.
25. _____ My friends think very highly of me.

3, 4, 5, 6, 7, 14, 15, 18, 21, 22, 23, 25.

FIGURE 6.1   Hudson's Index of Self-Esteem

Using the scale from one to five described below, please indicate on the line to the left of each item the number that comes closest to how you feel.

1 Strongly agree
2 Agree
3 Undecided
4 Disagree
5 Strongly disagree

_____

_____	1	The social worker took my problems very seriously.
_____	2	If I had been the social worker, I would have dealt with my problems in just the same way.
_____	3	The worker I had could never understand anyone like me.
_____	4	Overall the agency has been very helpful to me.
_____	5	If friends of mine had similar problems I would tell them to go to the agency.
_____	6	The social worker asks a lot of embarrassing questions.
_____	7	I can always count on the worker to help if I'm in trouble.
_____	8	The agency will help me as much as it can.
_____	9	I don't think the agency has the power to really help me.
_____	10	The social worker tries hard but usually isn't too helpful.
_____	11	The problem the agency tried to help me with is one of the most important in my life.
_____	12	Things have gotten better since I've been going to the agency.
_____	13	Since I've been using the agency my life is more messed up than ever.
_____	14	The agency is always available when I need it.
_____	15	I got from the agency exactly what I wanted.
_____	16	The social worker loves to talk but won't really do anything for me.
_____	17	Sometimes I just tell the social worker what I think she wants to hear.
_____	18	The social worker is usually in a hurry when I see her.
_____	19	No one should have any trouble getting some help from this agency.
_____	20	The worker sometimes says things I don't understand.
_____	21	The social worker is always explaining things carefully.
_____	22	I never looked forward to my visits to the agency.
_____	23	I hope I'll never have to go back to the agency for help.
_____	24	Every time I talk to my worker I feel relieved.
_____	25	I can tell the social worker the truth without worrying.
_____	26	I usually feel nervous when I talk to my worker.
_____	27	The social worker is always looking for lies in what I tell her.
_____	28	It takes a lot of courage to go to the agency.
_____	29	When I enter the agency I feel very small and insignificant.
_____	30	The agency is very demanding.
_____	31	The social worker will sometimes lie to me.
_____	32	Generally the social worker is an honest person.
_____	33	I have the feeling that the worker talks to other people about me.
_____	34	I always feel well treated when I leave the agency.

FIGURE 6.2   Reid-Gundlach Social Service Satisfaction Scale

INSTRUCTIONS: Listed below are people and groups that often times are helpful to members of a family raising a young child. This questionnaire asks you to indicate how helpful each source is to your family. Please circle the response that best describes how helpful the sources have been to your family during the past 3 to 6 months. If a source of help has not been available to your family during this period of time, circle NA (Not Available) response.

How helpful has each of the following been to you in terms of raising your child(ren):	Not Available	Not at all helpful	Sometimes helpful	Generally helpful	Very helpful	Extremely helpful
My parents...	NA	1	2	3	4	5
My spouse or parnter's spouse...	NA	1	2	3	4	5
My relatives/kin...	NA	1	2	3	4	5
My spouse or partner's relatives/kin...	NA	1	2	3	4	5
My friends...	NA	1	2	3	4	5
My spouse or partner's friends...	NA	1	2	3	4	5
My own children...	NA	1	2	3	4	5
Other parents...	NA	1	2	3	4	5
Coworkers...	NA	1	2	3	4	5
Parent groups...	NA	1	2	3	4	5
Social groups/clubs...	NA	1	2	3	4	5
Church members/minister...	NA	1	2	3	4	5
My family or child's physician...	NA	1	2	3	4	5
Early childhood intervention program...	NA	1	2	3	4	5
School/daycare center...	NA	1	2	3	4	5
Professional helpers (social workers, therapists, teachers, etc.)...	NA	1	2	3	4	5
Professional agencies (public health, social services, mental health, etc.)...	NA	1	2	3	4	5
_____	NA	1	2	3	4	5
_____	NA	1	2	3	4	5

FIGURE 6.3 Family Support Scale

For example, Figure 6.2 is a multidimensional summative measuring instrument that contains three unidimensional instruments:

1. Relevance of received social services (Items 1–11)
2. The extent to which the services reduced the problem (Items 12–21)
3. The extent to which services enhanced the client's self-esteem and contributed to a sense of power and integrity (Items 22–34)

Goal Attainment Scaling (GAS)

As seen in Chapters 3 and 4, social workers ultimately try to achieve program objectives with their clients. They do this by creating practice objectives which, if resolved, will accomplish the program objective. The underlying program objective is not the direct focus of a worker's attention. Instead, workers create and focus their attention on the practice objectives that are directly linked to the program's objectives. A useful medical analogy is to think of a disease as a program objective and the symptoms of the disease as practice objectives.

Creating Practice Objectives from Program Objectives

By way of example, suppose that a residential home for children who are delinquent accepts a boy, Ron, who is experiencing trouble at school as well as with the police. Ron's teacher reports that he is two grade levels behind on every subject, he has violent temper outbursts in the classroom, and acts as a negative leader to other students. The worker sets three practice objectives for Ron: first, that he should perform academically at his own grade level; second, that he should express anger in appropriate ways; third, that he should display positive leadership behaviors. In using the medical analogy above, delinquency is the disease and Ron's poor grades, inappropriate anger expression, and few leadership skills are symptoms of the disease—the practice objectives. It should be noted that Ron could have displayed other ways in which delinquent behavior could be exhibited (e.g., skipping school, criminal behavior, joining a street gang).

Weighting Practice Objectives   Each of the three practice objectives for Ron presented in Figure 6.4 is assigned a weight between 1 and 10, based on the worker's perception of its clinical importance. The first practice objective receives a weighting of 7, the second of 3, and the third of 9. These practice objectives, with their weights, are shown at the top of Ron's goal attainment scale (Alter & Evens, 1990).

   Next, each practice objective is operationalized; that is, a precise meaning is assigned to such phrases as "displays positive leadership" and "expresses anger in appropriate ways" so that the objective is measurable. Each objective is then rated on a 5-point scale ranging from −2 to + 2 (see left-hand column of Figure 6.4) where:

   −2 = Much less than expected level of outcome
   −1 = Somewhat less than expected level of outcome
    0 = Expected level of outcome
   + 1 = Somewhat more than expected level of outcome
   + 2 = Much more than expected level of outcome

   As can be seen from Figure 6.4, each point on the scale is anchored; that is, each of the five possible outcomes is operationalized in fairly precise terms. For example, the first practice objective, "Much more than expected level of outcome," is defined as an increase from Ron's present grade level of two years behind to a level of only one year behind, that is, a gain of one year. Similarly, the second practice objective, "Somewhat more than expected level of outcome," is defined in terms of a decrease in number of tantrums, and specifically, their becoming "rare."

   The Generation of Data   Once the scale has been established, a baseline score is obtained. As we will see in the following chapter, a baseline measure is a measure of the client's state before any intervention. Without this measure, it is impossible to know whether change has occurred, and so a baseline measurement is always critically important to any series of repeated measurements.

   Ron's baseline score is determined by rating him on the scale very soon after he enters the home, when nothing in his behavior will have yet changed. The worker assigns him a score of −1 on the first practice objective, −1 on the second, and −2 on the third. Because the objectives are weighted, the goal attainment score is determined by multiplying each rating by the assigned weight and summing the results. Ron's baseline goal attainment score would then be calculated as follows:

Levels of Predicted Attainment	Scale 1 Ron Achieves Appropriate Grade (Weight = 7)	Scale 2 Ron Expresses Anger Appropriately (Weight = 3)	Scale 3 Ron displays Positive Leadership (Weight = 9)
Much less than expected level of outcome (−2)	Falls behind current grade level	Acts out in more destructive ways	Uses others all the time to achieve negative goals
Somewhat less than expected level of outcome (−1)	Stays at current grade level	Stays the same	Sometimes uses others to achieve negative goals
Expected level of outcome (0)	Gains three months	Shows some signs expresses anger in acceptable ways	Sometime functions as a positive leader
Somewhat more than expected level of outcome (+1)	Gains six months	Rarely has tantrums	Has become a strong but inconsistent leader
Much more than expected level of outcome (+2)	Gains a year	Always expresses anger in acceptable ways	Never functions as a negative leader

FIGURE 6.4   Ron's Goal Attainment Scale

First Practice Objective
Weight = 7
Rating = −1
Score = 7 (−1) = **−7**
Second Practice Objective
Weight = 3
Rating = −1
Score = 3 (−1) = **−3**
Third Practice Objective
Weight = 9
Rating = −2
Score = 9 (−2) = **−18**

Total Goal Attainment Score = (−7) + (−3) + (−18) = **−28**

As the ratings reflect the opinion of the rater, it is always preferable to have two or more people simultaneously rate the client. Let us say that Ron's teacher gives him the same rating as his worker on the first two practice objectives, but on the third she gives him a –1 instead of a –2. Ron's score on the third practice objective is then 9 (–1) = –9 according to his teacher, bringing his total score to –19 from the teacher's point of view. Ron's baseline goal attainment score is then calculated as the average of the two scores, that is, (–28) + (–19)/2 = –23.5.

If the scores assigned by the two raters differ greatly, this is a sign that the anchor points on the scale have not been defined with sufficient precision. They will then have to be redefined and the ratings redone. The calculation of a baseline score therefore serves two purposes: It provides an initial score against which change can be measured, and it serves as a test of the measuring instrument.

Once a baseline score is established, the intervention is implemented and the client is repeatedly rated at whatever intervals seem appropriate. If the scale becomes outdated in light of the client's achievements, a new scale can be constructed for one or more practice objectives.

Advantages of GAS   The advantages of goal attainment scaling lie in its flexibility and its individualized approach. It can be used to measure process as well as outcome; that is, it can be used to evaluate what takes place during an intervention as well as the intervention results. It is readily adapted to any client in any situation, to any human service worker who wishes to assess the level of his or her own skills, and to any agency or organization undertaking an outcome evaluation. Further, although the example given above was qualitative in that the anchor points on the scale were defined descriptively, quantitative anchor points such as scores on standardized measuring instruments or frequency counts can also be used. The term *quantitative,* as its name suggests, has to do with quantity or numbers, and so any measure involving a number rather than a description counts as quantitative.

Another advantage of goal attainment scaling is that the data obtained can be aggregated across a number of clients and put to various uses. For example, suppose the practitioners in Ron's home noticed that most of those who obtained a score of 5 or higher on the scales after a three-month stay succeeded in the program, whereas those with lower scores tended to fail. Goal attainment scores after the first three months might then be used to indicate whether a particular child should remain in the program or be referred to a different facility. In addition, aggregation of a number of individual scores will indicate the degree to which the program is successful as a whole.

STANDARDIZED MEASURING INSTRUMENTS

A *standardized measuring instrument is* one that has been constructed by researchers to measure a particular knowledge level, attitude or feeling, or behavior of clients (Jordan, Franklin, & Corcoran, 2001). It is a paper-and-pencil instrument and may take the form of a questionnaire, checklist, inventory, or rating scale. Two factors differentiate a standardized instrument from any other instrument, such as the basic recording forms previously discussed: the effort made to attain uniformity in the instrument's application, scoring, and interpretation; and the amount of work that has been devoted to ensuring that the instrument is valid and reliable (Hudson, 1993).

Every instrument, whether standardized or not, is designed to measure some specific quality; if it is valid, it will measure only that quality. The information sheet that usually accompanies a standardized instrument will state the instrument's purpose: to measure anxiety about academic achievement, say, or to measure three aspects of assertiveness (Corcoran, 1988). In addition, the sheet will usually describe how the questions (items) on the instrument relate to that purpose and will say something about the clinical implications of the quality being measured (e.g., Hudson, 1982).

The information sheet may also indicate what the instrument does not measure. A description of an instrument to measure aggression, for example, may specifically state that it does not measure hostility. This statement of purpose and the accompanying description improve chances that the instrument will be used as it was intended, to measure what it was designed to measure. In other words, it is more likely that the application of the instrument will be uniform.

The information sheet may also discuss the research studies done to ensure the instrument's validity, often including the instrument's ability to discriminate between clinical and nonclinical populations. It may mention instruments or criteria with which the instrument was compared, so that users will better understand what validity means in this particular instance. Information about reliability will usually be given via descriptions of the research studies undertaken to ensure reliability, and their results. Again, this information will help the worker who uses the instrument to know what kind of reliability can be expected.

Information will also be given about the characteristics of people on whom the instrument was tested. For example, an instrument to measure loneliness may be accompanied by the information that it was tested on a sample of 399 undergraduate students (171 males, 228 females) from three university campuses. An instrument to measure self-esteem may have been tested on a sample of 240 eighth graders—110 African American and 130 Caucasian. In each case, scores will be given for the tested group and subgroups, so that the user can see what the norms are for people with particular demographic characteristics. A *norm is* an established score for a particular group against which the score of a client can be measured (Jordan, Franklin, & Corcoran, 2001).

Let us say, for example, that the mean score of African American eighth graders on the self-esteem instrument was 40, with a small range in scores about the mean given in terms of a standard deviation. In comparison, the mean score for Caucasian eighth graders was 60. A practitioner who read this information on the sheet accompanying the instrument would know that an African American client's score should be compared with the African American average score of 40, and a Caucasian client's score should be compared with the Caucasian average of 60. Without this information, the worker might think that an African American client who scored 42 was suffering from low self-esteem—although, in such a case 42 is really close to the average self-esteem score for African American eighth graders.

The concept of norms has an important place in the human services, particularly in the administering of measuring instruments. What is normal for an African American child from a poor, urban neighborhood is not necessarily normal for a Caucasian child from a prosperous rural neighborhood; what is normal for one ethnic group may not be normal for another; what is normal for an adolescent female may not be normal for an adolescent male. It is very important that a client's score be compared with the average score of people with similar demographic characteristics. If this information is not available, as it sometimes is not, the social worker should bear in mind that an "unusual" score may not be at all unusual; it may be normal for the type of client being measured. Conversely, a normal-looking score may turn out to be unusual when the demographic characteristics of the client are taken into account.

The documentation sheet should also explain how to score the instrument and how to interpret the score. Scoring may be simple or relatively complex; it may involve summing specific items, reversing entered scores, or following a preset template. Often, it may also be accomplished on a computer. Some instruments may yield one global score while others may provide several scores, each representing a dimension such as self-esteem or assertiveness. Interpretation of the scores also varies depending on the instrument. When interpreting scores, it is particularly important to be aware that some scores represent the magnitude of problems, while others indicate the magnitude of positive attributes such as skills or knowledge. Depending on what is measured, increasing scores may indicate improvement or deterioration; the same is true for decreasing scores.

A standardized measuring instrument, then, should be accompanied by at least six kinds of information:

1. The purpose of the instrument
2. A description of the instrument
3. The instrument's validity
4. The instrument's reliability
5. Norms
6. Scoring and interpretation procedures

The amount and quality of information provided may be taken as an indicator of whether an instrument is standardized or not and, if it is, to what degree.

LOCATING STANDARDIZED MEASURING INSTRUMENTS

Once the need for measurement has been established, the next consideration is locating appropriate standardized measuring instruments from which to choose. The two general sources for locating such instruments are commercial or professional publishers and professional literature (Jordan, Franklin, & Corcoran, 1993, 1997, 2001).

Publishers

Numerous commercial and professional publishing companies specialize in the production and sale of standardized measuring instruments for use in the human services. A selected list of publishers is provided by Jordan, Franklin, and Corcoran (1993) below. The ☞ represents a good first place to look.

Academic Therapy Publications, 20 Commercial Boulevard, Novato, CA, 94947; (415) 883-3314.
Behavior Science Press, P.O. Box BV, University, AL, 35486; (205) 759-2089.

Biometrics Research, Research Assessment and Training Unit, New York State Psychiatric Institute, 722 West 168th Street, Room 341, New York, NY, 10032; (212) 960-5534.

Bureau of Educational Measurements, Emporia State University, Emporia, KS, 66801; (316) 343-1200.

Center for Epidemiologic Studies, Department of Health and Human Services, 5600 Fishers Lane, Rockville, MD, 20857; (301) 443-4513.

Consulting Psychologists Press, Inc., 577 College Avenue, P.O. Box 11636, Palo Alto, CA, 94306; (415) 857-1444.

Educational and Industrial Testing Service (EDITS), P.O. Box 7234, San Diego, CA, 92107; (619) 222-1666.

Family Life Publications, Inc., Box 427, Saluda, NC, 28773; (704) 749-4971.

☞ http://ericae.net/testcol.htm

Institute for Personality and Ability Testing, Inc. (IPAT), P.O. Box 188, 1062 Coronado Drive, Champaign, IL, 61820; (213) 652-2922.

Merrill Publishing Company, 1300 Alum Creek Drive, Box 508, Columbus, OH, 43216; (614) 258-8441.

Personnel Research Institute (PRI), Psychological Research Services, Case Western Reserve University, 11220 Bellflower Road, Cleveland, OH, 44106; (216) 368-3546.

Professional Assessment Services Division, National Computer Systems, P.O. Box 1416, Minneapolis, MN, 55440; (800) 328-6759.

Psychological Assessment Resources, Inc., P.O. Box 98, Odessa, FL, 33556; (813) 920-6357.

Psychological Services, Inc., Suite 1200, 3450 Wilshire Boulevard, Los Angeles, CA, 90010; (213) 738-1132.

Research Concepts, A Division of Test Maker, Inc., 1368 East Airport Road, Muskegon, MI, 49444; (616) 739-7401.

Research Press, Box 317760, Champaign, IL, 61820; (217) 352-3273.

Science Research Associates, Inc. (SRA), 155 North Wacker Drive, Chicago, IL, 60606; (800) 621-0664, in Illinois (312) 984-2000.

Scott, Foresman, & Company, Test Division, 1900 East Lake Avenue, Glenview, IL, 60025; (847) 729-3000.

U.S. Department of Defense, Testing Directorate, Headquarters, Military Enlistment Processing Command, Attention: MEPCT, Fort Sheridan, IL, 60037; (847) 926-4111.

University Associates, Inc., Learning Resources Corporation, 8517 Production Avenue, P.O. Box 26240, San Diego, CA, 92126; (714) 578-5900.

☞ WALMYR Publishing Company, Post Office Box 6229, Tallahassee, FL 32314; (850) 656-2787.

Western Psychological Services, 12031 Wilshire Boulevard, Los Angeles, CA, 90025; (213) 478-2061.

The cost of instruments purchased from a publisher varies considerably, depending on the instrument, the number of copies needed, and the publisher. The instruments generally are well developed and their psychometric properties are supported by the results of several research studies. Often they are accompanied by manuals that include the normative data for the instrument. As well, publishers are expected to comply with professional standards such as those established by the American Psychological Association. These standards apply to claims made about the instrument's rationale, development, psychometric properties, administration, and interpretation of results.

Standards for the use of some instruments have been developed to protect the interests of clients. Consequently, purchasers of instruments may be required to have certain qualifications, such as possession of an advanced degree in a relevant field. A few publishers require membership in particular professional organizations. Most publishers will, however, accept an order from a human service student if it is cosigned by a qualified person, such as an instructor, who will supervise the use of the instrument.

Professional Journals and Books

Standardized measuring instruments are most commonly reproduced in human service journals; in fact, most commercially marketed instruments first appear in one of these publications. The instruments usually are supported by evidence of their validity and reliability, although they often require cross-validation and normative data from more representative samples and subsamples. A selected list of professional books and journals is provided by Jordan, Franklin, and Corcoran (1993, 1997, 2001) below. The ☞ represents a good first place to look.

Books

☞ Bloom, M., Fischer, J., & Orme, J. (1999). *Evaluating practice: Guidelines for the accountable professional* (3rd ed.). Englewood Cliffs, NJ: Prentice-Hall.

Cautela, J.R. (1988). *Behavior analysis forms for clinical intervention* (Vols. 1 & 2). Champaign, IL: Research Press.

☞ Corcoran, K.J., & Fischer, J. (2000). *Measures for clinical practice* (3rd ed). *Volume 1: Couples, families, and children. Volume 2: Adults.* New York: Free Press.

Goldman, B.A., & Busch, J.C. (1997). *Directory of unpublished experimental mental measures.* Washington, DC: American Psychological Association.

Hudson, W.W. (1982). *The clinical measurement package: A Field Manual.* Newbury Park, CA: Wadsworth.

Jordan, C., & Franklin, C. (1995). *Clinical assessment for social workers.* Chicago: Lyceum.

Krysik, J., Hoffart, I., & Grinnell, R.M., Jr. (1993). *Student study guide* to accompany the fourth edition of *Social Work Research and Evaluation.* Itasca, IL: Peacock.

Mash, E.J., & Terdal, L.G. (Eds.). (1976). *Behavior therapy assessment.* New York: Springer.

Nurius, P.S., & Hudson, W.W. (1993). *Human services: Practice, evaluation, and computers.* Pacific Grove, CA: Brooks/Cole.

Robinson, J.R., & Shaver, P.R. (1973). *Measures of social psychological attitudes* (rev. ed.). Ann Arbor, MI: Institute for Social Research.

☞ Sederer, L.I., & Dickey, B. (Eds.). (1996). *Outcomes assessment in clinical practice.* Baltimore: Williams & Wilkins.

Journals

Applied Behavioral Measurement
Behavioral Therapy
Behavior Assessment
Educational and Psychological Measurement
Evaluation
Family Process

Journal of Behavioral Assessment and Psychopathology
Journal of Clinical Psychology
Journal of Consulting and Clinical Psychology
Journal of Personality Assessment
☞ *Research on Social Work Practice*
Measurement and Evaluation in Counseling and Development

Locating instruments in journals or books is not easy. Of the two most common methods, computer searches of data banks and manual searches of the literature, the former is faster, unbelievably more thorough, and easier to use. Unfortunately, financial support for the development of comprehensive data banks has been limited and intermittent. Another disadvantage is that many articles on instruments are not referenced with the appropriate indicators for computer retrieval. These limitations are being overcome by the changing technology of computers and information retrieval systems. Several services now allow for a complex breakdown of measurement need; data banks that include references from over 1,300 journals, updated monthly, are now available from a division of Psychological Abstracts Information Services and from Bibliographic Retrieval Services.

Nevertheless, most human service professionals will probably rely on manual searches of references such as Psychological Abstracts. Although the reference indices will be the same as those in the data banks accessible by computer, the literature search can be supplemented with appropriate seminal (original) reference volumes.

EVALUATING MEASURING INSTRUMENTS

A literature search should produce several instruments suitable for measuring a particular program or practice objective. As one might expect, some measuring instruments are better than others. There are six main features that distinguish a good instrument from a poor one: (1) validity, (2) reliability, (3) sensitivity, (4) nonreactivity, (5) representativeness of sample, and (6) utility.

Validity

A human service worker who cannot find an instrument to measure a particular practice or program objective—to decrease social isolation, for example—may be tempted to use an instrument that measures something closely related, say, loneliness. If instruments and concepts were really as interchangeable as that, no one would ever be quite sure what was being measured. Note how the objective to "decrease social isolation" can be a practice objective as well as a program objective.

It is important to most human service professionals to know that the instrument they choose will measure what they want it to measure and not anything else. An instrument that measures what it is supposed to measure, and measures only that, is called a *valid* instrument.

If a number of questions on a measuring instrument are intended to measure the degree of loneliness, and if the instrument is valid, these questions should adequately reflect the true substance of loneliness. For instance, people who are lonely tend to feel that they have no one to turn to; they feel misunderstood and out of tune with the people around them; they feel withdrawn and are unhappy about being withdrawn; and they feel that their relationships are superficial. Each of these feelings, common to lonely people, contributes to the overall concept of loneliness.

If a measuring instrument is to truly measure loneliness, it must tap each one of these feelings, or at least an adequate sample of them. That is, it must reflect what loneliness really is and enable the client to measure his or her feelings of loneliness against the entire spectrum of loneliness. For example: a person who feels misunderstood is lonely; a person who feels misunderstood and also feels withdrawn is more lonely; a person who feels misunderstood and withdrawn and has no one to talk to is still lonelier. The measure is all a matter of degree.

Note that in order to construct an instrument to measure loneliness, one has first to operationalize the concept of loneliness—that is, to decide what specific feelings comprise that concept. An instrument purporting to measure loneliness will therefore be valid to the extent that its authors have identified all the requisite feelings and have included an adequate sample of them in the instrument. An instrument containing such an adequate sample is said to be *content valid*. Because it is almost impossible to identify all of the feelings that make up a complex concept such as loneliness or depression, no instrument will be entirely content valid, only more or less so. In sum, Jordan, Franklin, and Corcoran (1993, 1997, 2001) present a few validity concerns that need to be addressed when assessing an instrument:

1. Is the content domain clearly and specifically defined?
2. Was there a logical procedure for including the items?
3. Is the criterion measure relevant to the instrument?
4. Was the criterion measure reliable and valid?
5. Is the theoretical construct clearly and correctly stated?
6. Do the scores converge with other relevant measures?
7. Do the scores discriminate from irrelevant variables?
8. Are there cross-validation studies that conform to the above concerns?

Reliability

We have seen that, in testing for change, at least two and preferably more measurements are required. A human service worker who uses the same instrument more than once with the same client wants to assume that differences in the results (first measurement – second measurement = difference) are due to changes in the client. If this assumption is false—if the differences instead reflect, say, boredom with the questions—the instrument's results will give a false impression of the client's progress. It is therefore important that a measuring instrument gives the same result with the same unchanged client every time it is administered. An instrument that can do this is said to be *reliable*.

Of course, no client remains completely unchanged from one day to the next. The problem level may not have changed—the client may be just as depressed—but she may be more tired or less anxious about taking the test, or more physically uncomfortable because the day is hotter. These random and irrelevant changes will probably affect his or her score to some degree, but if the instrument is reliable, this degree will not be large. In fact, an instrument is said to be reliable to the extent that results are not affected by random changes in the individual. In sum, Jordan, Franklin, and Corcoran (1993, 1997, 2001) present a few reliability concerns that need to be addressed when assessing an instrument:

1. Is there sufficient evidence of internal consistency?
2. Is there equivalence between various forms?
3. Is there stability over a relevant time interval?

Sensitivity

Because changes in a client's problem level are often small, it is important that a measuring instrument be able to detect small changes. What is needed, in fact, is an instrument that is stable or reliable enough to ignore irrelevant changes and *sensitive* enough to detect small changes in the level of the real problem.

The key to achieving such subtlety of discrimination is to select an appropriate measurement method. For example, suppose that a practice objective is to reduce the number of nights on which a child wets his bed. The measure selected might be a count of the number of mornings on which the bed is dry. If the bed is wet every morning for a month despite the worker's intervention, we could assume that the intervention is ineffective. But, if before the intervention started the child was wetting his bed five times a night and after intervention only once a night, the intervention has been successful in reducing the wetting episodes. However, this success was overlooked because the measurement method selected was in this context insensitive. It measured whether the problem occurred, which it either does or does not; there are no degrees of change in between.

The same considerations apply when a problem is indicated by more than one behavior. For example, a child may indicate problems with his teacher both by skipping the particular teacher's class and by being rude to the teacher when he or she is in class. If the rudeness occurs more often than the skipping, it is sensible to count incidents of rudeness rather than of skipping, because the high-frequency behavior is more likely to reveal small changes in the child's attitude toward his teacher than the low-frequency behavior.

Nonreactivity

Sometimes the very act of measurement affects the behavior, feeling, or knowledge level objective that is being measured. For example, cigarette smokers who begin to count the number of cigarettes they smoke may smoke fewer cigarettes simply as a result of the counting, without any other intervention being involved. Staff being evaluated may change their routine because they know they are being evaluated. A child who knows his television watching is being monitored by his mother may watch television less to please her or more to spite her, but in either case, the amount of television watching will have changed. It is therefore important that the instrument chosen be *nonreactive* or not affect the behavior, feeling, or knowledge objective being measured. A synonym for *nonreactive* is *unobtrusive*. Put another way, a worker's aim is to record a measurement as unobtrusively as possible.

Representativeness of the Sample

One aspect of evaluating standardized instruments is the extent to which the data collected in setting the norms for the instrument represent the same types of individuals who are being measured. For example, if the instrument being considered was formulated and tested on a sample drawn from a white Anglo-Saxon population, it might give perfectly valid results when administered to white Anglo-Saxons, but not if it is administered to Native Americans, African Americans, or social minorities such as women. In general terms, the samples used in setting the norms for an instrument must reflect a population that is similar to those who will complete that instrument. Demographic characteristics such as age, gender, race, and socioeconomic status must also be considered.

Another consideration is the size of the sample: the larger the sample, the better. A further concern is when the data were collected from the sample. Data based on samples selected a long time ago may not be an adequate basis for accepting the instrument as psychometrically sound for contemporary use. In sum, Jordan, Franklin, and Corcoran (1993, 1997, 2001) present a few sample concerns that need to be addressed when assessing an instrument:

1. Are the samples representative of pertinent populations?
2. Are the sample sizes sufficiently large?
3. Are the samples homogeneous?
4. Are the subsamples pertinent to respondents' demographics?
5. Are the data obtained from the samples up to date?

Utility

Utility means usefulness. If a measuring instrument is to be useful, it also has to be practical in a particular situation with a particular client. For example, the best way to demonstrate to the client such changes as improved posture or more frequent eye contact may be by making video recordings of successive

The following is a list of questions regarding resources available in the Calgary area. Please write down as many resources as you know about in responding to each question.

1. Where would you go for help in caring for your children?
2. Where would you go for financial assistance?
3. Where would you go for help with parenting?
4. Where would you go for medical assistance or information?
5. Where would you go for information on improving your education?
6. Whom would you call to help at home?
7. Where would you go for help in finding a job?
8. Where would you go to get help in finding a place to stay?
9. Who would you call if you had an immediate crisis?
10. Where would you go for assistance for food or clothing?
11. Where would you go for legal assistance?
12. Where would you go for counseling?

FIGURE 6.5   Questionnaire on Support
                  Systems in Calgary

interviews. However, if the client refuses to be videotaped, this particular measurement method cannot be used. It may be a perfectly valid and reliable measure, but it lacks utility.

To give another example, a practitioner may discover a perfect instrument for measuring depression: It is valid, reliable, nonreactive, and sensitive to small changes, but it is also five pages long. In addition, it takes a long time to score, and the numerical score, once obtained, is difficult to translate into a meaningful assessment of the client's depression. This instrument, though perfect in every other respect, is useless in practice because it takes too long to complete and too long to score and interpret. Instruments that have utility are acceptable to the client; they are easy and quick to administer and score; and they give results that reveal the client's current state.

Naturally, an instrument that is short enough to have utility may be too short to be entirely valid. It may be impossible, for example, to sample loneliness adequately in a 10-item questionnaire. As is often the case, this is a

1. Alberta Social Services, Community Daycare/Day Home, City of Calgary Social Services, Children's Cottage
2. Alberta Social Services, church, Alberta Consumer Corporate Affairs, Alberta Student Finance Board
3. Calgary Health Services, family doctor, Parent Support Association, Calgary Association of Parents, Parent Aid, City of Calgary Social Services, Children's Hospital
4. Family doctor, hospitals, Calgary Birth Control Association, Calgary Health Services, Birthrite
5. Alberta Vocational College, Viscount Bennet School, SAIT, Mount Royal College, Canada Manpower, Alberta Social Services, Women's Career Center, Louise Dean School, University of Calgary
6. Homemaker Services (FSB), Landlord & Tenant Board, Calgary Housing Authority, Relief Society (Mormon Church), Alberta Social Services, City of Calgary Social Services
7. Alberta Social Services, Canada Manpower, Career Center, Volunteer Center, Hire-A-Student, newspapers, 12 Avenue, job boards
8. Alberta Social Services, YWCA Single Mother Program, Renfrew Recovery, Women's Emergency Shelter, Park Wood House, Discovery House, church, Avenue 15, Single Men's Hostel, JIMY Program, Alpha House, Sheriff King, McMan Youth Services, Birthrite
9. Emergency Social Services, Distress Center, Sexual Assault Center, Suicide Line (CMH), Children's Cottage, Wood's Stabilization Program, Alberta Children's Hospital, church, police/fire department
10. Interfaith Food Bank, Milk Fund, Salvation Army, church, Emergency Social Services, Alberta Social Services
11. Legal Aid, Legal Guidance, University of Calgary Legal Line, Women's Resource Center, Women's Shelter, Dial-A-Law
12. Family Service Bureau, church, Alberta Mental Health, Pastoral Institute, Sexual Assault Center, Children's Cottage, Alberta Social Services, City of Calgary Social Services, Catholic Family Services, Parents Anonymous, Distress Center

Note: Clients may respond to the questionnaire with answers not listed above but which may be entirely appropriate to their own unique situations and thus be evaluated as correct.

FIGURE 6.6   Answers to Questionnaire on Support Systems in Calgary (Figure 6.5)

matter for compromise: a situation in which the instrument developer's best judgment is the only real guide. An instrument's practicality of application depends on its ease of implementation and ease of analysis of the data it generates.

A longer instrument is usually more reliable than a shorter one, but it is also more time-consuming and so may not be completed by the client. This fact is especially important in case-level designs where multiple measures are needed, to be discussed in the following chapter.

The social acceptability of a measuring instrument turns on the client's, not the worker's, view of the appropriateness of the content. The content's perceived appropriateness as a measure of the program or practice objective of interest—not what the instrument in fact measures but what it *appears* to measure—is referred to as *face validity*. In addition, an instrument that is offensive or insulting to clients will not be completed. Instruments should also be easy for clients to complete, with content and instructions that are neither above nor below their typical level of functioning, as well as questions that can be easily answered.

Program and practice objectives that can be measured directly are often behavioral. Other practice objectives, such as self-esteem or depression, can be measured only indirectly, or through some behavior that is believed to be associated with the objective. An instrument is considered to have utility if the results provide some practical advantage or useful data. The significance of the results is obviously influenced by whether the instrument is reactive. The instrument has to be sensitive enough to pick up small changes in the program or practice objective being measured.

A final consideration is what is done with the instrument after it has been completed. It may seem self-evident that if an instrument is to provide meaningful data it must be possible to score it. However, the scoring procedures of many instruments are too complicated and time-consuming to be practical in practice situations. Even though they are psychometrically sound, they should be eliminated in favor of others that can more easily be scored. In sum, Jordan, Franklin, and Corcoran (1993, 1997, 2001) present a few utility concerns that need to be addressed when assessing an instrument:

1. Is the instrument an appropriate length?
2. Is the content socially acceptable to respondents?
3. Is the instrument feasible to complete?
4. Is the instrument relatively direct?
5. Does the instrument have utility?
6. Is the instrument relatively nonreactive?

7. Is the instrument sensitive to measuring change?

8. Is the instrument feasible to score?

Another important characteristic of utility is that the measurement fits within the program's structure and logic model. For example, below are the goal and one of eight program objectives for a social service program that helps pregnant teenagers in high school. Also included is the measurement of the program objective. In addition, two practice objectives (A and B) are outlined and their corresponding measurements are given.

Practice activities that are believed to achieve the two program objectives are also delineated. Notice the consistency between the concepts of the program's goal, the stated program's objective, the two practice objectives related to the program's objective, the various activities, and the two measurements.

— **Program Goal**: To provide social services to pregnant teenagers in high school who have elected to keep their babies in an effort for them to become adequate mothers when they graduate from high school.

— **Program Objective**: To increase the self-sufficiency of pregnant adolescents after they have their babies.

• *Measurement of Program Objective:* Self-Sufficiency Inventory.

— **Practice Objective (A)**: To increase parenting skills.

• *Measurement of Practice Objective (A):* Adult-Adolescent Parenting Inventory.

Practice Activities (A): Teach specific child-rearing skills, role-model/role play effective parenting skills, teach effective child/adult communication skills, teach and model alternative discipline measures, teach age-appropriate response of children, and establish family structure (e.g., meal times, bath times, and bed times).

— **Practice Objective (B)**: To increase the number of support systems knowledgeable to the client.

• Measurement of Practice Objective (B): Instrument specially constructed for the particular city. To show how simple measuring instruments can be, Figure 6.5 presents one that was used with this practice objective. Figure 6.6 presents the correct answers.

Practice Activities (B): Review the city's information resource book with the client, provide information sheet on key resources relevant to the client, provide brochures on various agencies, escort client to needed resources (e.g., career resource center, health clinic), and go through specific and appropriate sections of the Yellow Pages with the client.

SUMMING UP AND LOOKING AHEAD

This chapter has discussed the concept of measurement: what measurement is, what a measuring instrument is, what will be measured, and by what method it will be measured. We also presented a few examples of different types of measurements. In addition, we considered the features required of a good measuring instrument. The next chapter focuses on case-level evaluations where the principles of measurement as presented in this chapter will be utilized.

KEY TERMS

Graphic Rating Scale: A type of measuring instrument that describes an attribute on a continuum from one extreme to the other, with points of the continuum ordered in equal intervals and assigned numbers.

Measure: A label, usually numerical, assigned to an observation that has been subjected to measurement.

Measurement: The process of systematically assigning labels to observations; in statistics, measurement systems are classified according to level of measurement and usually produce data that can be represented in numerical form; the assignment of numerals to objects or events according to specific rules.

Measuring Instruments: Instruments such as questionnaires or rating scales used to obtain a measure for a particular client or client group.

Nonreactivity: An unobtrusive characteristic of a measuring instrument; nonreactive measuring instruments do not affect the behavior being measured.

Norm: In measurement, an average or set group standard of achievement that can be used to interpret individual scores; normative data describing statistical properties of a measuring instrument, such as means and standard deviations.

Rating Scales: A type of measuring instrument in which responses are rated on a continuum or in an ordered set of categories, with numerical values assigned to each point or category.

Reliability: (1) The degree of accuracy, precision, or consistency of results of a measuring instrument, including the ability to reproduce results when a variable is measured more than once or a test is repeatedly filled out by the same individual. (2) The degree to which individual differences on scores or in data are due either to true differences or to errors in measurement.

Response Bias: The tendency for individuals to score items on a measuring instrument in such a manner that one score is reported for the majority of all items.

Self-Anchored Rating Scale: A type of measuring instrument in which respondents rate themselves on a continuum of values, according to their own referents for each point.

Standardized Measurement Instrument: A paper and-pencil tool, usually constructed by researchers and used by human service professionals, to measure a particular area of knowledge, behavior, or feeling; provides for uniform administration and scoring and generates normative data against which later results can be evaluated.

Summated Scale: A multi-item measuring instrument in which respondents provide a rating for each item. The summation of items provides an overall score.

Utility: A characteristic of a measuring instrument that indicates its degree of usefulness (e.g., how practical is the measuring instrument in a particular situation?).

Validity: The degree to which a measuring instrument accurately measures the variable it claims to measure.

Variable: A characteristic that can take on different values for different individuals; any attribute whose value, or level, can change; any characteristic (of a person, object, or situation) that can change value or kind from observation to observation.

STUDY QUESTIONS

1. How can demographic information used in developing a standardized measurement instrument influence the interpretation of scores obtained by a single client?

2. A social work practitioner who has 10 years of clinical experience with depressed clients develops a 10-item scale to measure depression. What are the issues of validity and reliability that this person must consider?

3. In groups of four, have each member list his or her biases or beliefs about the use of measuring instruments in the human services. As a group, discuss the nature of each individual bias and determine how such biases affect client service delivery.

4. In groups of four, develop a hypothetical practice objective for a client who has difficulty in managing anger. Assign one type of measuring instrument to each member of the group, and have each individual develop a scale to measure the stated practice objective. Discuss the advantages and disadvantages of each type of scale, and select the best one. Present your decision to the class.

5. Your colleagues wonder why measurement of the practice objectives they have established for their clients is necessary. How do you respond?

6. Why are objective methods of assessment so important in the human services? Why are objective definitions of program and practice objectives important in the human services?

7. What are standardized measuring instruments? What types of information should accompany them?

8. You are a worker at a local immigrant society. You submit all Asian American clients to a standardized instrument measuring self-esteem. They all perform poorly on the instrument. Would you immediately specify increased self-esteem as a practice or program objective with your clients? Why or why not?

9. What do rating scales measure?

10. Specify a practice objective that can be described on a continuum from one extreme to another. Develop a graphic rating scale for this objective.

11. Develop a summated rating scale to measure the practice objective you specified in the above question.

12. Suppose you are a member of a self-help group designed to enhance your ability to interact with others and overcome your shyness. Define your practice objective and develop a 9-point self-anchored rating scale to measure this objective. Why would it

be important for your group leader to cross-validate the data gathered from your scale with other sources? What are other possible sources of data?

13. Under what circumstances would a worker measure a practice objective with a summated scale? Why? Explain in detail.

14. As a practitioner you will want to choose good measuring instruments when measuring a particular objective. How will you be able to distinguish good instruments from poor ones?

15. When measuring program or practice objectives, why is it important to choose the instrument that will measure the objective and not anything else?

16. What is the optimum time interval between repeated measurement of program and practice objectives? How is this determined? Provide an example in your discussion.

REFERENCES AND FURTHER READINGS

Alter, C., & Evens, W. (1990). *Evaluating your practice: A guide to self-assessment*. New York: Springer.

Bloom, M., Fischer, J., & Orme, J. (1999). *Evaluating practice: Guidelines for the accountable professional* (3rd ed.). Englewood Cliffs, NJ: Prentice-Hall.

Corcoran, K.J. (1988). Selecting a measuring instrument. In R.M. Grinnell, Jr. (Ed.), *Social work research and evaluation* (3rd ed., pp. 137–155). Itasca, IL: F.E. Peacock Publishers.

Corcoran, K.J., & Fischer, J. (2000). *Measures for Clinical Practice* (3rd ed). *Volume 1: Couples, Families, and Children. Volume 2: Adults.* New York: Free Press.

http://ericae.net/testcol.htm

Hudson, W.W. (1981). Development and use of indexes and scales. In R.M. Grinnell, Jr. (Ed.), *Social work research and evaluation* (pp. 130–155). Itasca, IL: F.E. Peacock Publishers.

Hudson, W.W. (1982). *The Clinical Measurement Package: A Field Manual.* Newbury Park, CA: Wadsworth.

Hudson, W.W. (1985). Indexes and scales. In R.M. Grinnell, Jr. (Ed.), *Social work research and evaluation* (2nd ed., pp. 185–205). Itasca, IL: F.E. Peacock Publishers.

Hudson, W.W. (1993). Standardized measures. In J. Krysik, I. Hoffart, & R.M. Grinnell, Jr. *Student study guide for the fourth edition of Social work research and evaluation* (pp. 243–263). Itasca, IL: F.E. Peacock Publishers.

Jordan, C., Franklin, C., & Corcoran, K. (1993). Standardized measuring instruments. In R.M. Grinnell, Jr. (Ed.), *Social work research and evaluation* (4th ed., pp. 198–220). Itasca, IL: F.E. Peacock Publishers.

Jordan, C., Franklin, C., & Corcoran, K. (1997). Measuring instruments. In R.M. Grinnell, Jr. (Ed.), *Social work research and evaluation: Quantitative and qualitative approaches* (5th ed., pp. 184–211). Itasca, IL: F.E. Peacock Publishers.

Jordan, C., Franklin, C., & Corcoran, K. (2001). Measuring instruments. In R.M. Grinnell, Jr. (Ed.), *Social work research and evaluation: Quantitative and qualitative approaches* (6th ed., pp. 151–180). Itasca, IL: F.E. Peacock Publishers.

Kidder, L.H., & Judd, C.M. (1986). *Research methods in social relations* (5th ed.). New York: Holt, Rinehart & Winston.

Kyte, N.S., & Bostwick, G. (2001). Measuring variables. In R.M. Grinnell, Jr. (Ed.), *Social work research and evaluation: Quantitative and qualitative approaches* (6th ed., pp. 129–150). Itasca, IL: F.E. Peacock Publishers.

Mindel, C.H. (2001). Designing measuring Instruments. In R.M. Grinnell, Jr. (Ed.), *Social work research and evaluation: Quantitative and qualitative approaches* (6th ed., pp. 181–203). Itasca, IL: F.E. Peacock Publishers.

7

Chapter Outline

Case-Level Evaluations

THE PREVIOUS CHAPTER discussed the measurement process: what and how program and practice objectives can be measured, who should measure them, when and where they can be measured, and what measuring instruments can be used. This chapter considers how the measurement process can help human service professionals to evaluate their practice efforts at the case level with the use of consultations and case conferences, and with the use of case-level evaluation designs. The advantages and limitations of these designs are also discussed.

INFORMAL CASE-LEVEL EVALUATIONS

An empirical method of evaluation is one in which the evaluation is based on the analysis of systematically collected valid and reliable data, that is, on the collation and interpretation of data generated by standardized measuring instruments. Correspondingly, nonempirical evaluations are derived from information developed from theories and descriptions considered relevant by the practitioner. Because nonempirical information collection is relatively less formal and rigorous than its empirical data collection counterpart, it is also known as *informal evaluation*. There are two informal methods that we can use to evaluate our cases at the case level: (1) private case consultations, and (2) case conferences.

Case Consultations

Many professionals consult informally with others regarding their cases. These requests for advice are usually accompanied by a description of the client's circumstances, the interventions the worker has tried so far, and the present condition of the client as perceived by the practitioner. Sometimes these descriptions are written, but more often than not, communication is verbal. In either case the consultation is informal because no authority structure mandates or controls it. And it is nonempirical because the information exchanged is not derived from data obtained through standardized measurement.

The disadvantages of case consultations lie in their lack of objectivity and precision, or in other words, in their nonempirical nature. Their main advantage is their efficiency, which is a function of their informal nature: Rapid exchange of ideas and information are facilitated by the absence of formal documentation and procedures.

Case Conferences

Case conferences tend to be more formal than private consultations in that the human service worker and other professionals are usually required to attend, and minutes may be taken and disseminated to participants. Nevertheless, the presentation of the case tends to remain nonempirical, a description reflecting the practitioner's point of view. Concurring and opposing viewpoints are generally couched in the same lack of precision. Although much information of value may be exchanged, it is not data derived from standardized measurements and, therefore, its reliability and validity are unknown.

The major advantage of a case conference is that all human service workers involved with a particular client can meet face to face, share their perceptions or concerns, and perhaps leave the conference feeling that they have been heard, something has been resolved, and future problems can be addressed with the help of people who have already shown themselves to be caring and cooperative.

As before, the disadvantages are lack of objectivity and lack of precision. While private consultations and case conferences are a very important part of professional practice, these two informal evaluation methods should be used in conjunction with formal case-level evaluations.

FORMAL CASE-LEVEL EVALUATIONS

Formal case-level evaluation designs can be used by social workers in many ways. Unlike case consultations and case conferences previously mentioned, they are formal, empirical methods of evaluation, based on the analysis of collected data usually generated by standardized measuring instruments. They are sometimes known as single-system research designs, single-subject research designs, idiographic research designs, $N = 1$ research designs, time-series designs, and subject replication research designs.

Whatever name is used, a case-level evaluation is a study of one entity—a single client, a single group, a single couple, a single family, a single organization, or a single community—involving repeated measurements over time in order to measure change. As we will see in later chapters in this book, the results of a number of formal case-level evaluations can be aggregated to assess the effectiveness of a program as a whole. In general, case-level evaluations can be used to measure the obtainment of practice-level objectives and program-level objectives. However, they are mostly used to measure practice-level objectives.

Formal case-level evaluations focus on practitioners' activities and their clients' practice objective outcomes so that cause-effect relationships can be established in some cases. There are a large number of case-level evaluation designs, ranging from the qualitative to the quantitative and from the exploratory to the explanatory, as illustrated below.

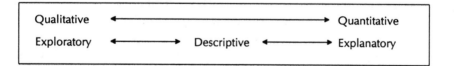

We have seen that the term *qualitative refers* to a description in words, which is less precise than a *quantitative* description, or one given in numbers. An *explanatory* study is one in which the worker manipulates certain factors in order to gain a greater degree of control over the intervention process. A *descriptive* study involves less manipulation and hence less control, and an *exploratory* study involves no manipulation and virtually no control. The case consultations and case conferences mentioned earlier in this chapter fall into the qualitative, exploratory category at the far left of the range.

It should be stressed that the characterization is a *continuum;* that is, there is no point at which qualitative becomes quantitative or descriptive becomes explanatory. Various evaluation designs are placed on the continuum according to the degree to which they manifest descriptive and manipulative qualities. These degrees tend to merge and blend, so that it is often difficult to place a particular design in a particular category.

Formal case-level designs are one of the most promising evaluative tools available to line-level practitioners (Thyer, 2001). A number of features are integral to these designs: (1) establishing baselines, (2) measurable practice objectives, (3) repeated measurements, (4) graphic data displays, and (5) comparisons across phases.

Establishing Baselines

A baseline is essentially a measure of the client's practice objective *before* the professional provides services. By establishing a baseline, the worker attempts to find out how long the problematic event lasts, how often it occurs, its intensity, and whether it occurs at all in the client's normal life.

For example, suppose that a young child throws temper tantrums. Before intervening, the worker will want to know how frequent and intense these tantrums are, when and where they occur, and for how long they last, in addition to trying to gain insight into the events that precipitate or alleviate them. An obvious way to gain such knowledge is to do nothing in the way of intervention while collecting the necessary data. The parents might be asked to keep a client log in which they record the day, date, and start and finish time of each episode, together with the events that occurred immediately preceding, during, and after it.

Alternatively, a standardized measure might be used, over a period of time, to measure the magnitude of the problem. In either case, at the end of the period, the practitioner will have baseline data on the tantrums as well as some data about possible precipitating events. These data provide a standard against which change can be measured and provide some indication of the most effective interventive method to use.

Measurable Practice Objectives

We have stressed in previous chapters that program and practice objectives must be measurable; they should be defined in a way that allows their degree of achievement to be observed and measured.

For example, three distinct practice objectives can be set for the child with the tantrums:

— To reduce the *frequency of* the episodes
— To reduce their *intensity*
— To reduce their *duration*

In each case, it must be clear exactly what is meant by a "temper tantrum." What behaviors, specifically, are observable when a temper tantrum occurs? How can the tantrum be measured when it occurs?

The frequency and duration of tantrums can be easily measured using techniques described in Chapters 4 and 5. The intensity, for example, might be measured using a self-anchored rating scale. The idea that practice (and program) objectives must be measurable thus has two conceptual components: The objective must be specifically defined and measurable.

Repeated Measurements

Formal case-level evaluation designs rely on repeated valid and reliable measurements: Change is perceived and measured by repeated administrations of the same measuring instrument under the same conditions. Repeated measurements document trends (if any), and how the practice objective is changing over time.

Graphic Data Displays

A *data display is* the way in which the collected data are set out on the page; the manner in which they are set out in turn depends on how the original data were grouped or collated. For example, the respective numbers of African American, Caucasian, or Asian clients attending a particular program may be presented merely as a list of numerals. For ease of interpretation, these numbers can also be presented in the form of a bar graph or line diagram, or they may be converted into percentages and displayed as a pie chart.

Most people find it easier to see what data mean when they are displayed as a graph or chart rather than as a list. Data collected in formal case-level studies are usually presented graphically, with the level of the practice

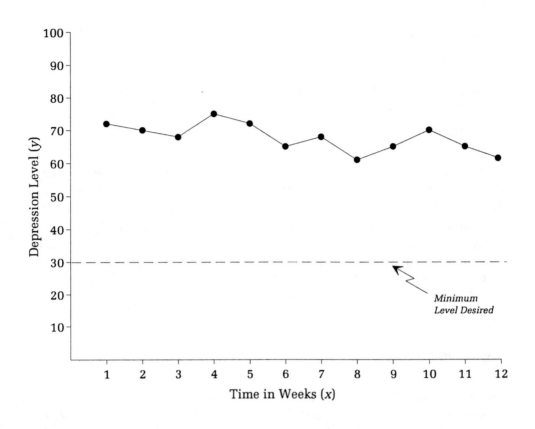

FIGURE 7.1   Magnitude of Ms. Jarrett's Depression
                       Levels over a 12-Week Period

objective plotted on the vertical line and time plotted on the horizontal line.
Let us take as an example Ms. Jarrett, who suffers from depression. The practitioner measures the magnitude of her depression every week for twelve weeks
using a standardized measuring instrument for depression. No intervention is
attempted during this time; the object is to obtain a baseline measure of Ms.
Jarrett's depression. The first time the instrument is administered, Ms. Jarrett
scores 72; the second time, 70; the third time, 69. The practitioner might plot
these scores on a simple graph as illustrated in Figure 7.1. (In Figure 7.1, high
scores equal high depression levels.)

   The vertical axis of the graph is labeled "Depression Level." What is really
being plotted is the magnitude of Ms. Jarrett's depression. The horizontal axis
of the graph is labeled "Time in Weeks." This indicates that changes in the
magnitude of Ms. Jarrett's depression are being monitored over a period of

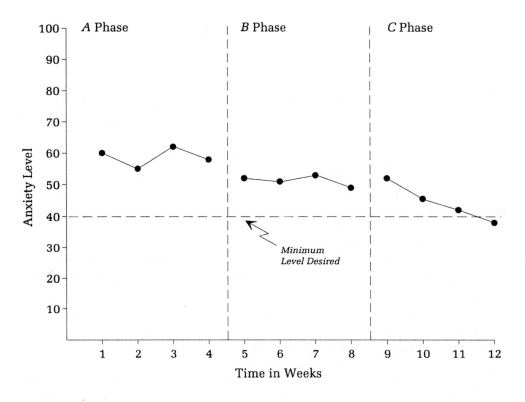

FIGURE 7.2   *ABC* Design: Magnitude of Barbara's
                      Anxiety Level Before and After Two
                      Interventions, Indicating an Improvement
                      with the *C* Intervention

time, measured in weeks. The practice objective, then, is what the practitioner
and client are trying to change. Repeated measurement of the objective will
show any change that has occurred during the course of the intervention; that
is, it will show an *effect*. The Length of intervention (activity), undertaken to
achieve the effect, is plotted on the horizontal line.

Comparison Across Phases

A phase is any distinct part of the contact between a social worker and a client. For example, the first few weeks of service may be spent collecting baseline data: This is one phase. Then an intervention (services) may be tried: This is the second phase. If the services do not seem to be effective, a different intervention may be tried: This is the third phase. Phases are usually represented on a graph by dashed vertical lines, as shown in Figure 7.2.

It is customary to use letters to designate the different phases. The letter A represents the baseline phase. Successive interventions are represented by successive letters: B for the first, C for the second, D for the third, and so on. A case-level evaluation design in which a baseline phase is followed by an interventive phase is therefore called an AB design. Similarly, an ABC design is one in which a baseline phase (A) is followed by two different interventive phases $(B$ and $C)$. A simple ABC design is illustrated in Figure 7.2 and will be discussed in more detail later in this chapter.

If an intervention is not really different but is merely a slight variation of one tried before, it is represented by the original letter plus a subscript. For example, one way of improving knowledge in a certain area may be to set homework assignments. This may be the first intervention tried, or Phase B. If understanding does not improve to the desired degree, the number of homework assignments set may be increased. This second intervention is merely an intensified version of the first and would be designated Phase B_2, with the first intervention (B) now considered B_1. A design in which a baseline phase is followed by three versions of the same intervention would thus be written $AB_1B_2B_3$.

EVALUATION DESIGN CONTINUUM

There are essentially three types of case-level designs: exploratory, descriptive, and explanatory. All three types of designs can be used for purposes of quality improvement as well as for purposes of knowledge building. Exploratory case-level designs are the most commonly used for quality improvement purposes because they involve continuous monitoring of client progress. Nevertheless, the other two types of designs, descriptive and explanatory designs, also produce data that can be valuable for quality improvement purposes. While exploratory designs can contribute to knowledge development, descriptive and explanatory designs are the most useful for this purpose.

Exploratory Designs

The purposes of exploratory case-level designs is to explore, to assess how things are going, and to build a foundation of general ideas and tentative theories that can be confirmed or abandoned later, using more rigorous designs. Exploratory designs will not produce conclusive or statistically definitive results. When an exploratory design is used, it is not possible to prove that the intervention caused the outcome; although it may be assumed that if an intervention is followed by a desired client outcome, then the intervention had something to do with the outcome. In general, exploratory designs measure and monitor the outcome of practice objectives without attempting to prove a causal link between those outcomes and the activities believed to have engendered them.

Although exploratory designs have their limitations from a scientific perspective, they are highly useful for quality improvement purposes. These designs can provide ongoing feedback about client progress, allowing the practitioner to make intervention decisions based on empirical data. This makes it likely that ineffective services will be quickly discontinued or modified and that effective interventions will be maintained—in short, that the most appropriate services will be provided to clients. In addition, these designs are less intrusive, less disruptive, and easier to implement than descriptive and explanatory designs.

There are three kinds of exploratory case-level evaluation designs: the *B* design, the *BC* design, and the *BCD* design.

The *B* Design

The first type of exploratory case-level evaluation designs is the *B* design. The *B* design tells us whether the client's practice objective is changing in the desired direction. If the level of the client's practice objective is not changing in the way that it should, we can at least wonder whether other interventions should be tried. The *B* design can monitor the level of the client's practice objective over time.

Figure 7.3 provides an example of a *B* design that was used by a practitioner to measure the practice objective "to reduce David's and Donna's interruptions of each other as the other one is talking." The data from Figure 7.3 are extremely useful since a worker will be better able to judge whether the intervention should be continued, modified, or abandoned in favor of a

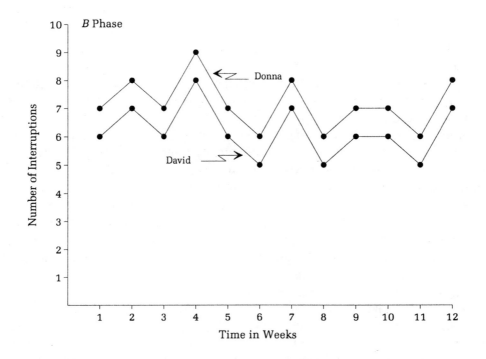

FIGURE 7.3   *B* Design: Frequency of Interruptions for a
                    Couple During One Intervention,
                    Indicating No Improvement

different interventive strategy. The *B* design monitors the effectiveness of an intervention over time and indicates when the desired level of the target problem has been reached.

The *B* design is useful in showing changes in the level of a problem or need. While a *B* design may provide clues about the degree to which a client is achieving his or her practice objectives, no extraneous factors are accounted for, and no suggestion of a causal relationship is possible. Consequently, no conclusions can be easily drawn regarding the relative merits and efficacy of the worker's interventions. The value of the *B* design, therefore, lies in two basic areas. First, it is quick and simple to implement. Second, it allows for the systematic monitoring of changing levels in the achievement of practice objectives.

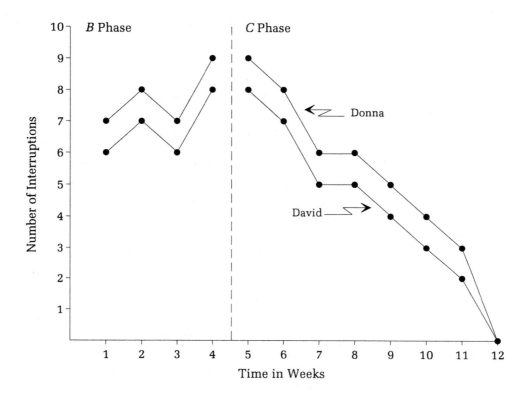

FIGURE 7.4   *BC* Design: Frequency of Interruptions for
Donna and David After Two Interventions,
Indicating an Improvement with the Second
Intervention

The *BC* and *BCD* Designs

The second and third types of exploratory case-level evaluation designs are the *BC* and *BCD* designs. As we know, the *B* design represents a single interventive strategy. Suppose now that a *B* intervention, such as an anger control training package, is implemented with David and Donna, and a graph like the one shown in Figure 7.4 is obtained.

The left side of Figure 7.4 indicates that David and Donnas' target problem is not being resolved with the implementation of only the *B* intervention (i.e., an anger control training package), and the worker may feel that a new intervention—say a communication skills training package—is needed, so a *C* intervention (i.e., communication skills training package) is introduced in the fifth week.

As indicated in Figure 7.4, the worker implemented the communication skills training package (Intervention C) in the fifth week. The worker also measured the target problem in the same way as before, by making weekly recordings of the number of times that each partner interrupts the other during the course of therapy sessions. Figure 7.4 shows that no change occurred in the target problem after Intervention B was implemented, but that the target problem was resolved following the implementation of Intervention C. Since the BC and BCD designs involve successive, different interventions, they are sometimes known as successive interventions designs. It is conceivable that an E intervention might be necessary, forming a BCDE design, and even an F, forming a BCDEF design.

Descriptive Designs

Descriptive designs are often called quasi-experimental designs. The prefix quasi means "having some resemblance." Thus, a quasi-experiment is one that resembles a true experiment but is lacking some essential ingredient. To understand what the essential ingredient is, it is necessary to say something about the characteristics of a true experiment.

The purpose of a true experiment is to demonstrate with certainty that something causes something else, or, in the cases that concern us, that a certain activity caused an observed change in a client's practice objective. We can demonstrate this causal connection by proving that nothing else could have caused the observed change. For example, suppose that Ms. Jarrett is still being treated for depression. Repeated measurement has shown that Ms Jarrett's depression level underwent a marked decrease over a period of one month.

To prove that the interventive strategy alone caused the observed decrease, we must prove that she did not win a lottery during that month, did not have a joyful reunion with her long-lost son, did not find a satisfying job. In short, we have to prove that nothing, aside from the intervention, happened that could have decreased her depression. All of the things that might have happened to Ms. Jarrett are called extraneous variables because they might also have influenced the attainment of the practice objective; they could have confounded the desired establishment of a cause-effect relationship between the intervention and the client outcome.

Because the number of extraneous variables that may have lightened Ms. Jarrett's depression is so enormous, the best way of testing for causality is to have two identical Ms. Jarretts, one experiencing only the extraneous variables and the other experiencing both the extraneous variables and the intervention. Comparison of the state of mind of the two Ms. Jarretts will then reveal how much of the reduced depression was due to the extraneous variables and how much to the intervention. Or, the equivalent of a comparison of two Ms. Jarretts can be obtained by comparing groups, as will be discussed in the following chapter. However, in case-level evaluation there is only one Ms. Jarrett; some other solution to the difficulty must be found.

The best solution, with only one case (client), is to repeat the experiment: to obtain baseline data, implement an intervention, measure the resulting change, and then bring the client back to the baseline level and do it all again. If the intervention succeeds in bringing about the desired change the second time, it is more probable that the intervention, rather than extraneous variables, was the causal agent.

As should be obvious, there are several problems associated with this procedure. In the first place, it is hardly ethical to return a client deliberately to an original problematic condition; in the second place, it is rarely possible to do so because a useful intervention does not cease to have an effect when it is stopped. For these reasons, it is difficult to implement all the features of a true experiment. Specifically, returning the client to baseline and repeating the treatment are rarely implemented in practice. However, the remaining aspects of these designs, which are more practical to apply, are incorporated in the descriptive designs described in this section.

Two basic descriptive evaluation designs can be used in formal case-level evaluations: (1) the *AB* design, and (2) the *ABC* design.

The *AB* Design

As indicated earlier, an *AB* design is one in which a baseline phase (*A*) is followed by a single interventive phase (*B*). The assumption underlying this design is that the level of the practice objective in the baseline phase (*A*) will continue unchanged if the worker does not intervene (*B*) to change it. On the face of it, this seems like a reasonable assumption but, if the practice objective happens to be Ms. Jarrett's depression, innumerable extraneous variables are waiting in the wings. In fact, one can argue that the first contact with the professional is in itself an extraneous variable, and will already have had an effect. Ms. Jarrett may feel more hopeful or more understood; her depression may have been lifted to some extent by the very act of leaving the house to attend the interview, by being offered coffee by the secretary, by seeing a new face.

A partial answer to these concerns about measurement impurity can be found in the nature of the baseline itself. A single measure of her depression level before the intervention was initiated does not constitute a baseline. After all, a line is defined as the shortest distance between two points—there cannot be a line if there are not at least two points. Preferably, three or more measurements of the original problem level should be made, and in these repeated measures there is some security.

The first contact with the practitioner may have lifted. Ms Jarrett's depression temporarily, but the effect is unlikely to last for the length of time it takes to establish a baseline. Any effect of extraneous variables is also likely to be temporary. If a stable baseline is established, or a baseline shows the depression to be worsening, it may be assumed that nothing in Ms. Jarrett's life aside from the intervention will decrease her level of depression.

Figure 7.5 shows a graph of Ms. Jarrett's depression levels, plotted against time, through the baseline phase (A) and the interventive phase (B). Note that higher scores indicate a higher level of depression, so the practice objective in this case is "to decrease Ms. Jarretts depression."

The AB design is a basic component of many more complex designs. It shows only that change has occurred; with a stable or worsening baseline, it supports the assumption that the intervention caused the change. If the intervention includes a number of activities, such as role-plays, films, and discussions, the design will not show which of these activities (or what combination) was most effective in promoting change. Nevertheless, the AB design lies within the reach of every social worker, and it fulfills the major function of a case-level evaluative design: It allows workers to know to what degree their clients are reaching their practice objectives. These data, in turn, help them to decide upon the most appropriate interventions.

$AB_1B_2B_3$ Designs   An important extension of the AB design is the $AB_1B_2B_3$ design, which consists of a baseline phase (A) followed by three variations on one intervention. The $AB_1B_2B_3$ design, also called the changing intensity design, may take either of two forms. One involves increasing the expectations of the client's desired outcome over time, and the other involves changing the intensity of the intervention over time.

For example, suppose that a boy receives a monthly reward of, say, two dollars if he achieves a grade in English that is 5 percent higher than his grade the month before. Here the intervention remains the same—providing the two

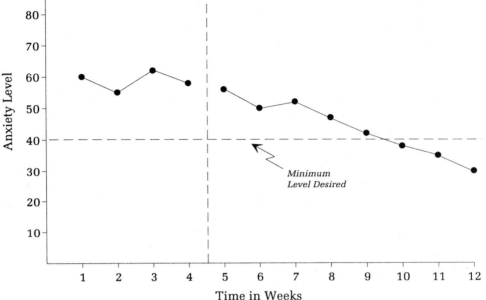

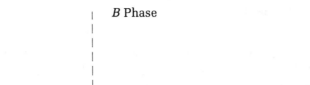

FIGURE 7.5   *AB* Design: Magnitude of Ms. Jarrett's
Anxiety Level Before and After an
Intervention, Indicating an Improvement

dollars—but the boy must perform at a higher level every month in order to receive the money. Because the criterion for success has changed, the $AB_1B_2B_3$ design used in this context is called the changing criterion design. Its main advantage is that it allows the client to move in graduated steps toward a final practice objective.

The second form of the changing intensity design involves changing the intensity of the intervention. If a practice objective has failed to reach the desired level, a practitioner may offer more varied or more intense reinforcement, increase the number of tasks per week, or increase the number of weekly sessions. If termination is imminent, we may want to reduce the number of contacts or provide more intermittent reinforcement. In either case, the basic intervention remains the same, but its intensity is increased or diminished.

The *ABC Design*

The *ABC* (and *ABCD, ABCDE,* and so on) designs are extensions of the basic *AB* design and involve a baseline phase (*A*) followed by two, three, or more different interventions (*B* and *C*). Successive interventions are often employed by professionals when data indicate that the first or second interventions are not working satisfactorily and something new needs to be tried.

Another application of the *ABC* designs is the introduction of a maintenance phase, when an intervention has been successful, but the client now needs to be taught to use new skills, without the aid of the worker. For example, the worker may have succeeded in reducing stress (practice objective) with the aid of relaxation techniques (activities) applied in weekly sessions, but the client now needs to begin to use these techniques at home. Figure 7.2 shows a client's anxiety level over time. *A* represents the baseline phase, *B* an unsuccessful interventive phase, and *C,* a successful interventive phase. Higher scores indicate greater stress, so the desired change is in a downward direction.

The disadvantage of successive intervention designs is that *C* or *D* phases cannot be compared with the baseline phase because an intervening *B* phase has occurred. In addition, the effect of the *C* phase alone cannot readily be distinguished from the combined effects of the *B* phase and the *C* phase, so that the practitioner will not know whether the *C* intervention would have worked without the introduction of *B*. Of course, the more interventions there are, the more confused the picture becomes and the harder it is to ascribe the observed result to any particular interventive strategy.

Explanatory Designs

Explanatory designs are often called experimental designs. They try to demonstrate causality; they show that an activity—the intervention—caused the observed changes in the practice objective—the problem level. As mentioned, explanatory designs are the most rigorous case-level designs. They help to further our understanding of the relationship between interventions and their outcomes; these designs are powerful tools from a scientific perspective. Nevertheless, they also provide information that can be used in the quality improvement process. Five basic explanatory designs used to measure practice objectives are: (1) the *ABA* design, (2) the *ABAB,* design, (3) the *BAB* design, and (4) the *BCBC* design.

The *ABA* Design

The *ABA* design involve establishing a baseline in Phase *A*, intervening in Phase *B*, and then removing the intervention, *A*. As a deliberate procedure, this is rarely permissible, but it happens by chance quite often. A client may come for assistance, receive it, and terminate when the problem is apparently resolved. However, when the intervention stops, the problem reappears at its former level; the client returns to the professional, and Phase *A* is in place again. This second time, though, the worker knows that the *B* intervention did resolve the problem, if only temporarily. The fact that the problem returned when the intervention was stopped makes it more likely that the intervention caused the resolution of the problem; thus, the worker will be more confident in trying the same intervention again.

The *ABAB* Design

When the same *B* intervention is tried again, the *ABA* design becomes an *ABAB* design. If the intervention works for the second time, the practitioner can be still more confident that it was the intervention, and only the intervention, that resolved the problem. However, if the client is not to spend a lifetime on the *ABABAB* treadmill, obviously something further needs to be done. The worker will probably introduce a *C* phase in which the intervention is intended to maintain the progress already made. The *ABABAB* design now becomes an *ABABABC* design.

There are other circumstances in which a successful intervention may be halted, and so an *ABAB* design (or some variant thereof) may be employed. Perhaps a client has completed a successful *B* phase with respect to one particular problem when a crisis erupts in another problem area. The worker's efforts are refocused on the crisis; by the time it has been resolved, the success in the *B* phase has been lost.

In general, it is a common problem in the human services that success, where achieved, is not maintained. One possible reason for this is that termination is initiated prematurely, before the desired change has had a chance to stabilize. It must be stressed that repeated measurements are necessary not just to establish a baseline, but also to establish that a desired outcome has been achieved and maintained. To illustrate, Figure 7.6 shows Barbara's anxiety levels plotted against time through an *ABAB* succession.

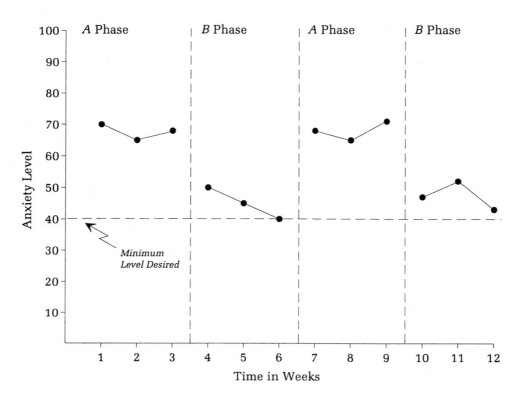

FIGURE 7.6   *ABAB* Design: Magnitude of Barbara's
Anxiety Level Before and After an
Intervention, Indicating High Deterioration
in the Second *A* Phase

The *BAB* Design

There are some occasions, especially in crisis work, when taking the time
to establish a baseline before intervening would be harmful to the client. On
these occasions, a *B*, or interventive phase, is initiated immediately and
terminated when the problem appears to be resolved. As before, the problem
may reemerge without the continued service, and the client may then return
to the baseline level.

Of course, because the baseline level was never measured, it cannot be
known that the client has returned to it. It is also possible that the *B* interven-

tion continued to have some effect but not enough to prevent the problem from flaring up again.

Practitioners are not entirely defenseless in the face of these different causal possibilities. Initial measurements in the first *B* phase will give some indication of the problem level at the very beginning of intervention, and, if the intervention takes some time to have an effect, these measurements might even constitute a baseline phase. That is, a pseudo-*A* phase may be established merely because the intervention is not immediately effective. In addition, whether or not the client returns to the same level after the first *B* intervention , comparisons between the two *B* phases and the *A* phase can still be made. One can at least state that when the intervention was removed, the problem returned, and when the intervention was reinstated, the problem was resolved. This in itself is enough to show causality, although causality is more fully demonstrated if two *A* phases can also be compared, as in the *ABAB* design. To illustrate, Figure 7.7 shows Barbara's anxiety levels plotted against time through a *BAB* succession.

The *BCBC* Design

Often a worker may consider two different interventions, but is unsure of which one to try. The *BCBC* design allows both to be introduced sequentially: The *B* intervention is tried and its effectiveness is assessed. It is then removed and the *C* intervention is tried in its place; again, measures of effectiveness are made and the *C* intervention is removed. The original *B* intervention is then reinstated, to be followed once more by a second *C* phase.

This design allows us to compare the effectiveness of two interventions. It is also useful when no baseline data can be obtained, as with the *BAB* design. To see this, suppose that members of the support staff in a hospital are bringing a large number of grievances directly to department heads. The hospital already has a system in place to deal with grievances:

Support staff are supposed to take them to their own representatives, who meet with department heads to resolve the issues. This system does not seem to be working well, but the administrator does not want to replace it with an alternative system, which may be even worse, without some preliminary testing.

Using a *BCBC* design, the administrator asks department heads to record for three weeks how many grievances support staff bring to their personal attention. This is the first *B* phase and the "intervention" is the original grievance system. After three months, the administrator discontinues the system

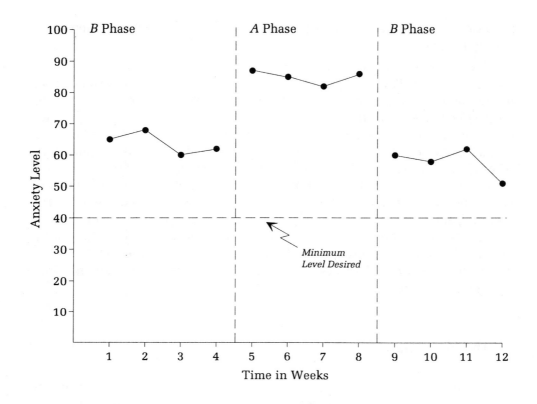

FIGURE 7.7   *BAB* Design: Magnitude of Barbara's Anxiety
                    Level During and After an Intervention

in favor of twice monthly meetings in which hospital administrators, department heads, and all support staff meet to discuss issues.

This is the first *C* phase and, once again, department heads are asked to
note the number of grievances brought by individuals. Three months later, the
administrator reinstates the original system, and three months after that, returns
to the twice monthly meetings.

ADVANTAGES OF CASE-LEVEL DESIGNS

By now it should be clearly evident that formal case-level designs provide the
methods by which social workers can evaluate their success with individual

clients. This approach has advantages for the worker, the client, and the social service program itself.

The Practitioner Is Responsible for Data Collection

Although data may be collected by the client or others in the client's environment, the practitioner has both control over and responsibility for the data. That is, the social worker decides what data should be collected where, when, under what conditions, and by whom. Given this, it is possible to organize data collection so that if confirmational data are needed (from, say, a teacher or relative), they can be obtained efficiently in time to assist decision making. In addition, workers are free to follow their own theoretical approaches to practice. The data collected will not determine the practice approach utilized but will be determined by it.

The Focus Is on the Client

All formal case-level designs are developed for or can be adapted to an individual case. Measuring instruments can be chosen that are specific to the client's practice objective or, if no instruments exist, the worker and client can develop them together. Many types of existing scales discussed in Chapters 4 and 5 are a good example of this individualized approach to measurement.

Usually, clients are able to recognize that the interventions and measuring methods are specially tailored to them. Their belief that something relevant is being done will often increase their motivation, allowing them to participate more fully in solving their own practice objectives.

Formal case-level designs can also be adapted to the client. For example, it may be necessary to intervene with a particular client at once, without establishing a baseline. However, if the client can provide reliable data about the duration, frequency, or intensity of the problem prior to the interview, a retroactive baseline may be established on the strength of the client's recollection. The design is adaptable in a further sense: It may begin as *AB* (because a practitioner obviously hopes the first intervention will be effective), but if measurements indicate that it is not effective, it may become *ABC* or *ABCBC*, or *ABCD*, depending on the professional's judgment and the client's response.

Clinical Decisions Are Based on the Data Collected

Formal case-level evaluation designs provide continuous data to social workers so that they can monitor clients' progress and alter their interventions if that progress is slower than expected. In addition, the collected data can be useful in making decisions to terminate or initiate different treatment interventions.

Problem Analysis Is Facilitated

Formal case-level evaluation designs require that measurable practice objectives be set. Formulating a specific measurable objective compels the worker to think the client's problem through. What is it precisely about Mike's aggression that needs to be measured? Is Mike aggressive in the sense that he is hostile or in the sense that he is overassertive? It is obviously necessary to decide this, as interventions aimed at reducing hostility will differ from those intended to reduce overassertiveness. If Mike is hostile, is he hostile only to certain people in certain situations—for example, his mother or peers—or is he *generally* hostile? Again, we need to know this in order to plan.

Once the problem is defined, the worker will be able to devise an appropriate intervention. If a similar problem has occurred with another client, the worker may well have formed a hunch about the most effective intervention. The intervention can be used again and its effectiveness measured; in other words, the hunch can be *tested*. Data serving to strengthen or weaken the hunch will enable the worker to reassess his or her own theoretical bases or practice approaches.

The Cost Is Small in Time and Disruptiveness

There is no doubt that making measurements takes more time than not making them. However, this time must be compared to time that is inevitably wasted when the practitioner does not really know how the practice objective is progressing, whether the intervention is working, and whether or not it is time to try something else. Nor should measurement be considered disruptive. A disruption is, by definition, something that disturbs the normal course of events; if measurement is a part of the normal course of events, it is not a disruption, but only a continuous record of progress made.

The Client's Situation Is Taken into Account

One of the major advantages of formal case-level designs is that they are infinitely flexible and the client's unique situation can always be taken into account. For example, a rating scale that the practitioner knows will be completed by the client's mother can be designed to fit the mother's capabilities; instruments can be completed at home at times convenient for the client; and designs can always be adapted to fit the client's individual needs.

Data Can Be Used in Program-Level Evaluations

As we know, data collected on individual clients can be aggregated or clustered to provide program evaluation data. For example, a charitable organization that funds a number of social service programs might require its members to document a minimum level of verified successful case outcomes in order to qualify for further funding. The operative word here is *verified*. Individual practitioners would have to provide evidence of successful case outcomes, complete with data clearly displayed on graphs. Formal case-level designs lend themselves to such documentation. A social service program staffed with professional social workers who all use case-levels designs will have less difficulty in demonstrating success and obtaining future funding than those programs that do not use them.

Data collected on clients over time can also be useful in determining eligibility criteria for a social service program as a whole. For example, it may have been found that clients who achieved a certain score on a particular standardized measuring instrument tended to do better in the program than clients who achieved a lower score. A minimum score might then be set as a criterion for admittance.

LIMITATIONS OF CASE-LEVEL DESIGNS

There are advantages and disadvantages to most things in life, and case-level evaluation designs are no exception. Two disadvantages are listed below.

Limited Generalizability

As will be discussed in the next chapter, when a study is conducted at the explanatory level with such controls as random sampling and random assignment to groups, the results of the study apply not just to the group being tested but to the entire population from which the sample was drawn. When a case-level study is conducted with an individual client, the results apply only to that client. Thus, they have limited generalizability from one client to the next or from one practice objective to the next. This is a major drawback of case-level evaluation designs.

A number of similar results obtained in similar situations with similar clients make it more likely that the findings are generally applicable; but an individual worker may not have such comparative data available. Workers should therefore resist the temptation to assume that because an intervention worked once it must necessarily work again.

Explanatory Designs Are Difficult to Implement

Only in exceptional circumstances is it ethical to deliberately implement such explanatory designs as the *ABA* and *ABAB* designs, where a successful intervention is removed and the problem allowed to return to the baseline level. Because of ethical difficulties, such designs usually come into being accidentally; consequently, rigor suffers. Very often, measurement of the problem level does not continue between the first *B* phase and the second *A* phase, as a client who believes that a problem has been solved will not continue to keep records between the apparent solution and the reappearance.

There is, therefore, a gap in the data, and it is not possible to say with certainty that the reappearance of the problem had anything to do with the removal of the intervention. Perhaps the problem would have reappeared even if the intervention had been continued. An accidental application of an *ABAB* design thus eliminates one argument for causality: that the problem reappears when the intervention is removed.

Descriptive formal case-level designs are easier to implement than explanatory designs because they require only a baseline phase followed by as many intervention phases as are necessary to solve the client's problem. However, they do not provide causal data, and practitioners who want to know whether a particular intervention solved a particular problem cannot rely on these more practical designs.

SUMMING UP AND LOOKING AHEAD

This chapter has discussed various kinds of case-level evaluations that included informal and formal case-level evaluation designs. It highlighted their use by providing brief introductions to exploratory, descriptive, and explanatory case-level designs. The next chapter provides a complementary discussion of evaluation designs that can be used in program-level evaluations.

KEY TERMS

A Phase: In case-level evaluation designs, a phase (A Phase) in which the baseline measurement of the target problem is established before the intervention (B Phase) is implemented.

Axes: Straight horizontal and vertical lines in a graph upon which values of a measurement, or the corresponding frequencies, are plotted.

Baseline Measure: A numerical label assigned to a client's level of performance, knowledge, or affect prior to any intervention; the first measure to be made in any series of repeated measurements; designated as the A phase in formal case-level designs.

B Phase: In case-level evaluation designs, the intervention phase, which may, or may not, include simultaneous measurements.

Case: The basic unit of social work practice, whether it be an individual, a couple, a family, an agency, a community, a county, a state, or a country.

Case Conferences: An informal, or nonempirical, method of case evaluation that requires professionals to meet and exchange descriptive client information for the purposes of making a case decision.

Case Study: Using research approaches to investigate a research question or hypothesis relating to a specific case; used to develop theory and test hypotheses; an in-depth form of research in which data are gathered and analyzed about an individual unit of analysis, person, city, event, society, etc.; it allows more intensive analysis of specific details; the disadvantage is that it is hard to use the results to generalize to other cases.

Causal Relationship: A relationship between two variables for which we can state that the presence of, or absence of, one variable determines the presence of, or absence of, the other variable.

Data Display: The manner in which collected data are set out on a page.

Descriptive Design: A design that approximates a true experiment, but the worker does not have the same degree of control over manipulation of the intervention process; also known as quasi-experimental designs.

Empirical Evaluation: A method of appraisal based on the analysis of data collected by measuring instruments.

Explanatory Design: An attempt to demonstrate with certainty that specific activities caused specific reported changes in practice objectives. The professional manipulates certain factors in the intervention to gain a greater degree of control over the proceedings; also known as experimental designs.

Exploratory Design: A process in which a professional assesses the effects of an intervention process for the purpose of building a foundation of general ideas and tentative theories that can later be examined by more rigorous evaluative methods.

Extraneous Variables: Outside factors that occur at the same time as the intervention and thus may account for some of the measured change in practice objectives.

Formal Case-Level Evaluation: An empirical method of appraisal in which a single client is monitored via repeated measurements over time in order to examine change in a practice objective.

Horizontal Axis: The horizontal dimension of a two-dimensional graph; represents values of the independent variable in frequency distributions; sometimes called the x-axis or the abscissa.

Ideographic Research: Research studies that focus on unique individuals or situations.

Nonempirical Evaluation: An informal method of appraisal that is not based on empirical data; it depends on theories and descriptions that a professional considers to be relevant to the case.

Ordinate: See Vertical Axis.

Origin: The point of a graph at which the abscissa and ordinate intersect.

Phase: Any relatively distinct part of the contact between a professional and a client; A represents a baseline phase and B an intervention phase.

Private Consultation: An informal method of case evaluation in which a professional exchanges descriptive information about a client with another helping human service worker to obtain solid advice.

Qualitative: A description of data that is given in words.

Quantitative: A description of data that is given in numbers.

Repeated Measurements: The administration of one measuring instrument (or set of instruments) a number of times to the same client, under the same conditions, over a period of time.

Vertical Axis: The vertical dimension of a two-dimensional graph; it usually represents frequency in frequency distributions, relative frequency in relative frequency distributions, and cumulative proportion in cumulative proportion graphs.

STUDY QUESTIONS

1. In your own words, identify the advantages of using case-level evaluation designs.

2. In groups of four, design an explanatory case-level evaluation design. Describe how you would carry out the study. In your description, define the testable assertion, or hypothesis, to be examined by your design. What instruments would you use to collect the data? What sources of data would you use? Present your design to the class.

3. In groups of four, design a descriptive case-level evaluation design. Describe how you would carry out the study. In your description, define the testable assertion, or hypothesis, to be examined by your design. What instruments would you use to collect the data? What sources of data would you use? Present your design to the class.

4. In groups of four, design an exploratory case-level evaluation design. Describe how you would carry out the study. In your description, define the testable

assertion, or hypothesis, to be examined by your design. What instruments would you use to collect the data? What sources of data would you use? Present your design to the class.

5. List and discuss the advantages and disadvantages of using informal and formal case-level evaluations. How can they be used together? Explain your rationale in detail. Use a single human service example throughout your discussion.

6. List and discuss the advantages and disadvantages of using only formal case-level evaluation designs to replace case consultations and case conferences. Use a human service example in your discussion.

7. What are some of the disadvantages of using case conferencing to evaluate a client's achievement of his or her practice objective?

8. Jose, a fellow student in your program, is experiencing problems at school. He is doing poorly in every class, receiving the minimum marks necessary to pass. He is also very shy and has a difficult time forming friendships with classmates. Moreover, he does not attend classes on a regular basis. Jose asks for your help. Set three practice objectives for Jose.

9. Next, operationalize each of your practice objectives with Jose.

10. What is a baseline measure? Why is it important in your evaluation of Jose's problem?

11. Another student also provides a rating for Jose. Why is this important and necessary to the evaluative effort?

12. Jose decides that he wants to work on his self-esteem; that is, his practice objective is to increase his self-esteem. Why is it important to establish a baseline for Jose's practice objective before an intervention takes place?

13. Why are repeated measurements of Jose's practice objectives necessary to a successful evaluation of his progress?

14. In order to obtain a baseline, you measure Jose's self-esteem for three weeks. He scores 62, 58, and 63. Graphically display the scores. Remember to plot measures of your practice objective on the vertical axis of the graph and time on the horizontal axis. Why is it important to display your data graphically?

15. You decide to use an intervention strategy to increase Jose's self-esteem. Repeated measurement may show that his self-esteem problems have declined over the course of a month. Can you prove that your intervention strategy alone caused this increase? Why or why not?

16. You decide to evaluate Jose's case using an *AB* design. What are the benefits of using such a design? Why is an established baseline of Jose's level of self-esteem so important? Under what circumstances would you decide to use a successive intervention design with Jose's case? What are some of the advantages and disadvantages of such a design?

17. How can you increase your confidence in the effects of your intervention strategy? Why is this sometimes not ethical or possible?

18. Under what circumstances would you deliberately not establish a baseline with Jose? If you fail to establish a baseline, can you still demonstrate that your intervention strategy caused Jose's self-esteem to increase? Why or why not?

19. You have just been hired by a human service agency and propose the incorporation of formal and informal case-level evaluations in practice. Summarize the main points of your argument. Be very clear and concise.

REFERENCES AND FURTHER READINGS

Alter, C., & Evens, W. (1990). *Evaluating your practice: A guide to self-assessment*. New York: Springer.

Barlow, D.H., Hayes, S.C., & Nelson, R.O. (1984). *The scientist-practitioner: Research and accountability in applied settings*. Elmsford, NY: Pergamon.

Barlow, D.H., & Hersen, M. (1984). *Single-case experimental designs: Strategies for studying behavior change* (2nd ed.). Elmsford, NY: Pergamon.

Bloom, M., Fischer, J., & Orme, J. (1999). *Evaluating practice: Guidelines for the accountable professional* (3rd ed.). Englewood Cliffs, NJ: Prentice-Hall.

Blythe, B.J., & Tripodi, T. (1989). *Measurement in direct practice*. Thousand Oaks, CA: Sage.

Gilgun, J. (2001). Case research designs. In R.M. Grinnell, Jr. (Ed.), *Social work research and evaluation: Quantitative and qualitative approaches* (6th ed., pp. 260–273). Itasca, IL: F.E. Peacock Publishers.

Mutschler, E. (1979). Using single-case evaluation procedures in a family and children's service center: Integration of practice and research. *Journal of Social Service Research, 2,* 115–134.

Nelsen, J.C. (1988). Single-subject research. In R.M. Grinnell, Jr. (Ed.), *Social work research and evaluation* (3rd ed., pp. 362–399). Itasca, IL: F.E. Peacock Publishers.

Thyer, B.A. (2001). Single-system designs. In R.M. Grinnell, Jr. (Ed.), *Social work research and evaluation: Quantitative and qualitative approaches* (6th ed., pp. 455–480). Itasca, IL: F.E. Peacock Publishers.

8

Chapter Outline

Program-Level Evaluations

THE LAST CHAPTER discussed simple approaches to case-level evaluations. This chapter is a logical extension of the previous one in that it presents various approaches to program-level evaluations that emphasize the use of groups of clients or cases instead of one client (e.g., one individual, one couple, one family, one group, one community, one organization). As the previous chapter pointed out, case-level evaluations are used mainly to evaluate practice objectives. Program-level evaluations are used to evaluate program objectives. The key difference between case-level and program-level evaluations is the kind of objectives they measure.

THE EVALUATION CONTINUUM

When the focus and purpose of an evaluation have been determined, the program objectives have been formulated, and instruments have been selected to measure the objectives, it is time to select a program-level evaluation design. Essentially, a design is selected for the specific purpose of an evaluation, or the use to which the results will be put. If the purpose is to make decisions about continuing, abandoning, or replicating the program, the decision makers will need to be very confident about the validity and reliability of the evaluation, and a rigorous design may be required.

Like formal case-level designs, there are three levels of program-level evaluation designs: explanatory, descriptive, and exploratory. All three design levels can focus on the evaluation of a program's objectives to some degree; that is, they all can be used to generate useful data that can help human service programs deliver better services to the clients they serve.

Explanatory Designs   *less powerful design*

Explanatory evaluation designs are sometimes called "ideal" evaluative experimental designs. They involve random assignment of clients (or case files) to groups. It is rarely possible to implement them in agency settings, and less powerful designs, such as descriptive and exploratory designs that are usually less intrusive, will have to be chosen.

Explanatory program-level evaluation designs have the largest number of "design requirements." They are best used in confirmatory or causal evaluation studies where the program objective being evaluated is well developed, theories abound, and testable hypotheses can be formulated on the basis of previous work or existing theory. These designs usually seek to establish causal relationships between the program objectives and the activities the workers perform to achieve them (interventions).

Descriptive Designs

Descriptive program-level evaluation designs have the advantage of being practical when conditions prevent implementation of an explanatory evaluation design They do not control as strictly for the effects of extraneous factors as explanatory designs and are thus less "rigorous." Nevertheless, they are very useful and practical in the evaluation of the human services.

Exploratory Designs

A third type of program-level evaluation design is the exploratory design. These designs only provide an estimate of the relationship between the program objectives and the workers' activities (interventions) with no defense at all against the effects of extraneous factors. However, such a design can be used for a preliminary, "nonscientific" look at their relationship to see if it is worthwhile using more rigorous, and also more costly and time-consuming, designs.

Exploratory designs do not produce statistically definitive data or conclusive results; they are not intended to. Their purpose is to build a foundation of general ideas and tentative theories that can be explored later with more precise and hence more complex evaluation designs and their corresponding data-gathering techniques. As is stressed throughout this book, monitoring designs, a form of exploratory designs, are extremely useful in determining if interventive efforts are having an effect on a program's objectives.

Choosing a Design

(1) purpose
(2) how data collected will be used

The two most important considerations in choosing a program-level evaluation design are the purpose of the evaluative effort and how the data obtained will be used. In addition, ethical issues must be taken into account, along with political, social, and practical considerations.

Before a discussion of using program-level evaluation designs can occur, it is necessary to distinguish what comprises an "ideal" evaluation, (explanatory design) because any evaluation design finally selected should come as close to an "ideal" evaluation as possible given the social, political, ethical, and practical constraints that surround any evaluative effort. In short, it is useful to understand what an "ideal" evaluation is, so comparisons can be made between the program-level evaluation design selected and the requirements of an "ideal" evaluation. Or, to put it another way, it is always helpful to know how far the evaluation design selected is from an "ideal" evaluation.

CHARACTERISTICS OF "IDEAL" EVALUATIONS

An "ideal" evaluation is one in which a study approaches certainty about the relationship between the workers' activities and the program objectives they are trying to achieve. The purpose of doing any "ideal" evaluation is to ascertain whether the conclusions derived from the findings that the workers' activities (their interventions or independent variables) are or are not the only cause of the change they are trying to achieve in the program objectives (dependent variables).

This concept is introduced with the word "ideal" in quotes because an "ideal" evaluation study is rarely achieved in the human services. On a general level, in order to achieve this high degree of certainty and qualify as an "ideal" evaluation, a design must meet the following six conditions:

1. The time order of the intervention (independent variable) must be established.
2. The intervention must be manipulated.
3. The relationship between the intervention and program objective(s) must be established.
4. The design must control for rival hypotheses.
5. At least one control group should be used.
6. Random sampling and random assignment procedures must be employed in choosing the sample for the study.

6 conditions for "ideal" eval

Time Order of the Intervention

In an "ideal" program-level evaluation, the independent variable must precede the dependent variable. Time order is crucial if the evaluation is to show that one variable causes another, because something that happens later cannot be the cause of something that occurred earlier. Thus X, the independent variable, or intervention, must occur before Y, the dependent variable, or degree of the achievement of the program objective.

Suppose we want to find out if a specific treatment intervention, Intervention X (independent variable), reduces our clients' depression levels (dependent variable) and formulate the following hypothesis:

Intervention X will cause a reduction in our clients' depression levels.

In this hypothesis, the independent variable is the intervention, and the program's objective, or the dependent variable, is the clients' depression levels. The intervention must come *before* a reduction in the clients' depression, because the hypothesis states that the intervention will *cause* a reduction of depression in our clients.

Manipulation of the Intervention

Manipulation of the intervention, or independent variable, means that something must be done with the intervention to at least one group of clients in the evaluation study. In the general form of the hypothesis if X occurs then Y will result, the intervention (X) must be manipulated in order to effect a variation in the program's objective (Y). There are essentially three ways in which human service interventions can be manipulated:

1. X present versus X absent. If the effectiveness of a specific treatment intervention is being evaluated, an experimental group and a control group could be used. The experimental group would be given the intervention (presence of X) and the control group would not (absence of X).
2. A small amount of X versus a larger amount of X. If the effect of treatment time (independent variable) on client outcomes (dependent variable) is being evaluated, two experimental groups could be used, one of which would be treated for a shorter period of time (small amount of X) and the other being treated for a longer period of time (larger amount of X).
3. X versus something else. If the effectiveness of two different treatment interventions is being evaluated, Intervention X_1 could be used with Experimental Group 1 and Intervention X_2 with Experimental Group 2.

There are certain demographic characteristics, such as the sex or race of clients participating in evaluations, that obviously cannot be manipulated because they are fixed. They do not vary, so they are called constants, not variables. Other constants, such as socioeconomic status or IQ, may vary for clients over their life spans, but they are fixed quantities at the beginning of the study, probably will not change during the study, and are not subject to alteration by the evaluator.

Any variable that is subject to alteration by the evaluator (treatment time, for example) is an independent variable. At least one independent variable must be manipulated in a "true" evaluation.

Relationships Between Interventions and Objectives

The relationship between the intervention and the attainment of the program's objective(s) must be established in order to infer a cause-effect relationship within a "true" evaluation. If the intervention is considered to be the cause in the change of the program objective, there must be some pattern in the relationship between them. An example is the hypothesis: "The more time clients spend in treatment (the intervention or the independent variable), the better the program objective will be (the dependent variable)."

Control of Rival Hypotheses

Rival, or alternative, hypotheses must be identified and eliminated in an "ideal" program-level evaluation. The logic of this requirement is extremely important, because this is what makes cause-effect statements possible in "ideal" evaluations.

The prime question to ask when trying to identify a rival hypothesis is, "What other independent variables might affect the dependent variable?" (What else might affect the client's outcome besides treatment time?) With the risk of sounding redundant, "What else besides X might affect Y?" Perhaps the client's motivation for treatment, in addition to the time spent in treatment, might affect the client's outcome. If so, motivation for treatment is another independent variable; it could be used to form the rival hypothesis, "The higher the client's motivation for treatment, the better his or her progress."

Perhaps the practitioner's attitude toward the client might have an effect on the client's outcome, or the client might win the state lottery and ascend abruptly from depression to ecstasy. These and other potential independent variables could be used to form rival hypotheses. They must all be considered and eliminated, before it can be said with reasonable certainty that a client's outcome resulted from the length of treatment time and not from any other independent variables contained within the rival hypotheses.

Control over rival hypotheses refers to efforts on the evaluator's part to identify and, if at all possible, to eliminate the independent variables in these hypotheses. Three of the ways most frequently used to deal with rival hypotheses are (1) to keep the variables in them constant, (2) to use correlated variation, or (3) to use analysis of covariance. This text will not discuss how to control for rival hypotheses, as this discussion can be found elsewhere (e.g., Weinbach & Grinnell, 2001).

Use of a Control Group

An "ideal" program-level evaluation should use at least one control group in addition to the experimental group. This is one of the principal differences between an "ideal" evaluation and formal case-level designs discussed in the previous chapter. Instead of controlling for rival hypotheses and achieving internal validity by comparing baseline and intervention phases as in case-level designs, program-level evaluation designs can accomplish the same purposes by comparing outcomes between two or more equivalent groups. The experimental group may receive an intervention that is withheld from the control group, or an equivalent group may receive a different intervention.

A human service worker who initiates a treatment intervention is often interested in knowing what would have happened if the intervention had not been used or if some different intervention had been substituted. Would Ms. Gomez have recovered from alcoholism anyway without the worker's efforts? Would she have recovered faster or more completely had family counseling (Intervention A) been used instead of a support group (Intervention B)?

The answer to these questions will never be known if only Ms. Gomez is studied, because there is only one of her and it is not possible, at the same time, to treat her, not treat her, and treat her in different ways. But if more than one group of alcoholics is studied, we have a better idea of the outcome of the treatment, because groups can be made equivalent in respect to important variables. Random assignment procedures (see next section) may be used to assure that the groups are not only equal but are representative of all others with similar problems of alcoholism.

In a typical program-level evaluation design with a control group, two equivalent groups, 1 and 2, can be formed, and both are administered the same pretest to ensure that they are the same in all important respects. Then an intervention is initiated with Group 1 but not with Group 2. The group treated, Group 1 or the experimental group, receives the independent variable (the intervention). The group not treated, Group 2 or the control group, does not receive it. At the conclusion of the treatment, both groups are given a posttest (the same measure as the pretest). Some kind of standardized measuring instrument can be used for the pretest and posttest.

Like formal case-level designs, program-level evaluation designs can also be written in symbols. With the notation scheme used later in this chapter, this design can be written as follows:

Experimental Group: R O_1 X O_2
Control Group: R O_1 O_2

Where:

R = Random selection from a population and random assignment to group
O_1 = First measurement of the dependent variable
X = Independent variable, the intervention
O_2 = Second measurement of the dependent variable

The two *Rs* in this design indicate that the clients are to be randomly assigned to each group. The symbol *X*, which, as usual, stands for the interventive efforts, or the independent variable, indicates that an intervention, or service, is to be given to the experimental group after the pretest (O_1) and before the posttest (O_2). The absence of *X* in the control group indicates that the intervention is not to be given to the control group. Thus, one group receives the services (the experimental group) and the other group does not receive them (the control group).

Table 8.1 displays results from a program-level evaluation study of this type. If the experimental group is equivalent to the control group, the pretest results should be approximately the same for both groups. Within an acceptable margin of error, 24 can be considered approximately the same as 26. Since the control group has not been given any services, the posttest results for this group would not be expected to differ appreciably from the pretest results. In fact, the posttest score, 27, differs little from the pretest score, 26, for the control group.

Because the experimental and control groups are considered equivalent, any rival hypothesis that affected the experimental group would have affected the control group in the same way. No rival hypothesis affected the control group, as indicated by the fact that without the intervention, the pretest and posttest scores did not differ. Therefore, it can be concluded that no rival hypothesis affected the experimental group, either, and the difference (– 44) between pretest and posttest scores for this group was probably due to the intervention and not to any other factor.

TABLE 8.1   Clients' Outcomes
                 by Group

Group	Pretest	Posttest	Difference
Experimental	24	68	– 44
Control	26	27	– 1

Random Sampling and Random Assignment

Random sampling and assignment procedures are essential to assure that the results derived from a program-level evaluation study apply not only to the clients who actually took part in the program but to a much larger population. This makes it possible to generalize the findings to other program settings or other clients with similar characteristics, provided that the sample—those who are chosen to take part in a study—is representative of the population to whom the findings are to be generalized. A sample may also consist of cases or elements chosen from a set or population of objects or events, but most human service evaluations deal with people, individually or in groups.

Random sampling is the procedure used to select a sample from a population in such a way that the individuals (or objects or events) chosen accurately represent the population from which they were drawn (see Chapter 5). Once a sample has been randomly selected, the individuals in it are randomly assigned either to an experimental or to a control group in such a way that the groups are equivalent. This procedure is known as *random assignment* or randomization.

In random assignment, the word *equivalent* means equal in terms of variables that are important to the evaluation study, such as the clients' motivation for treatment or level of parenting skills.

If the effect of treatment time on clients' outcomes is being evaluated, for example, the evaluation design might use one experimental group which is treated for a comparatively longer time, a second experimental group which is treated for a shorter time, and a control group which is not treated at all. If we are concerned that the clients' motivation for treatment might also affect their outcomes, the clients can be assigned so that all the groups are equivalent (on the average) in terms of their motivation for treatment.

The process of random sampling from a population, followed by random assignment of the sample to groups, is illustrated in Figure 8.1. The design calls for a sample size of one-tenth of the population. From a population of 10,000, therefore, a random sampling procedure is used to select a sample of 1,000

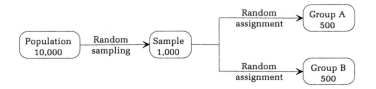

FIGURE 8.1   Random Sampling and
                     Random Assignment
                     Procedures

individuals. Then random assignment procedures are used to place the sample of 1,000 into two equivalent groups of 500 individuals each. In theory, Group A will be equivalent to Group B, which will be equivalent to the random sample, which will be equivalent to the population in respect to all important variables studied.

Matched Pairs

Another more deliberate method of assigning clients or other units to groups involves matching. The matched pairs method is suitable when the composition of each group consists of variables with a range of characteristics.

Sometimes trios and quartets can also be matched if more groups are required, but the matching process grows more complex and uncertain as the numbers in the matched set increase. It is usually not practical to match more than four clients. One of the disadvantages of matching is that some individuals cannot be matched and so cannot participate in the evaluation project. When available clients are few, this can be a serious drawback.

Suppose a new intervention program for depression is being evaluated, and it is important that the experimental and control groups have an equal number of more severely and less severely depressed clients. The clients chosen for the sample are matched in pairs according to level of depression; the two most severely depressed clients are matched, then the next two, and so on. One person in each pair of approximately equally depressed clients is then randomly assigned to the experimental group, and the other is placed in the control group.

An example of this procedure is as follows: A standardized measuring instrument that measures depression is administered to a sample of ten clients.

Their scores are then rank ordered, and one of the clients with the two highest scores is selected to be assigned either to the experimental group or the control group. It does not make any difference which group the first client is randomly assigned to, as long as there is an equal chance that the client will go to either the control group or the experimental group. In this example the first person is randomly chosen to go to the experimental group, as illustrated below:

Rank Order of Depression Scores (in parentheses)
— *First Pair*
   (69) Randomly assigned to the experimental group
   (68) Assigned to the control group
— *Second Pair*
   (67) Assigned to the control group
   (66) Assigned to the experimental group
— *Third Pair*
   (65) Assigned to the experimental group
   (64) Assigned to the control group
— *Fourth Pair*
   (63) Assigned to the control group
   (62) Assigned to the experimental group
— *Fifth Pair*
   (61) Assigned to the experimental group
   (60) Assigned to the control group

The client with the highest score (69) is randomly assigned to the experimental group, and this client's "match," with a score of 68, is assigned to the control group. This process is reversed with the next matched pair, where the first client is assigned to the control group and the match is assigned to the experimental group. If the assignment of clients according to scores is not reversed for every other pair, one group will be higher than the other on the variable being matched.

To illustrate this point, suppose the first person (highest score) in each match is always assigned to the experimental group. The experimental group's average score would be 65 (69 + 67 + 65 + 63 + 61 = 325/5 = 65), and the control group's average score would be 64 (68 + 66 + 64 + 62 + 60 = 320/5 = 64). If every other matched pair is reversed, however, as in the example, the average scores of the two groups are closer together— 64.6 for the experimental group (69 + 66 + 65 + 62 + 61 = 323/5 = 64.6) and 64.4 for the control group (68 + 67 + 64 + 63 + 60 = 322/5 = 64.4). In short, 64.6 and 64.4 (difference of 0.2) are closer together than 65 and 64 (difference of 1).

INTERNAL AND EXTERNAL VALIDITY

In addition to the six characteristics of "ideal" program-level evaluation designs described above, an "ideal" evaluation study must also have both internal and external validity. Internal validity has to do with the provisions of the evaluation design for establishing that the introduction of the independent variable (such as a treatment intervention) alone can be identified as the cause of change in the dependent variable (such as the client's outcome). In contrast, external validity has to do with the extent to which the evaluation design allows for generalization of the findings of the study to other groups and other situations.

Both internal and external validity are achieved in a design by taking into account various threats that are inherent in the evaluation effort. A program-level evaluation design for a study with both types of validity will recognize and attempt to control for potential factors that could affect the study's outcome or findings.

Threats to Internal Validity

In an "ideal" program-level evaluation, the evaluator should be able to conclude from the findings that the intervention (independent variable) is or is not the only cause of change in the program's objective (dependent variable). If a study does not have internal validity, such a conclusion is not possible, and the study is not interpretable (Campbell & Stanley, 1963).

Internal validity is concerned with one of the requirements for an "ideal" evaluation—the control of rival hypotheses, or alternative explanations for what might bring about a change in the program's objective(s). The higher the internal validity of an evaluation study, the greater the extent to which rival hypotheses can be controlled; the lower the internal validity, the less they can be controlled. We must be prepared to rule out the effects of factors other than the intervention that could influence any changes in the program's objective(s). The various factors that are relevant to internal validity are described in Box 8.1 (pages 221-226).

BOX 8.1

THREATS TO INTERNAL VALIDITY

In any explanatory research study, we should be able to conclude from our findings that the independent variable is, or is not, the only cause of change in the dependent variable. If our study does not have internal validity, such a conclusion is not possible, and the study's findings can be misleading.

Internal validity is concerned with one of the requirements for an "ideal" experiment—the control of rival hypotheses, or alternative explanations for what might bring about a change in the dependent variable.

The higher the internal validity of any research study, the greater the extent to which rival hypotheses can be controlled; the lower the internal validity, the less they can be controlled. Thus, we must be prepared to rule out the effects of factors other than the independent variable that could influence the dependent variable.

History

The first threat to internal validity, history, refers to any outside event, either public or private, that may affect the dependent variable and was not taken into account in our research design. Many times, it refers to events occurring between the first and second measurement of the dependent variable (the pretest and the posttest).

If events occur that have the potential to alter the second measurement, there would be no way of knowing how much (if any) of the observed change in the dependent variable is a function of the independent variable and how much is attributable to these events.

Suppose, for example, we are investigating the effects of an educational program on racial tolerance. We may decide to measure the dependent variable, racial tolerance in the community, before introducing the independent variable, the educational program.

The educational program is then implemented. Since it is the independent variable, it is represented by X. Finally, racial tolerance is measured again, after the program has run its course. This final measurement yields a posttest score, represented by O_2. The one-group pretest-posttest study design can be written as:

$$O_1 \quad X \quad O_2$$

Where:

O_1 = First measurement, or pretest score, of racial tolerance
X = Educational program (independent variable) (see Box 8.3)
O_2 = Second measurement, or post-test score, of racial tolerance

The difference between the values O_2 and O_1 represent the difference in racial tolerance in the community before and after the educational program. If the study is internally valid, $O_2 - O_1$ will be a crude measure of the effect of the educational program on racial tolerance; and this is what we were trying to discover. Suppose before the posttest could be administered, an outbreak of racial violence, such as the type that occurred in Los Angeles in the summer of 1992, occurred in the community.

Violence can be expected to have a negative effect on racial tolerance, and the posttest scores may, therefore, show a lower level of tolerance than if the violence had not occurred. The effect, $O_2 - O_1$, will now be the combined effects of the educational program *and* the violence, not the effect of the program alone, as we intended.

Racial violence is an extraneous variable that we could not have anticipated and did

BOX 8.1 CONTINUED

not control for when designing the study. Other examples might include an earthquake, an election, illness, divorce, or marriage—any event, public or private that could affect the dependent variable. Any such variable that is unanticipated and uncontrolled for is an example of history.

Maturation

Maturation, the second threat to internal validity, refers to changes, both physical and psychological, that take place in our research participants over time and can affect the dependent variable. Suppose that we are evaluating an interventive strategy designed to improve the behavior of adolescents who engage in delinquent behavior.

Since the behavior of adolescents changes naturally as they mature, the observed changed behavior may have been due as much to their natural development as it was to the intervention strategy.

Maturation refers not only to physical or mental growth, however. Over time, people grow older, more or less anxious, more or less bored, and more or less motivated to take part in a research study. All these factors and many more can affect the way in which people respond when the dependent variable is measured a second or third time.

Testing

The third threat to internal validity, testing, is sometimes referred to as the initial measurement effect. Thus, the pretests that are the starting point for many research designs are another potential threat to internal validity.

One of the most utilized research designs involves three steps: measuring some dependent variable, such as learning behavior in school or attitudes toward work; initiating a program to change that variable (the independent variable); then measuring the dependent variable again at the conclusion of

the program. This simple one-group pretest-posttest design can be written as follows:

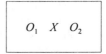

$$O_1 \quad X \quad O_2$$

Where:

O_1 = First measurement of the dependent variable, or pretest score

X = Independent variable (see Box 8.3)

O_2 = Second measurement of the dependent variable, or posttest score

The testing effect is the effect that taking a pretest might have on posttest scores. Suppose that Roberto, a research participant, takes a pretest to measure his initial level of racial tolerance before being exposed to a racial tolerance educational program. He might remember some of the questions on the pretest, think about them later, and change his views on racial issues before taking part in the educational program.

After the program, his posttest score will reveal his changed opinions, and we may incorrectly assume that the program was responsible, whereas the true cause was his experience with the pretest.

Sometimes, a pretest induces anxiety in a research participant, so that Roberto receives a worse score on the posttest than he should have; or boredom with the same questions repeated again may be a factor. In order to avoid the testing effect, we may wish to use a design that does not require a pretest.

If a pretest is essential, we then must consider the length of time that elapses between the pretest and posttest measurements. A pretest is far more likely to affect the posttest when the time between the two is

BOX 8.1 CONTINUED_____

short. The nature of the pretest is another factor. Questions dealing with factual matters, such as knowledge levels, may have a larger testing effect because they tend to be more easily recalled.

Instrumentation Error

The fourth threat to internal validity is instrumentation error, which refers to all the troubles that can afflict the measurement process. The instrument may be unreliable or invalid, as presented in Chapter 6. It may be a mechanical instrument, such as an electroencephalogram (EEG), that has malfunctioned.

Occasionally, the term *instrumentation error* is used to refer to an observer whose observations are inconsistent; or to measuring instruments, such as the ones presented in Chapter 6, that are reliable in themselves, but not administered properly.

"Administration," with respect to a measuring instrument, means the circumstances under which the measurement is made: where, when, how, and by whom. A mother being asked about her attitudes toward her children, for example, may respond in one way in the social worker's office and in a different way at home when her children are screaming around her feet.

A mother's verbal response may differ from her written response; or she may respond differently in the morning than she would in the evening, or differently alone than she would in a group.

These variations in situational responses do not indicate a true change in the feelings, attitudes, or behaviors being measured, but are only examples of instrumentation error.

Statistical Regression

The fifth threat to internal validity, statistical regression, refers to the tendency of extremely low and extremely high scores to regress, or move toward the average score for everyone in the research study. Suppose that a student, named Maryanna, has to take a multiple-choice exam on a subject she knows nothing about.

There are many questions, and each question has five possible answers. Since, for each question, Maryanna has a 20 percent (one in five) chance of guessing correctly, she might expect to score 20 percent on the exam just by guessing. If she guesses badly, she will score a lot lower; if well, a lot higher. The other members of the class take the same exam and, since they are all equally uninformed, the average score for the class is 20 percent.

Now suppose that the instructor separates the low scorers from the high scorers and tries to even out the level of the class by giving the low scorers special instruction. In order to determine if the special instruction has been effective, the entire class then takes another multiple-choice exam. The result of the exam is that the low scorers (as a group) do better than they did the first time, and the high scorers (as a group) worse. The instructor believes that this has occurred because the low scorers received special instruction and the high scorers did not.

According to the logic of statistical regression, however, both the average score of the low scorers (as a group) and the average score of the high scorers (as a group) would move toward the total average score for both groups (i.e., high and low).

Even without any special instruction and still in their state of ignorance, the low scorers (as a group) would be expected to have a higher average score than they did before. Likewise, the high scorers (as a group) would be expected to have a lower average score than they did before.

It would be easy for the research instructor to assume that the low scores had increased because of the special instruction and the high scores had decreased because of the lack of it. Not necessarily so, however; the instruction may have had nothing to do with it. It may all be due to statistical regression.

BOX 8.1 CONTINUED

Differential Selection of Research Participants

The sixth threat to internal validity is differential selection of research participants. To some extent, the participants selected for a research study are different from one another to begin with. "Ideal" experiments, however, require random sampling from a population (if at all possible) and random assignment to groups.

This assures that the results of a study will be generalizable to a larger population, thus addressing threats to external validity. In respect to differential selection as a threat to internal validity, "ideal" experiments control for this since equivalency among the groups at pretest is assumed through the randomization process.

This threat is, however, present when we are working with preformed groups or groups that already exist, such as classes of students, self-help groups, or community groups. In terms of the external validity of such designs, because there is no way of knowing whether the preformed groups are representative of any larger population, it is not possible to generalize the study's results beyond the people (or objects or events) that were actually studied.

The use of preformed groups also affects the internal validity of a study, though. It is probable that different preformed groups will not be equivalent with respect to relevant variables, and that these initial differences will invalidate the results of the posttest.

A child abuse prevention educational program for children in schools might be evaluated by comparing the prevention skills of one group of children who have experienced the educational program with the skills of a second group who have not. In order to make a valid comparison, the two groups must be as similar as possible, with respect to age, gender, intelligence, socioeconomic status, and anything else that might affect the acquisition of child abuse prevention skills.

We would have to make every effort to form or select equivalent groups, but the groups are sometimes not as equivalent as might be hoped—especially if we are obliged to work with preformed groups, such as classes of students or community groups. If the two groups are different before the intervention was introduced, there is not much point in comparing them at the end.

Accordingly, preformed groups should be avoided whenever possible. If it is not feasible to do this, rigorous pretesting must be done to determine in what ways the groups are (or are not) equivalent, and differences must be compensated for with the use of statistical methods.

Mortality

The seventh threat to internal validity is mortality, which simply means that individual research participants may drop out before the end of the study. Their absence will probably have a significant effect on the study's findings because people who drop out are likely to be different in some ways from the other participants who stay in the study. People who drop out may be less motivated to participate in the intervention than people who stay in, for example.

Since dropouts often have such characteristics in common, it cannot be assumed that the attrition occurred in a random manner. If considerably more people drop out of one group than out of the other, the result will be two groups that are no longer equivalent and cannot be usefully compared. We cannot know at the beginning of the study how many people will drop out, but we can watch to see how many do. Mortality is never problematic if dropout rates are five percent or less *and* if the dropout rates are similar for the various groups.

Reactive Effects of Research Participants

The eighth threat to internal validity is reactive effects. Changes in the behaviors or

BOX 8.1 CONTINUED _____

feelings of research participants may be caused by their reaction to the novelty of the situation or the knowledge that they are participating in a research study. A mother practicing communication skills with her child, for example, may try especially hard when she knows the social worker is watching. We may wrongly believe that such reactive effects are due to the independent variable.

The classic example of reactive effects was found in a series of studies carried out at the Hawthorne plant of the Western Electric Company in Chicago many years ago. Researchers were investigating the relationship between working conditions and productivity. When they increased the level of lighting in one section of the plant, productivity increased; a further increase in the lighting was followed by an additional increase in productivity.

When the lighting was then decreased, however, production levels did not fall accordingly but continued to rise. The conclusion was that the workers were increasing their productivity not because of the lighting level but because of the attention they were receiving as research participants in the study.

The term *Hawthorne effect* is still used to describe any situation in which the research participants' behaviors are influenced not by the independent variable but by the knowledge that they are taking part in a research project. Another example of such a reactive effect is the placebo given to patients, which produces beneficial results because they believe it is medication.

Reactive effects can be controlled by ensuring that all participants in a research study, in both the experimental and control groups, appear to be treated equally. If one group is to be shown an educational film, for example, the other group should also be shown a film—some film carefully chosen to bear no relationship to the variable being investigated. If the study involves a change in the participants' routine, this in itself may be enough to change behavior, and care must be

taken to continue the study until novelty has ceased to be a factor.

Interaction Effects

Interaction among the various threats to internal validity can have an effect of its own. Any of the factors already described as threats may interact with one another, but the most common interactive effect involves differential selection and maturation.

Let us say we are studying two groups of clients who are being treated for depression. The intention was for these groups to be equivalent, in terms of both their motivation for treatment and their levels of depression. It turns out that Group A is more generally depressed than Group B, however. Whereas both groups may grow less motivated over time, it is likely that Group A, whose members were more depressed to begin with, will lose motivation more completely and more quickly than Group B. Inequivalent groups thus grow less equivalent over time as a result of the interaction between differential selection and maturation.

Relations Between Experimental and Control Groups

The final group of threats to internal validity has to do with the effects of the use of experimental and control groups that receive different interventions. These effects include: (1) diffusion of treatments, (2) compensatory equalization, (3) compensatory rivalry, and (4) demoralization.

Diffusion of Treatments

Diffusion, or imitation of treatments, may occur when the experimental and control groups talk to each other about the study. Suppose a study is designed that presents a new relaxation exercise to the experimental

BOX 8.1 CONTINUED

group and nothing at all to the control group. There is always the possibility that one of the participants in the experimental group will explain the exercise to a friend who happens to be in the control group. The friend explains it to another friend, and so on. This might be beneficial for the control group, but it invalidates the study's findings.

Compensatory Equalization

Compensatory equalization of treatment occurs when the person doing the study and/or the staff member administering the intervention to the experimental group feels sorry for people in the control group who are not receiving it and attempts to compensate them.

A social worker might take a control group member aside and covertly demonstrate the relaxation exercise, for example. On the other hand, if our study has been ethically designed, there should be no need for guilt on the part of the social worker because some people are not being taught to relax. They can be taught to relax when our study is "officially" over.

Compensatory Rivalry

Compensatory rivalry is an effect that occurs when the control group becomes motivated to compete with the experimental group. For example, a control group in a program to encourage parental involvement in school activities might get wind that something is up and make a determined effort to participate too, on the basis that "anything they can do, we can do better." There is no direct communication between groups, as in the diffusion of treatment effect—only rumors and suggestions of rumors. However, rumors are often enough to threaten the internal validity of a study.

Demoralization

In direct contrast with compensatory rivalry, demoralization refers to feelings of deprivation among the control group that may cause them to give up and drop out of the study, in which case this effect would be referred to as mortality. The people in the control group may also get angry.

Threats to External Validity

External validity is the degree to which the results of a program-level evaluation study are generalizable to a larger population or to settings outside the evaluative context, situation, or setting. If an evaluative design is to have external validity, it must provide for selection of a sample of clients for the study that is representative of the population from which it was drawn.

Generalizability is difficult to establish in case-level evaluations; we would have to be able to demonstrate that the clients on whom the intervention is to be tested are representative of a larger group of clients to whom the intervention might be applied. Program-level evaluation designs provide a much broader basis for generalization; if two or more groups are used, we must be able to demonstrate that groups formed for the evaluation project are not only representative of a larger population but are equivalent in all important variables.

Moreover, it is necessary to establish that nothing happened during the course of the evaluation—except for the introduction of the intervention, the independent variable—to change either the representativeness of the sample or the equivalence of the groups. The factors that constitute threats to external validity are described in Box 8.2 on pages 228 and 229.

PROGRAM-LEVEL EVALUATION DESIGNS

Examples of simple evaluation designs were introduced in the previous chapter with case-level designs, because they represent a class of designs that is comparatively consistent and uncomplicated. Many of these designs have the same purpose: to evaluate the effects of interventions on clients. Many have the same independent variable—the intervention—and the same dependent variable—the attainment of the practice objective. The study is done at the individual level—a single person, a single couple, a single group, a single family, a single community or a single organization.

Understanding formal case-level designs, therefore, lays a good foundation for understanding more complex program-level evaluation designs that use groups of clients rather than single clients. But only some of the program-level evaluation designs discussed in this chapter are complex; a design that is unnecessarily complex costs more, takes more time, and probably will not serve its purpose nearly as well as a simpler one.

In choosing an evaluation design, therefore, the principle of parsimony must be applied. As in formal case-level designs discussed in the previous chapter, the simplest and most economical route to gather the necessary data is the best choice. The order for the lists of group evaluation designs in Table 8.2 (page 231) goes from simplest to most complex. A simple notation is used to write these designs in symbol form. Only three basic symbols are used:

X = Intervention, the independent variable

O = Measurement of the program objective, the dependent variable

R = Random selection from a population or random assignment to a group

BOX 8.2

THREATS TO EXTERNAL VALIDITY

External validity is the degree to which the results of our research study are generalizable to a larger population or to settings outside the research situation or setting.

Pretest-Treatment Interaction

The first threat to external validity, pretest-treatment interaction, is similar to the testing threat to internal validity. The nature of a pretest can alter the way research participants respond to the experimental treatment, as well as to the posttest. Suppose, for example, that an educational program on racial tolerance is being evaluated.

A pretest that measures the level of tolerance could well alert the participants to the fact that they are going to be educated into loving all their neighbors, but many people do not want to be "educated" into anything. They are satisfied with the way they feel and will resist the instruction. This will affect the level of racial tolerance registered on the posttest.

Selection-Treatment Interaction

The second threat to external validity is selection-treatment interaction. This threat commonly occurs when a research design cannot provide for random selection of participants from a population. Suppose we wanted to study the effectiveness of a family service agency staff, for example. If our research proposal was turned down by 50 agencies before it was accepted by the 51st, it is very likely that the accepting agency differs in certain important aspects from the other 50.

It may accept the proposal because its workers are more highly motivated, more secure, more satisfied with their jobs, or more interested in the practical application of the study than the average agency staff member.

As a result, we would be assessing the research participants on the very factors for which they were unwittingly (and by default) selected—motivation, job satisfaction, and so on. The study may be internally valid, but, since it will not be possible to generalize the results to other family service agencies, it would have little external validity.

Specificity of Variables

Specificity of variables has to do with the fact that a research project conducted with a specific group of people at a specific time and in a specific setting may not always be generalizable to other people at a different time and in a different setting.

For example, a measuring instrument developed to measure the IQ levels of upper-socioeconomic level, Caucasian, suburban children does not provide an equally accurate measure of IQ when it is applied to lower-socioeconomic level children of racial minorities in the inner city.

Reactive Effects

The fourth threat to external validity is reactive effects which, as with internal validity, occur when the attitudes or behaviors of our research participants are affected to some degree by the very act of taking a pretest. Thus, they are no longer exactly equivalent to the population from which they were randomly selected, and it may not be possible to generalize our study's results to that population. Because pretests affect research participants to some degree, our results may be valid only for those who were pretested.

BOX 8.2 CONTINUED_____

Multiple-Treatment Interference

The fifth threat to external validity, multiple-treatment interference, occurs if a research participant is given two or more interventions in succession, so that the results of the first intervention may affect the results of the second one. A client attending treatment sessions, for example, may not seem to benefit from one therapeutic technique, so another is tried.

In fact, however, the client may have benefitted from the first technique but the benefit does not become apparent until the second technique has been tried. As a result, the effects of both techniques become commingled, or the results may be erroneously ascribed to the second technique alone.

Because of this threat, interventions should be given separately if possible. If our research design does not allow this, sufficient time should be allowed to elapse between the two interventions in an effort to minimize the possibility of multiple-treatment interference.

Researcher Bias

The final threat to external validity is researcher bias. Researchers, like people in general, tend to see what they want to see or expect to see. Unconsciously and without any thought of deceit, they may manipulate a study so that the actual results agree with the anticipated results. A practitioner may favor an intervention so strongly that the research study is structured to support it, or the results are interpreted favorably.

If we know which individuals are in the experimental group and which are in the control group, this knowledge alone might affect the study's results. Students who an instructor believes to be bright, for example, often are given higher grades than their performance warrants, while students believed to be dull are given lower grades.

The way to control for such researcher bias is to perform a double-blind experiment in which neither the research participants nor the researcher knows who is in the experimental or control group or who is receiving a specific treatment intervention.

EXPLORATORY DESIGNS

At the lowest level of the continuum of knowledge that can be derived from program-level evaluation studies are the exploratory studies. An exploratory study explores a program's objective about which little is already known, in order to uncover generalizations and develop hypotheses that can be investigated and tested later with more precise and hence more complex designs and data gathering techniques.

The three examples of exploratory designs given in this section do not use pretests; they measure the program objective only after the introduction of the intervention, or the independent variable.

BOX 8.3_____

TREATMENT: A VARIABLE OR A CONSTANT?

For instructional purposes, group designs are displayed using symbols where X is the independent variable (treatment) and O is the measure of the dependent variable. This presentation is accurate when studies are designed with two or more groups.

When one-group designs are used, however, this interpretation does not hold. In one-group designs, the treatment, or program, cannot truly vary because all research participants have experienced the same event; that is, they all have experienced the program.

Without a comparison or control group, treatment is considered a constant because it is a quality shared by all members in the research study. In short, *time* is the independent variable.

One-Group Posttest-Only Design

The one-group posttest-only design (Design 1a) is sometimes called the one-shot case study or cross-sectional case study design. It is the simplest of all the program-level evaluation designs.

Suppose the effectiveness of a stop-smoking program is being evaluated. Did anyone who completed it actually stop smoking? To answer this question, all that needs to be done is to locate the last group of clients who completed the program and count the number of clients who no longer smoke.

This simple design can be written as:

$$X \quad O_1$$

Where:

X = Independent variable (Stop-Smoking Program, the intervention, see Box 8.3)

O_1 = First and only measurement of the dependent variable (number of participants who stopped smoking, the program's outcome, or program objective)

TABLE 8.2   Knowledge Levels and Corresponding
                   Research Designs

Knowledge Levels	Research Designs
1. Exploratory	*a:* One-group posttest-only
	b: Multigroup posttest-only
	c: Longitudinal case study
	d: Longitudinal survey
	—Trend Studies
	—Cohort Studies
	—Panel Studies
2. Descriptive	*a:* Randomized one-group posttest-only
	b: Randomized cross-sectional and longitudinal survey
	c: One-group pretest-posttest
	d: Comparison group posttest-only
	e: Comparison group pretest-posttest
	f: Interrupted time-series
3. Explanatory	*a:* Classical experimental
	b: Randomized posttest-only control group

This simple design only provides for a measure (O_1) of what happens when one group of clients is subjected to one treatment or experience (X). The group was not randomly selected from any particular population, and thus the results of the findings cannot be generalizable to any other group or population. This design will not ascertain whether the value of O_1 indicates any improvement, since a pretest was not conducted.

It is safe to assume that all the members of the group smoked before the treatment was introduced, since clients who do not smoke would not enroll in a quit-smoking program. Even if the value of O_1 indicates that some of the group did quit smoking after the treatment, it cannot be determined whether they quit *because* of the intervention (the program) or because of some other rival hypothesis. Perhaps a law was passed to limit smoking in public places, or an ultimatum was issued by the doctor leading the group.

Cross-Sectional Survey Design

Let us take another example of a one-group posttest-only design that *does not* have an independent or dependent variable. In survey research, this type of a group research design is called a cross-sectional survey design.

In doing a cross-sectional survey, we survey *only once* a cross-section of some particular population. Let us say that Susan wants to start a Drug Prevention Program within a local grade school. Before Susan starts the program, however, she wants to know what the parents think about her idea. She may send out questionnaires to all the parents or she may decide to personally telephone every second parent, or every fifth, or tenth, depending on how much time and money she has. The results of her simple survey constitute a single measurement, or observation (O_1), of the parents' opinions of her proposed Drug Prevention Program. This design is written as:

The symbol O_1 represents the entire cross-sectional survey design since such a design involves making only a single observation, or measurement, at one time period. Note that there is no X, as there is really no independent variable. Susan only wants to ascertain the parents' attitudes toward her proposed program being run at the local grade school—nothing more, nothing less.

Multigroup Posttest-Only Design

The multigroup posttest-only design (Design 1*b*) is an elaboration of the one-group posttest-only design in which more than one group is used. To check a bit further into the effectiveness of the stop-smoking program, for example, we might decide to locate several more groups who had completed the program and see how many of the clients in each group had stopped smoking. Any number of groups may be used in this design.

This simple design can be written as:

Experimental Group 1: X O_1
Experimental Group 2: X O_1
Experimental Group 3: X O_1
Experimental Group 4: X O_1

Where:

X = Independent variable (Stop-Smoking Program, the intervention, see Box 8.3)

O_1 = First and only measurement of the dependent variable (number of participants who stopped smoking, the program's outcome, or program objective)

With this design it cannot be assumed that all four Xs are equivalent because all four programs might not be exactly the same; one group might have had a different facilitator, the program might have been presented differently, or the material could have varied in important respects. It cannot be assumed that all four groups were equivalent either; the clients in one group might have been better motivated to stop smoking (on the average) than the clients in the other groups.

It certainly cannot be assumed that any of the groups were representative of the larger population who might wish to stop smoking in the future. Nothing is known about whether any of the clients would have stopped smoking anyway, without the program. Nothing is known as to the extent to which smoking was perhaps reduced, because a pretest was not conducted, and it is not known how heavily the group members smoked before they went through the program.

Longitudinal Case Study Design

The longitudinal case study design (Design 1c) is exactly like the posttest-only design, only it provides for more measurements of the program objective, or the dependent variable. This design can be written in symbols as follows:

$$X \quad O_1 \quad O_2 \quad O_3 \ldots$$

Where:

X = Independent variable (Stop-Smoking Program, the intervention, see Box 8.3)

O_1 = First measurement of the dependent variable (number of participants who stopped smoking, the program's outcome, or program objective)

O_2 = Second measurement of the dependent variable (number of participants who stopped smoking, the program's outcome, or program objective)

O_3 = Third measurement of the dependent variable (number of participants who stopped smoking, the program's outcome, or program objective)

Longitudinal Survey Design

Unlike cross-sectional surveys, where the variable of interest (usually the dependent variable) is measured only once, longitudinal surveys (Design 1d) provide data at various points so that changes can be monitored over time. A simple longitudinal survey design is written as follows:

$$\boxed{O_1 \quad O_2 \quad O_3}$$

Where:

O_1 = First measurement of some variable
O_2 = Second measurement of some variable
O_3 = Third measurement of some variable

In general, longitudinal survey designs do not contain independent and dependent variables. As indicated in Table 8.2, there are three types of longitudinal surveys: (1) trend studies, (2) cohort studies, and (3) panel studies.

Trend Studies

A trend study is used to find out how a population, or sample, changes over time. Susan, the school social worker who wanted to start a drug prevention program in a local grade school mentioned previously, may want to know if parents of young children enrolled in her school are becoming more receptive to the idea of the school teaching their children drug prevention education in the second grade. She may survey all the parents of third grade children this year, all the parents of the new complement of third grade children next year, and so on until she thinks she has sufficient data.

Each year the parents surveyed will be different, but they will all be parents of third grade children. Thus, Susan can determine whether parents are becoming more receptive, as time goes on, to the idea of introducing a drug prevention program to their children in the third grade. In a nutshell, Susan will be able to measure any parental attitudinal trends that may be occurring. A trend study research design is simply written as:

$$\boxed{O_1 \quad O_2 \quad O_3}$$

Where:

O_1 = First measurement of a variable for a sample (Sample 1)

O_2 = Second measurement of a variable for a different sample (Sample 2)

O_3 = Third measurement of a variable for yet another different sample (Sample 3)

Cohort Studies

Cohort studies are useful to study variables over time. Unlike trend studies, these designs follow a group of people who have shared a similar experience—for example, sexual abuse survivors, cancer survivors, or parents of grade-school children. Let us continue with the example of Susan, who is interested in knowing whether parents' attitudes toward the grade school offering a drug prevention program to third-grade students change as their children grow older. She may survey a sample of the parents who had third grade children enrolled in the grade school who attend a Parent Night this year, and survey a different sample of parents who attend a similar meeting for the same parents next year, when their children are in the fourth grade.

The following year, when the children are in the fifth grade, she will take another, different sample of those parents who attend Parent Night. Although different parents are being surveyed every year, they all belong to the same population of parents whose children are progressing through the grades together. The selection of the samples was not random, though, because parents who take the time to attend Parent Night may be different from those who stay at home. The simple research design is written as:

$$O_1 \quad O_2 \quad O_3$$

Where:

O_1 = First measurement of a variable for a sample drawn from some population

O_2 = Second measurement of a variable for a different sample drawn from the same population (one year later in our example)

O_3 = Third measurement of a variable for a still different sample, drawn from the same population (two years later in our example)

Panel Studies

In a panel study, the *same individuals* are followed over a period of time. Susan might select one particular sample of parents, for example, and measure their attitudes toward her drug prevention program in successive years. Again, the design can be written:

$$O_1 \quad O_2 \quad O_3$$

Where:

O_1 = First measurement of a variable for a sample of individuals

O_2 = Second measurement of a variable for the same sample of individuals (one year later in our example)

O_3 = Third measurement of some variable for the same sample of individuals (two years later in our example)

In summary, trend studies are interested in broad trends over time where cohort studies are interested in people over time who have shared a similar experience. In neither case do we know anything about *individual* contributions to the changes that are being measured. A panel study provides data that looks at change (if any) over time as experienced by particular individuals.

DESCRIPTIVE DESIGNS

At the midpoint of the knowledge continuum are descriptive designs, which have some but not all of the requirements of an "ideal" evaluation. They usually require specification of the time order of variables, manipulation of the intervention (independent variable), and establishment of the relationship between the intervention and the attainment of the program objectives (dependent variables). They may also control for rival hypotheses and use a second group as a comparison (not a control). The requirement that these designs lack most frequently is random selection of clients from a population and random assignment to groups.

We are rarely in a position to assign clients randomly to either an experimental or a comparison group (or control group). Sometimes the groups to be studied are already in existence; sometimes ethical issues are involved. For example, it would not be ethical to assign clients who need immediate help to two random groups, only one of which is to receive the intervention. Since a lack of random assignment will affect the internal and external validities of the evaluative effort, a descriptive evaluation design must try to compensate for this. The six examples of descriptive evaluation designs presented in this section do this in various ways.

Randomized One-Group Posttest-Only Design

[handwritten: Can't determine effectiveness on Pre & Post test]

The distinguishing feature of the randomized one-group posttest-only design (Design 2a) is that members of the group are deliberately and randomly selected for it. Otherwise, this design is identical to the exploratory one-group posttest-only design (Design 1a).

The randomized one-group posttest-only design is written as follows:

$$R \quad X \quad O_1$$

Where:

R = Random selection from a population

X = Independent variable (see Box 8.3)

O_1 = First and only measurement of the dependent variable

In our continuing example of the stop-smoking group, the difference in this design is that the group does not accidentally assemble itself by participating in a stop-smoking program. Instead, it is randomly selected from a population, say, of all the 400 people who smoke cigarettes in Twin Parks, Idaho (total population 567). These 400 people comprise the population of all the cigarette smokers in Twin Parks.

The total smoking population of 400 people (sampling frame) is used to select a simple random sample of 40 people. The stop-smoking program is administered (X) to these 40 people, and the number of people who quit smoking after the program is determined (O_1). If this design is written for this particular example, the symbols represent:

R =   Random selection of 40 people from the population of people who smoke cigarettes in Twin Parks

X =   Stop-smoking program, the intervention

O_1 =   Number of people in program who quit smoking, the program objective or dependent variable

Assume that the program fails to have the desired effect, and 39 of the 40 people continue to smoke cigarettes after participating in the program. Because the program was ineffective for the sample and the sample was randomly selected, it can be concluded that it would be ineffective for the entire cigarette smoking population of Twin Parks—the other 360 who did not go through the program. In other words, because a representative random sample was selected, it is possible to generalize the results to the population from which the sample was drawn.

Since no change in the program objective occurred, it is not sensible to consider the control of rival hypotheses. The evaluator need not wonder what might have caused the change—X, or an alternative explanation. However, if the program had been successful, it would not have been possible to ascribe success solely to "the program," because the evaluator would have no idea of what other factors might have contributed to it.

Randomized Cross-Sectional and Longitudinal Survey Design

These designs (Design 2*b*) are commonly used with surveys as the data collection method. The randomized cross-sectional survey design is written as follows:

$$R \quad O_1$$

Where:

R = Random sample drawn from a population
O_1 = First and only measurement of the dependent variable (see Box 8.3)

The randomized longitudinal survey design is written as;

$$R \quad O_1 \quad O_2 \ldots$$

Where:

R = Random sample drawn from a population
Os = Repeated measurements of the dependent variable (see Box 8.3)

The notation RO_1 describes what is done when a survey is carried out. For example, suppose a survey is conducted to find out how many people in Twin Parks smoke cigarettes. First, a representative random sample (R) is drawn of all the people in the town. Then personal interviews are conducted to determine how many of the people in this sample smoke cigarettes. The number of cigarette smokers uncovered is the O_1 part of the RO_1 notation; there is no X part in this design. Note that there does not have to be an intervention before a survey can be undertaken. This design is used quite often in needs assessments.

As discussed earlier, a cross-sectional survey obtains data only once from a sample of a particular population. If the sample is a random sample—that is, if it represents the population from which it was drawn—then the data obtained from the sample can be generalized to the entire population.

Explanatory surveys look for associations between variables. Often, the suspected reason for the relationship is that one variable caused the other. In Susan's case, she has two studies going on: her current Stop-Smoking Program, and her survey of parental attitudes toward the school offering a Drug Prevention Program that is geared toward teaching third grade children drug prevention strategies. The success of her stop-smoking program may have caused parents to adopt more positive attitudes toward the school in teaching their children drug prevention (her survey). In this situation, the two variables, her stop-smoking program and her survey, become commingled.

Demonstrating causality is frustrating because it is so difficult to show that nothing apart from the independent variable could have caused the observed change in the dependent variable. Even supposing that this problem is solved, it is impossible to demonstrate causality unless data are obtained from random samples that are generalizable to entire populations.

Suppose an initial survey of randomly selected people from Twin Parks uncovers that 99.44 percent of them smoke cigarettes (O_1). Six months later another randomly selected sample is surveyed, with results O_2. In another six months, a third survey is conducted, with results O_3. These results can be used to monitor the cigarette smoking behavior over time of the people in the population. This design thus provides a description of net change over time. It can be used to monitor the knowledge, behaviors, attitudes, or affects of any population.

One-Group Pretest-Posttest Design

The one-group pretest-posttest design (Design 2c) may also be referred to as a before-after design, because it includes a pretest of the program's objective (dependent variable), which can be used as a basis of comparison with the posttest results. This design is illustrated as:

$$O_1 \quad X \quad O_2$$

Where:

O_1 = First measurement of the dependent variable
X = Independent variable, the intervention (see Box 8.3)
O_2 = Second measurement of the dependent variable

The one-group pretest-posttest design, in which a pretest precedes the introduction of the intervention and a posttest follows it, can be used to determine precisely how the intervention affects a particular group in relation to program objectives. The design is used often in human service decision making—far too often, in fact, because it does not control for extraneous variables. The difference between O_1 and O_2 on which these decisions are based, therefore, could be due to other factors rather than the intervention.

In our stop-smoking example, history would be an extraneous variable or threat to internal validity, because all kinds of things could have happened between O_1 and O_2 to affect the clients, such as a new tax on cigarettes that raises the price. Testing also would be a problem; just the experience of taking the pretest could motivate some clients to quit smoking. There also could be other threats or interactions among threats.

Comparison Group Posttest-Only Design

The comparison group posttest-only design (Design 2d) improves on the exploratory one-group and multigroup posttest-only designs by introducing a comparison group that does not receive the intervention but is subject to the same posttest as those who do (the experimental group). A group used for purposes of comparison is usually referred to as a comparison group in an exploratory or descriptive program-level evaluation design and as a control group in an explanatory program-level evaluation design. While a control group is always randomly assigned, a comparison group is not.

This design is written as follows:

$$\boxed{\begin{array}{l} \text{Experimental Group:} \quad X \quad O_1 \\ \text{Comparison Group:} \qquad\qquad O_1 \end{array}}$$

Where:

X = Independent variable, the intervention

O_1 = First and only measurement of the dependent variable

In the stop-smoking program, if January, April, and August sections are scheduled and the August sections are canceled for some reason, those who would have been clients in that section could be used as a comparison group. If the values of O_1 were similar for the experimental and comparison groups, it could be concluded that the program was of little use, since those who had experienced it (those receiving X) were not much better or worse off than those who had not.

There would not be a real basis for this conclusion, however, because there is no evidence that the groups were equivalent to begin with. Therefore the comparison group cannot be used to control for such threats to internal validity as maturation, testing, and history, since these factors could have affected each group differently.

Comparison Group Pretest-Posttest Design

The comparison group pretest-posttest design (Design 2e) elaborates on the one-group pretest-posttest design (Design 2c) by adding a comparison group. This second group receives both the pretest (O_1) and the posttest (O_2) at the same time as the experimental group, but it does not receive the intervention.

In symbols, it is written as follows:

> Experimental Group: O_1 X O_2
> Comparison Group: O_1 O_2

Where:

O_1 = First measurement of the dependent variable

X = Independent variable, the intervention

O_2 = Second measurement of the dependent variable

The experimental and comparison groups formed under this design will probably not be equivalent, because members are not randomly assigned to them. The pretest, however, will indicate the extent of their differences. If the differences are likely to affect the posttest, the statistical technique of analysis of covariance can be used to compensate for them (Weinbach & Grinnell, 2001).

Interrupted Time-Series Design

In the interrupted time-series design (Design 2f), a series of pretests and posttests are conducted on a group of research participants over time, both before and after the independent variable is introduced. The basic elements of this design are illustrated as follows:

> O_1 O_2 O_3 X O_4 O_5 O_6

Where:

Os = Measurements of the dependent variable

X = Independent variable (see Box 8.3)

This design takes care of the major weakness in the descriptive one-group pretest-posttest design (Design 2c), which does not control for rival hypotheses. Suppose, for example, that a new policy is to be introduced into an agency whereby all promotions and raises are to be tied to the number of educational credits acquired by social workers. Since there is a strong feeling among some workers that years of experience should count for more than educational credits, the agency's management decides to examine the effect of the new policy on morale.

Because agency morale is affected by many things and varies normally from month to month, it is necessary to ensure that these normal fluctuations are not confused with the results of the new policy. Therefore, a baseline is first established for morale by conducting a number of pretests over, say, a six-month period before the policy is introduced. Then, a similar number of posttests is conducted over the six months following the introduction of the policy. This design would be written as follows:

$$O_1 \quad O_2 \quad O_3 \quad O_4 \quad O_5 \quad O_6 \quad X \quad O_7 \quad O_8 \quad O_9 \quad O_{10} \quad O_{11} \quad O_{12}$$

The same type of time-series design can be used to evaluate the result of a treatment intervention with a client or client system, as in case-level designs described in the previous chapter. Again, without randomization, threats to external validity still could affect the results, but most of the threats to internal validity are addressed.

EXPLANATORY DESIGNS

Explanatory program-level evaluation designs approach an "ideal" evaluation most closely. They are at the highest level on the knowledge continuum, have the most rigid requirements, and are most able to produce results that can be generalized to other clients and situations. Explanatory designs, therefore, are most able to provide valid and reliable evaluation results that can add to our theoretical knowledge base.

The purpose of most explanatory designs is to establish a causal connection between the intervention (the independent variable) and the program objectives (the dependent variable). The attainment of the objectives could always result from chance rather than from the influence of the intervention, but there are statistical techniques for calculating the probability that this will occur (see Weinbach & Grinnell, 2001).

Classical Experimental Design

The classical experimental design (Design 3a), or classical evaluation design, is the basis for all explanatory designs. It involves an experimental group and a control group, both created by random sampling and random assignment methods. Both groups take a pretest (O_1) at the same time after which the intervention (X) is given only to the experimental group, and then both groups take the posttest (O_2).

This design is written as follows:

Experimental Group: R O_1 X O_2
Control Group: R O_1 O_2

Where:

R = Random selection from a population and random assignment to group

O_1 = First measurement of the dependent variable

X = Independent variable, the intervention

O_2 = Second measurement of the dependent variable

Because the experimental and control groups have been randomly assigned, they are equivalent with respect to all important factors. This group equivalence in the design helps control for extraneous variables, because both groups would be affected by them in the same way.

Randomized Posttest-Only Control Group Design

The randomized posttest-only control group design (Design 3*b*) is identical to the descriptive comparison group posttest-only design (Design 2*e*), except that in this explanatory design clients are randomly assigned to groups. This design, therefore, has a control group rather than a comparison group.

The randomized posttest-only control group design usually involves only two groups, one experimental and one control. There are no pretests. The experimental group receives the intervention and takes the posttest; the control group takes only the posttest.

This design is written as:

Where:

R = Random selection from a population and random assignment to group

X = Independent variable, the intervention

O_1 = First and only measurement of the dependent variable

In addition to measuring change in a group or groups, a pretest also helps to ensure equivalence between the control and experimental groups. This design does not have a pretest. However, the groups have been randomly assigned, as indicated by R, and this in itself is often enough to ensure equivalence without the need for a confirming pretest. This design is useful in situations where it is not possible to conduct a pretest or where the pretest is expected to influence the results of the posttest strongly, due to the effects of testing.

SUMMING UP AND LOOKING AHEAD

Program-level evaluation designs are conducted with groups of cases rather than on a case-by-case basis. They cover the entire range of evaluation concerns and provide designs that can be used to gain knowledge on the exploratory, descriptive, and explanatory levels. The chapter presented the threats to internal and external validity and demonstrated how these threats can affect various evaluation designs.

The prior chapter described how formal case-level evaluations can be used to enhance quality improvement at the line level; that is, it presented various evaluative designs that can be used to evaluate (or monitor) clients' practice objectives. This chapter presented various designs that can be used to evaluate program objectives. Thus, the two chapters complement one another as they both describe how evaluations can be used in the quality improvement process at the case level (practice objectives) and at the program level (program objectives). All of the evaluative designs presented in the last chapter and this one can be used to enhance the delivery of human services.

Most of the designs described in these two chapters can be used in the project and monitoring approaches to quality improvement, depending on when the evaluation takes place. Designs that reflect the project approach usually take place after a program is completed, whereas designs that reflect the monitoring approach usually take place while the program is underway.

KEY TERMS

Classical Experimental Design: An explanatory research design with randomly selected and randomly assigned experimental and control groups in which the program's objective (the dependent variable) is measured before and after the intervention (the independent variable) for both groups, but only the experimental group receives the intervention.

Comparison Group Posttest-Only Design: A descriptive research design with two groups, experimental and comparison, in which the program's objective (dependent variable) is measured once for both groups, and only the experimental group receives the intervention (the independent variable).

Comparison Group Pretest-Posttest Design: A descriptive research design with two groups, experimental and comparison, in which the program's objective (the dependent variable) is measured before and after the intervention (the independent variable) for both groups, but only the experimental group receives the intervention.

Compensation: Attempts by evaluators or staff members to counterbalance the lack of treatment for control group clients by administering some or all of the intervention (the independent variable); a threat to internal validity.

Compensatory Rivalry: Motivation of control group clients to compete with experimental group clients; a threat to internal validity.

Constants: A characteristic that has the same value for all clients in an evaluation.

Control Group: A group of randomly selected and randomly assigned clients in a study who do not receive the experimental intervention (the independent variable) and are used for comparison purposes.

Demoralization: Feelings of deprivation among control group clients that may cause them to drop out of the evaluation study; a form of mortality which is a threat to internal validity.

Dependent Variable: A variable that is dependent on or caused by another variable; an outcome variable that is not manipulated directly but is measured to determine if the independent variable has had an effect. Program objectives are dependent variables.

Differential Selection: The failure to achieve or maintain equivalency among the preformed groups; a threat to internal validity.

Diffusion of Treatment: Problems that may occur when experimental and control group clients talk to each other about a study; a threat to internal validity.

Experimental Group: In an experimental research design, the group of clients exposed to the manipulation of the intervention (the independent variable); also referred to as the treatment group.

External Validity: The extent to which the findings of an evaluation study can be generalized outside the evaluative situation.

Generalizability: Extending or applying the findings of an evaluation study to clients or situations that were not directly evaluated.

Hawthorne Effect: Effects on clients' behaviors or attitudes attributable to their knowledge that they are taking part in an evaluation project.

History in Research Design: Any event that may affect the second or subsequent measurement of the program's objectives (the dependent variables) and which cannot be accounted for in the evaluation design; a threat to internal validity.

Hypothesis: A theory-based prediction of the expected results in an evaluation study; a tentative explanation of a relationship or supposition that a relationship may exist.

Independent Variable: A variable that is not dependent on another variable but is said to cause or determine changes in the dependent variable; an antecedent variable that is directly manipulated in order to assess its effect on the dependent variable. Interventions are independent variables.

Instrumentation Error: Any flaws in the construction of a measuring instrument or any faults in the administration of a measuring instrument that affect the appraisal of program and practice objectives; a threat to internal validity.

Interaction Effect: Effects on the program's objective (the dependent variable) that are produced by the combination of two or more threats to internal validity.

Internal Validity: The extent to which it can be demonstrated that the intervention (the independent variable) in an evaluation is the only cause of change in the program's objective (the dependent variable); soundness of the experimental procedures and measuring instruments.

Interrupted Time-Series Design: An explanatory evaluation design in which there is only one group and the program objective (the dependent variable) is measured repeatedly before and after the intervention (the independent variable).

Longitudinal Case Study Design: An exploratory research design in which there is only one group and the program's objective (the dependent variable) is measured more than once; also referred to as a panel design, a developmental design, or a dynamic case study design.

Matched Pairs Method: A technique of assigning clients to groups so that the experimental and control groups are approximately equivalent in pretest scores or other characteristics, or so that all differences except the experimental condition are eliminated.

Maturation: Any unplanned change in clients due to mental, physical or other processes that take place over the course of the evaluation project and that affect the program's objective; a threat to internal validity.

Mortality: The tendency for clients to drop out of an evaluation study before it is completed; a threat to internal validity.

Multigroup Posttest-Only Design: An exploratory research design in which there is more than one group and the program's objective (the dependent variable) is measured only once for each group.

Multiple-Treatment Interference: When a client is given two or more interventions in succession, the results of the first intervention may affect the results of the second or subsequent interventions; a threat to external validity.

One-Group Posttest-Only Design: An exploratory design in which the program's objective (the dependent variable) is measured only once; the simplest of all group evaluation designs.

One-Group Pretest-Posttest Design: A descriptive research design in which the program's objective (the dependent variable) is measured before and after the intervention (the independent variable).

Pretest-Treatment Interaction: Effects of the pretest on the responses of clients to the introduction of the intervention (the independent variable); a threat to external validity.

Principle of Parsimony: A principle stating that the simplest and most economical route to evaluating the achievement of the program's objective (the dependent variable) is the best.

Random Assignment: The process of allocating clients to experimental and control groups so that the groups are equivalent; also referred to as randomization.

Randomized Cross-Sectional Survey Design: A descriptive research design in which there is only one group, the program's objective (the dependent variable) is measured only once, the clients are randomly selected from the population and there is no intervention (the independent variable).

Randomized Longitudinal Survey Design: A descriptive research design in which there is only one group, the program's objective (the dependent variable) is measured more than once, and clients are randomly selected from the population before the intervention (the independent variable).

Randomized One-Group Posttest-Only Design: A descriptive research design in which there is only one group, the program's objective (the dependent variable) is measured only once, and all members of a population have equal opportunity for participation in the evaluation.

Randomized Posttest-Only Control Group Design: An explanatory research design in which there are two or more randomly selected and randomly assigned groups; the control group does not receive the intervention (the independent variable), and the experimental groups receive different interventions.

Random Sampling: An unbiased selection process conducted so that all members of a population have an equal chance of being selected to participate in the evaluation study.

Reactive Effects: An effect on outcome measures due to the clients' awareness that they are participating in an evaluation study; a threat to internal and external validity.

Researcher Bias: The tendency of evaluators to find results that they expect to find; a threat to external validity.

Rival Hypothesis: A theory-based prediction that is a plausible alternative to the research hypothesis and might explain results as well or better; a hypothesis involving extraneous variables other than the intervention (the independent variable); also referred to as the alternative hypothesis.

Selection-Treatment Interaction: The relationship between the manner of selecting clients to participate in an evaluation study and their responses to the intervention (the independent variable); a threat to external validity.

Solomon Four-Group Design: An explanatory research design with four randomly assigned groups, two experimental and two control; the program's objective (the dependent variable) is measured before and after the intervention (the independent variable) for one experimental and one control group, but only after the intervention for the other two groups, and only the experimental groups receive the intervention.

Specificity of Variables: An evaluation project conducted with a specific group of clients at a specific time and in a specific setting that may not always be generalizable to other clients at a different time and in a different setting; a threat to external validity.

Statistical Regression: The tendency for extreme high or low scores to regress, or shift, toward the average (mean) score on subsequent measurements; a threat to internal validity.

Testing Effect: The effect that taking a pretest might have on posttest scores; a threat to internal validity.

STUDY QUESTIONS

1. What are the differences between random selection and random sampling?

2. In groups of six, decide on a human service–related problem area. Design three hypothetical studies using one exploratory, one explanatory, and one descriptive evaluation design. For each

study determine what data need to be gathered. Provide the graphic representation of the study detailing the Rs, Os, and Xs. Present the three designs to the class with a detailed explanation of sampling procedures.

3. In groups of four, discuss each of the threats to external validity and the threats to internal validity in terms of how you would control for each one. What problems arise when attempting to control for all of the threats to internal and external validity? Present your discussion to the class.

4. Describe thoroughly in your own words the similarities and differences between formal case-level evaluation designs (Chapter 7) and program-level evaluations. Discuss in detail how they complement one another in contemporary human service practice.

5. Discuss how program-level designs provide data that are more generalizable than those data that are generated from formal case level designs (Chapter 7).

6. In your own words describe what an "ideal" program evaluation is. What is the purpose of conducting one? Why is an "ideal" evaluative study rarely achieved in the human services?

7. Time order of variables is crucial to an "ideal" evaluation, as is the manipulation of at least one independent variable and the establishment of a relationship between interventions and program objectives. Why?

8. "Ideal" evaluations also require the control of rival hypotheses, the use of a control group, and random sampling and assignment. Explain why this is so.

9. In addition to the six characteristics of "ideal" evaluations, an "ideal" evaluation study must have internal and external validity. What is the main difference between internal and external validity?

10. In an "ideal" evaluation, the evaluator should be able to conclude from the findings that the intervention is or is not the only cause of the change in the programs objective. What factors would threaten the ability of the evaluator to draw such a conclusion?

11. In an "ideal" evaluation, the results are generalizable to a larger group or setting outside of the evaluative context, situation, or setting. Why is generalizability so important to establish in evaluative studies? What factors would threaten the generalizability of the results of a particular study to a large population or group?

12. Why is the principle of parsimony so important in choosing an evaluative design?

13. Why are exploratory designs at the lowest level on the continuum of knowledge that can be derived from evaluation studies? What is meant by an exploratory design?

14. What are the characteristics of a one-group posttest-only design? Can the results of this design be generalized to another group or population? Why or why not? Can a causal relationship between the program or practice objectives and intervention be established with these designs?

15. What are the characteristics of a multigroup posttest-only design? Can we assume that all the groups in the study are equivalent? Can we assume that any of the groups are representative of the larger population? Why?

16. How is the longitudinal case-study design like the one-group posttest-only design? How is it different? What is the advantage of using this design?

17. Why are descriptive designs found at the midpoint on the continuum of knowledge that can be derived from evaluation studies? Explain what is meant by a descriptive design.

18. How is the randomized one-group posttest-only design similar to the exploratory one-group posttest-only design? How is it different? What is the advantage of using the randomized design? What is a major problem in its use?

19. What is the difference between a randomized cross-sectional survey design and a randomized longitudinal survey design? Under what conditions would you choose the use of one design over another?

20. Describe the characteristics of the one-group pretest-posttest design. Why is the design used so often in the human services? What are some of the shortcomings of this design? How is this design different from the comparison group pretest-posttest design?

21. How is the comparison group posttest-only design an improvement over the exploratory one-group and multigroup posttest-only designs?

22. What is the difference between a control group and a comparison group? How does the use of a comparison group affect the evaluator's ability to prove a causal relationship between the intervention and the program objectives?

23. Why are explanatory designs at the highest level on the continuum of knowledge that can be derived from evaluation studies? Explain what is meant by an explanatory design.

24. What is a classical experimental design? How does it fulfill the requirements of an "ideal" explanatory evaluative design?

REFERENCES AND FURTHER READINGS

Campbell, D.T., & Stanley, J.C. (1963). *Experimental and quasi-experimental designs for research*. Skokie, IL: Rand McNally.

Cournoyer, D.E., & Klein, W.C. (2001). Formulating research questions. In R.M. Grinnell, Jr. (Ed.), *Social work research and evaluation: Quantitative and qualitative approaches* (6th ed., pp. 73–87). Itasca, IL: F.E. Peacock.

Creswell, J.W. (1994). *Research design: Qualitative and quantitative approaches*. Newbury Park, CA: Sage.

Gabor, P.A., & Grinnell, R.M., Jr. (1994). *Evaluation and quality improvement in the human services*. Boston: Allyn & Bacon.

Gabor, P.A., Unrau, Y.A., & Grinnell, R.M., Jr. (1997). *Evaluation and quality improvement in the human services* (2nd ed.). Boston: Allyn & Bacon.

Grinnell, R.M., Jr., & Unrau, Y. (2001). Group research designs. In R.M. Grinnell, Jr. (Ed.), *Social work research and evaluation: Quantitative and qualitative approaches* (6th ed., pp. 224–259). Itasca, IL: F.E. Peacock.

Grinnell, R.M., Jr., & Williams, M. (1990). *Research in social work: A primer*. Itasca, IL: F.E. Peacock.

Reid, W.J., & Smith, A. (1989). *Research in social work* (2nd ed.). New York: Columbia University Press.

Schutt, R.K. (2001). Science, society, and research. In R.M. Grinnell, Jr. (Ed.), *Social work research and evaluation: Quantitative and qualitative approaches* (6th ed., pp. 20–40). Itasca, IL: F.E. Peacock.

Tripodi, T. (1981). The logic of research design. In R.M. Grinnell, Jr. (Ed.), *Social work research and evaluation* (pp. 198–225). Itasca, IL: F.E. Peacock.

Tripodi, T. (1985). Research designs. In R.M. Grinnell, Jr. (Ed.), *Social work research and evaluation* (2nd ed., pp. 231–259). Itasca, IL: F.E. Peacock.

Unrau, Y.A., Krysik, J., & Grinnell, R.M., Jr. (2001). *Student study guide for the sixth edition of social work research and evaluation: Quantitative and qualitative approaches*. Itasca, IL: F.E. Peacock.

Weinbach, R.W., & Grinnell, R.M., Jr. (2001). *Statistics for social workers* (5th ed.). Boston: Allyn & Bacon.

Weinbach, R.W., Grinnell, R.M., Jr., Taylor, L., & Unrau, Y.A. (1999). *Applying research knowledge: A workbook for social work students* (3rd ed.). Boston: Allyn & Bacon.

Williams, M., Unrau, Y.A., & Grinnell, R.M., Jr. (1998). *Introduction to social work research.* Itasca, IL: F.E. Peacock.

___

Part III

Issues of Evaluation

9

Chapter Outline

Politics, Ethics, and Standards

AS WE KNOW BY NOW, this book is intended to provide an approach to planning, implementing, reporting, and using evaluations. In previous chapters we have considered the research methods and approaches required to conduct evaluations. In subsequent chapters we will provide an approach to implementing evaluations. Implementation occurs in the real world and, therefore, is subject to the multiple influences and pressures that exist there. In this chapter, professional and ethical guidelines for evaluations are discussed and presented. They provide a way of ensuring that evaluations are properly and competently conducted and appropriately used.

POLITICS OF EVALUATION

The real world pressures that affect, and sometimes buffet, evaluation work exist because evaluations are often perceived to have serious consequences affecting people's interests. Consequently, people, factions, or groups sometimes seek to advance their interests by influencing the evaluation process. Politics may be at work within a program or outside of a program; these can result in very strong pressure on the evaluation process. Further, because politics often leads to personal contention, the actual conduct of the evaluation may become difficult.

Politically charged situations may emerge within a social service program, in which case individuals internal to the program are primarily involved. Administrators and staff are key players when it comes to internal politics. Program politics become apparent in situations where their interests are involved; the evaluation may lead to changes in philosophy, organization, or approach to service provision. An evaluation must be prudent in dealing with internal politics since the cooperation of administrators and staff needs to be maintained to facilitate the evaluation process. At other times, individuals who are *outside* of the program may wish to influence decisions about the future development or the allocation of resources. When individuals outside the program attempt to influence the evaluation, external politics are at work.

Further contention may develop when a program's staff members and external stakeholder groups hold different views about what events should take place and what decisions ought to be made. The nature of the decisions to be made, the invested interests of the respective parties, and the magnitude of potential change can all serve to raise the perceived consequences of the evaluation and the intensity of the political climate.

APPROPRIATE AND INAPPROPRIATE USES OF EVALUATION

Any human endeavor, including evaluation, can be appropriately or inappropriately used; when stakes are high, the probability of misuse increases. A good evaluation results in the production of fair, balanced, and accurate data about the program; appropriate use of these data is in the decision-making process. At its best, this should be an open, transparent process with decisions evolving from evaluation results. However, in politicized situations, there is little intention to use evaluation results in an open decision-making process; the intent is to use the evaluation process to further some other purpose. Inevitably, a misuse of evaluation results.

Misuses of Evaluation

Evaluations can be misused in various ways. Some of the more common misuses include: (1) justifying decisions already made, (2) public relations, (3) performance appraisal, and (4) fulfilling funding requirements.

Justifying Decisions Already Made

Perhaps the most frequent misuse of evaluation is justifying decisions that were made in advance of the evaluation. At the case level, for example, a worker may have decided, if only at the subconscious level, that a youngster in treatment foster care should be referred to a group care program. The worker may then select a standardized measuring instrument (Chapter 6) that is likely to show that the youngster's functioning is highly problematic, and then use these data to justify the previously taken decision.

At the program level, an administrator may already have decided that a certain program within the agency should be reduced in size. The administrator may then commission an evaluation in the hope that the results will show the program to be ineffective. Inevitably, any evaluation will uncover some shortcomings and limitations; the administrator can then use these to justify the decision to reduce the size of the program. Similarly, outside funders who have already decided to curtail or cancel funding for a program may first commission an evaluation in the hope that the results will justify the preformed decision.

Public Relations

A second misuse of evaluation is to distract attention from negative events. From time to time, problems and incidents occur that bring unwelcome publicity. A worker in a group home, for example, may be indicted for sexual abuse of residents, or a preschooler may be returned from a treatment foster home to her natural home and be subsequently physically abused. These types of incidents inevitably attract intense media scrutiny and public interest.

Some administrators may immediately respond to such incidents by commissioning an evaluation and then declining any comment. "I have today engaged Professor Rodriguez from the university to undertake a comprehensive evaluation of this program; until the evaluation results are available, I do not want to say anything further that might prejudge the findings," an administrator might announce. Although an evaluation may be an appropriate response in such a situation, it is so only to the extent that it will be used as data that can help to decide on changes that will reduce the likelihood that a similar problem will again occur. When an evaluation is commissioned merely to distract attention, to avoid having to comment, much of the time, effort, and resources invested will be wasted, as there is unlikely to be any genuine interest in the results. Evaluation in such a situation is mere window dressing—a diversion.

Performance Appraisal

The third serious misuse of evaluation occurs when it is used for purposes of performance appraisal. For example, data can be aggregated inappropriately across a worker's caseload, and the resulting "cumulative data" are then used for performance appraisal. At the program level, the contents of an evaluation report, which focuses on an operating unit, may be used to evaluate the performance of a supervisor or administrator. While administrators do have some responsibility for the performance of their unit, program, or department, other factors—beyond the control of the administrator—may also be involved; the point is that program evaluation is not meant to link program performance and outcomes to individual social workers and their performances.

When an evaluation is used for purposes of performance appraisal, the findings are likely to be used for political goals—to promote or undermine an individual. Such misuse of evaluation is destructive, as administrators and workers alike will undoubtedly become defensive and concentrate their efforts on ensuring that evaluation data show them in the best possible light. These efforts detract from the delivery of effective services and will also likely result in less reliable data. Performance appraisals and program evaluations are two distinct processes, with different purposes. Both are compromised if they are not kept separate.

Fulfilling Funding Requirements

Nowadays, funders are commonly requiring an evaluation of some kind as a condition of a program's funding, particularly in the case of new projects. Staff members who are trying to set up a new program, or maintain an old one, may see the evaluation requirement as a ritual without having direct relevance to them. They may thus incorporate an evaluation component into the funding proposal, or graft evaluation activities onto an existing program, obediently jumping through hoops in order to satisfy funders that they are in compliance with evaluation requirements.

Often, these evaluation plans are not even implemented, because they were designed for "show" only. At other times, the evaluation activities are undertaken, but without any intention of making use of the results. It is, of course, a serious misuse (not to mention a waste of time, effort, and resources) to undertake an evaluation only to obtain program funds, without any thought of using the data that were derived from the evaluation in any meaningful way.

Proper Uses of Evaluation

Having described a variety of possible misuses, it is appropriate to conclude this section of the discussion by reviewing the appropriate uses of evaluations. As discussed previously, evaluations are most properly used to guide an open and transparent decision-making process, where evaluation findings will be weighed and considered.

Internal Decision Making

The primary internal use of evaluation data is feedback; evaluation findings provide data about the degree to which objectives are being met. When these data are available in a timely fashion, administrators and workers alike can continually monitor the impacts of their decisions, and, where required, make adjustments to activities and program operations.

At the case level, for example, evaluation data can provide an objective basis for making clinical decisions. As has been described in Chapter 7, selected practice objectives are measured repeatedly while the client is receiving service. These data are then used as feedback on client progress and become an important consideration in decisions to maintain, modify, or change treatment interventions.

At the program level, staff members' interest is in a broader picture of how the program functions. The monitoring approach to evaluation allows a program to gather data continuously about its various components, practices, and procedures. The principal internal use for such data is developmental. The process is essentially as follows: Data are collected continuously and analyzed periodically, to provide ongoing feedback about the functioning of various aspects of the program. Where the program is not performing as desired, there is an opportunity to make changes in structures, procedures, and practices. Subsequent data will then provide information about the impact of these changes. Through this process, administrators and staff can continuously fine-tune and improve the program.

Since the purpose of the evaluation is development, not judgment, people are more likely to take risks, innovate, and experiment. In such an environment, growth and development are more likely to occur. When staff members and teams feel encouraged to grow and learn, the program itself grows and learns.

External Decision Making

External uses of evaluation data usually involve funders, policy makers, other stakeholder groups, and researchers. Appropriate uses include the demonstration of accountability, decision making about program and policy, and knowledge building.

Social service programs are, in a general sense, accountable to their clients, to their communities, and to professional peers. In a more specific way, they are also accountable to their funders. Accountability generally requires evidence that goals are consistent with community needs; that contracted services are provided; and that services are being provided effectively and efficiently. These are among the most common uses of evaluation data: to account for program activities and program results.

At the policy level, it is sometimes necessary to make decisions among various ways of meeting particular social needs. Or, policy makers may decide to encourage the development of programs that are organized along certain intervention models. For example, in many jurisdictions, the development of treatment foster homes has been encouraged in recent years, while group care facilities for young people are supported much more reluctantly. At other times, funders must make decisions regarding future funding for a specific program. In all three situations, evaluation will provide data that can help guide decisions.

Knowledge building is another way in which an evaluation's results may be used. Each completed evaluation study has the potential of adding to the knowledge base. Indeed, at times, evaluations are undertaken specifically for the purpose of acquiring knowledge. Because evaluations are conducted in field settings, they are a particularly useful method for testing the effectiveness of interventions and treatment models.

Evaluations for external purposes are usually initiated by people outside the program, typically funding bodies such as governments or foundations. They are often also externally conducted by evaluation specialists on a project-by-project basis. When evaluations are externally initiated and externally conducted, there is a higher potential for problems in the evaluation process and for the misuse of the findings. This is because an external evaluator may impose an evaluation framework that does not fit well with program operations or is not consistent with staff members' or administrators' expectations.

An effective safeguard is provided when administrators and staff are involved in decisions relating to the planning and execution of the evaluation. An alternative to the externally conducted project evaluation is available to programs that establish internal evaluation systems. When internal systems are developed with stakeholders participating, the data collected through them often satisfy many of the data needs of external stakeholders.

POLITICAL INFLUENCES ON THE EVALUATION PROCESS

We have seen how internal and external politics can lead to inappropriate reasons for conducting case- and program-level evaluations. Moreover, we should also be aware that political influences may have an impact once the evaluation is underway. Individuals may attempt to influence the evaluation process itself, in an attempt to obtain results that support their views and positions.

Manipulating the Evaluation Process

Stakeholders usually have legitimate interests in relation to a social service program and, quite appropriately, may attempt to further these interests. For example, some staff members may believe strongly that a new approach would work better than an existing intervention method. They may then try to convince and influence others that the new intervention approach should be adopted. Or, an administrator may believe that a certain approach to intake will produce better results.

Attempting to influence program development so that the new approach or intake method is adopted is quite natural and entirely appropriate. In the normal course of an evaluation, data may emerge that would, in fact, confirm the superiority of the intervention approach or the benefits of the new intake process.

However, people sometimes move beyond the legitimate use of influence and attempt to manipulate the evaluation process itself. Thus, staff members may selectively provide data that tend to show the benefits of their preferred approach or the shortcomings of the existing approach, hoping to influence the outcome of the evaluation. Or, an administrator may offer to an evaluator a comparison situation between two units, one using the old intake approach and one using the new intake approach.

However, the administrator might also know that the unit using the old intake approach has encountered large staff turnover recently and currently faces other difficulties as well. If the evaluator collected data from the two proposed units, the resulting comparison might well reflect the functioning of the units rather than the effectiveness of the intake processes. Any number of other examples could be cited, ranging from relatively mild examples of attempting to exert undue influence to very flagrant attempts at manipulating the process.

Misdirecting the Evaluation Process

We know that social service programs (including interventions) do not exist in a single static state. They exist in many states, or are multifaceted, and the particular state revealed by an evaluation depends on the purpose and focus of the evaluation and the methodology employed. Individuals and groups may attempt to further their interests by misdirecting the evaluation process, in the hope that the state of the program revealed in the evaluation will serve to promote their agenda. Misdirecting the process may be accomplished through: (1) program objectives, (2) the evaluation sample, (3) data collection methods, and (4) interpretation of findings

Evaluators have considerable latitude in establishing the methodology and process concerning these matters. However, these methodological and process choices are subject to political pressures from individuals and groups who hope to influence the findings. It is, therefore, particularly important that evaluators avoid becoming unwitting pawns in a manipulative political process; they need to be keenly aware of the implications of each choice they make. Let us now consider these four key decision-making points in evaluations and take a closer look at how politics may play within each.

Program Objectives

Unfortunately, many social service programs do not have clearly stated and measurable program objectives. How can a program be evaluated if its objectives are not explicitly stated? What is to be evaluated in such a situation? If specific objectives are lacking, they will need to be developed early in the evaluation process. The task of defining a program's objectives may heighten political contention because, in reality, a program's objectives define the criteria on which the program will be evaluated.

Administrators and workers, understandably, will wish to be evaluated against criteria that they feel reflect their program's philosophy, practices, and focus. They would also like to see the objectives set in a manner that takes into account the constraints imposed by mandate, resources, and context. In addition, they will wish to emphasize objectives that they believe they are meeting or exceeding. On the other hand, stakeholders from the outside may wish to set objectives around matters that are important to them. Funders, for example, may wish to define outcome objectives; other agencies may identify partnership-related objectives; service recipients may emphasize access.

Of course, the program will inevitably fare better on some objectives than on others; thus, if any of these groups have political goals or are trying to advance a hidden agenda, these may be furthered depending on the selection of the objectives that will frame the evaluation.

The evaluator thus has a responsibility to ensure that the program is evaluated against existing objectives, if there are any. If there are none, objectives need to be identified, and the evaluator must ensure that the objectives are fair and reasonable and include a balance of perspectives from all relevant stakeholder groups.

Sample Selection

As we know from Chapter 5, whom we decide to include in an evaluation sample influences the data that are collected and, ultimately, the findings that are derived from the evaluative effort. Since all social service programs have a number of stakeholder groups, it is possible to gather evaluation data from many different sources. In a family preservation program, for example, we could sample the program's workers (Data Source 1), other helping professionals involved with the clients (Data Source 2), the clients themselves (Data Source 3), or even the general public (Data Source 4) to obtain relevant data.

Further, after the sources are decided upon, questions often arise about the criteria for sample inclusion. Suppose, for example, it was agreed in a family preservation program that the families would be the main data source. Evaluation results may be influenced considerably by how a "family" is defined. Are data collected from parents only, or are children included as well? Sometimes data are collected from *available* family members. Data for one family, for example, can be collected from the mother, while data for another family can be collected from both parents, the children, and a live-in grandparent. Clearly, decisions regarding these matters will influence results.

Another consideration in sampling is whether all clients who started in the program are to be included in the sample. If, for example, clients complete a self-administered satisfaction survey at termination, those who have dropped out of the program early and who are presumably less satisfied will not be included. Thus, the results will likely reflect more satisfaction with the program than is actually the case.

Or, if a focus group is to be conducted, who will participate? Often, such groups are composed on the basis of recommendations of staff members, who tend to suggest their "best" clients, those who are articulate, cooperative, have made the most improvement, and generally hold the most favorable attitudes toward the program. Obviously, such a sample would not likely result in data that are representative of all clients.

Again, it is the evaluator's responsibility to consider the implications of how the sample is selected and to ensure that the sampling method is reasonable under the circumstances.

Data Collection Methods

The methods used to collect data may also influence results. For example, in an evaluation of the stability of changes brought about during a program, a follow-up of closed cases may be undertaken and telephone interviews may be conducted to collect data. Clearly, clients without telephones or those who have moved and not left forwarding information will be excluded. It is, however, likely that these clients may be different from those who are included; they are probably not doing as well as clients who have a stable residence and can be contacted through telephone calls. Thus, follow-up data collected by this method may tend to overstate the level of functioning of former clients.

The timing of data collection can also have a considerable effect on an evaluation's results. At both the case and program levels, different conclusions may be drawn about client success if progress is measured at the time of termination of services, rather than at some time after termination. In the case of adolescents discharged from a group care program, for example, deterioration often takes place subsequent to termination, because less structure and fewer supports are available in the community.

Outcome measures taken at the time of termination (as well as at follow-up) are both legitimate reflections of a program's objectives, but they represent different perspectives and may show different results. Clients, for example, may show considerable gains at posttest, immediately after exiting the program, but may show only marginal gains at follow-up, three months later.

Who collects the data is another important decision. As discussed in previous chapters, many programs use front-line workers to collect data in an effort to keep costs at a minimum. If the data are collected by their workers, service recipients may not feel free to express their true opinions, particularly if their opinions are somewhat critical. Alternatively, if workers are asked to rate their own clients' functioning, they may overstate the case, in a conscious or subconscious effort to reflect their own efforts in the best possible light.

Since data collection has implications for the results, evaluators have a responsibility to ensure that the methods used are appropriate, will provide for the integrity of the resulting data, and are without biasing effects.

Interpretation of Findings

In this book, evaluation is described as a way of monitoring interventions, program processes, and outcomes in order to provide feedback that can support a process of continuous improvement and development. As we know, the degree to which a program achieves its objectives is a measure of success. However, it is essentially a matter of opinion what level of achievement actually constitutes *success*. Suppose for a moment that 60 percent of the graduates of a job-training program find employment. This figure may be interpreted as indicating success, in that *fully* 60 percent of graduates are employed or it may be taken to indicate failure, in that *only* 60 percent of graduates find work.

Moreover, such data as the percentage of former clients who find employment represent only a part of the evaluative picture. Relevant contextual factors should also be considered; these could include the rate of unemployment in the community, the income earned by former participants, and the level of job satisfaction experienced by them. The way in which evaluation findings are interpreted is a process known as *valuation*.

Because criteria for a program's success are seldom predefined, evaluators often play an influential part in the valuation process; and depending on the judgment of an evaluator, the same result may be classified as either a success or a failure. It goes without saying that evaluators must ensure that the valuation process is fair and reasonable.

PROFESSIONAL STANDARDS FOR EVALUATION

To safeguard against the misdirection of the evaluation process or the misuse of the results, evaluators turn to professional standards for guidelines regarding the conceptualization and implementation of their work. There are various standards that exist; this section provides a description of one widely accepted set of standards for evaluation.

The oldest professional standards for evaluation are those issued by the Joint Committee on Standards of Educational Evaluation (1994). The Committee was formed in 1975 and now includes a large number of organizations concerned with maintaining high professional standards in evaluation practice. The Joint Committee has identified four overlapping criteria against which evaluation practice should be judged: (1) utility, (2) feasibility, (3) propriety, and (4) accuracy. Although the Committee standards were written specifically as guidelines for program-level evaluation, many of the standards are relevant and can be applied to case level evaluation as well.

Utility

The utility criteria are intended to ensure that evaluations will provide useful data to one or more of the program's stakeholder groups. In other words, evaluators are required to establish links between an evaluation's findings and the decisions to be derived from them. Data obtained from an evaluation must be relevant to decision makers and reported in a manner that decision makers can understand.

At the case level, the participant and the front-line worker are, in most cases, joint decision makers. Because workers usually carry out case-level evaluations, they will be able to decide on the type of data to be gathered, the method of analyses, and the way in which evaluation findings will impact case-level decision making.

At the program level, evaluation findings are usually documented in a written report. In a monitoring situation, the report may be one of a regular series, without formal recommendations; in a project evaluation there is likely to be a formal report, often ending with a series of recommendations. In either case, to ensure that an evaluation has utility, the evaluator is responsible for determining in advance, with as much clarity as possible, the decisions that are to be based on the evaluation's findings.

The evaluator is then responsible for reporting results in a manner that can inform the decisions to be taken. It is obviously important that the report be tailored to the decision makers, who usually do not have an extensive background in evaluation, research methods, or statistics. Thus, statistical results, for example, should be provided so they are comprehensible to the users. When drafting recommendations, it is important that evaluators keep in mind the social, political, economic, and professional contexts within which recommendations will be implemented. The challenge is to provide recommendations that can result in meaningful and feasible improvement within existing constraints.

Feasibility

Feasibility standards attempt to ensure that evaluations shall be conducted only when feasible, practical, and economically viable. These standards speak to minimizing disruption within the organization where the evaluation is conducted; evaluators need to consider the impacts of evaluation activities such as data collection and ensure that they do not impose an unreasonable burden on staff and on the organization itself.

As well, these standards address the issue of "political viability," suggesting that evaluators should anticipate political influence and possible attempts to misdirect the process or to misapply the results. These matters have already been discussed in detail in previous sections of this chapter. The standards require that the evaluators be aware of these possibilities and ensure that the integrity of the evaluation process is maintained throughout.

Propriety

As presented in detail in Box 9.1, propriety standards provide the framework for the legal and ethical conduct of evaluations and describe the responsibilities of evaluators to ensure due regard for the welfare of those involved in the evaluation, as well as of those affected by the evaluation.

These standards emphasize the obligation of those undertaking evaluations to act within the law, to respect those involved in the evaluation, and to protect the rights and well-being of all human subjects. These standards are similar to, but not as detailed as, the normal ethical standards that apply to the protection of human subjects in any research project.

Universities generally maintain Institutional Review Boards, or their equivalent, which are concerned with ensuring that research methods are implemented in an ethical manner and that human subjects are protected from harm or undue risk. Most professions also address research procedures in their ethical codes. An evaluation project usually entails the implementation of

BOX 9.1_____

ETHICAL GUIDELINES FOR EVALUATION

Ethics is concerned with the moral practice of evaluation or the "code of right and wrong" for deciding how to handle data, how to interact with clients, and, in a general sense, how to proceed in politically charged situations.

A variety of ethical codes applicable to evaluation have been published. Although the ethical guidelines in existence have been written specifically to apply to program evaluations, many of the provisions apply to case-level evaluation as well. Most of the ethical guidelines and principles found in published codes can be organized around the four following themes: (1) purpose of the evaluation, (2) confidentiality, anonymity, and informed consent, (3) designing an ethical evaluation, and (4) informing others about an evaluation's findings.

Purpose of the Evaluation

The purpose of an evaluation must be clearly spelled out to all those who are asked to participate, as well as to those who will be directly affected by the evaluation findings. Purpose includes information about who initiated and is funding the evaluation and the types of decisions to be based on the evaluation's findings. This is a time for clarity and frankness (see Figure 9.1 on page 274).

If the purpose of an evaluation is to obtain objective data that can help in making decisions about funding, this should be clearly spelled out. If specific aspects of program functioning are the primary concern and it is hoped that evaluation data will shed light on relevant procedures and practices, this, too, should be explicitly stated.

Although this guideline may seem obvious, it is frequently violated. Evaluations should be conducted to obtain data for pro-

gram development, but it sometimes turns out that they were really intended to provide data for a funding decision. It is clearly unethical to engage in evaluations with hidden agendas.

Confidentiality, Anonymity, and Informed Consent

Confidentiality and anonymity specifically relate to how data are analyzed and reported. Confidentiality means that we have asked individuals providing us with data to trust us that we will keep the data private and restrict their use. Anonymity, on the other hand, refers to the practice of keeping data nameless.

In case-level evaluations, we can guarantee confidentiality but not anonymity. In program-level evaluations, both conditions apply. The utmost care must be taken to preserve the promised anonymity and to keep confidential data out of the hands of unauthorized persons.

A promise that is of particular concern to many evaluation participants is that of anonymity. A drug offender, for example, may be very afraid of being identified; a person on welfare may be concerned whether anyone else might learn that he or she was on welfare.

Also, there is often some confusion between the terms "anonymity" and "confidentiality." Some evaluations are designed so that no one, not even the person doing the evaluation, knows which evaluation participant gave what response. An example is a mailed survey form, bearing no identifying mark and asking the respondent not to give a name. In an evaluation like this, the respondent is *anonymous*.

BOX 9.1 CONTINUED_____

However, it is more often the case that we do know how a particular participant responded and have agreed not to divulge the information to anyone else. In such cases, the information is *confidential*. Part of our explanation to a potential evaluation participant must include a clear statement of what information will be shared with whom.

As soon after data collection as practical, the identities of evaluation participants should be disguised by use of codes that make it impossible to associate specific data with any particular individual. Assigning codes will also provide an additional level of protection during the data analysis phase. The master code book, listing clients and their assigned codes, should be kept under lock and key, and preferably in a different location from the data.

An important consideration in any evaluation is to obtain the participants' *informed* consent. The word "informed" means that each participant fully understands what is going to happen in the course of the evaluation, why it is going to happen, and what its effect will be on him or her. If the participant is psychiatrically challenged, mentally delayed, or in any other way incapable of full understanding, the evaluation must be explained to someone else—perhaps a parent, guardian, social worker, or spouse, or someone to whom the participant's welfare is important.

Informed consent means that the program participant has voluntarily agreed to participate in the evaluation, knows what will happen in the program, and fully understands any possible consequences. This applies equally to evaluations conducted at the case and program level.

Again, this provision seems self-evident, but there are well-known instances in which relevant information has been withheld from participants for fear that they would decline to participate or that their knowing the true purposes of the evaluation would compromise the reliability of measurements.

Participants should also be informed that they can withdraw at any time without penalty, and evaluators should recognize that, even when so assured, many clients do not feel free to do so. This is particularly likely to be true of children, as well as residents in group homes, institutions, hospitals, prisons, and senior citizens' homes. In such settings, it is the evaluator's responsibility to ensure that the consent obtained has not been coerced, either explicitly or implicitly.

It is clear that no evaluation participant may be bribed, threatened, deceived, or in any way coerced into participating. Questions must be encouraged, both initially and throughout the course of the evaluation. People who believe they understand may have misinterpreted our explanation or understood it only in part.

They may say they understand, when they do not, in an effort to avoid appearing foolish. They may even sign documents they do not comprehend to confirm their supposed understanding, and it is our responsibility to ensure that their understanding is real and complete.

It is particularly important for participants to know that they are not signing away their rights when they sign a consent form. They can decide at any time to withdraw from the evaluation *without penalty*, without so much as a reproachful glance. The results of the evaluation will be made available to them as soon as it has been completed. No promise will be made to them that cannot be fulfilled.

All this seems reasonable in theory, but ethical obligations are often difficult to fulfill in practice. For example, there are times when it is very difficult to remove coercive influences because these influences are inherent in the situation. A woman awaiting an abortion may agree to provide private information about herself and her partner because she believes that, if she does not, she will be denied the abortion. It is of no use to tell her that this is not true: She feels she is not in a position to take any chances.

BOX 9.1 CONTINUED

There are captive populations of people in prisons, schools, or institutions who may agree out of sheer boredom to take part in an evaluation study. Or, they may participate in return for certain privileges, or because they fear some penalty or reprisal. There may be people who agree because they are pressured into it by family members, or they want to please the social worker, or they need some service or payment that they believe depends on their cooperation. Often, situations like this cannot be changed, but at least we can be aware of them and try to deal with them in an ethical manner.

A written consent form should be only part of the process of informing evaluation participants of their roles and their rights as volunteers. It should give participants a basic description of the purpose of the evaluation, its procedures, and their rights as voluntary participants. All information should be provided in simple language, without jargon.

A consent form should be no longer than two pages of single-spaced typing. All participants should be given a copy of the consent form. Questionnaires may have an introductory letter containing the required information, with the written statement that the completion of the questionnaire is the person's agreement to participate. In telephone surveys, the information below will need to be given verbally and must be standardized across all calls.

A written consent form should contain the following items, recognizing that the relevancy of this information and the amount required will vary with each evaluation project (Grinnell & Williams, 1990; Williams, Tutty, & Grinnell, 1995):

1. A brief description of the purpose of the evaluation, as well as its value to the general/professional social work community (probability and nature of direct and indirect benefits) and to the participants and/or others.

2. An explanation as to how and/or why participants were selected and a statement that participation is completely voluntary.

3. A description of experimental conditions (if any) and/or procedures. Some points that should be covered are:
   a. The frequency with which the participants will be contacted.
   b. The time commitment required by the participants.
   c. The physical effort required and/or protection from overexertion.
   d. Emotionally sensitive issues that might be exposed and/or follow-up resources that are available if required.
   e. Location of participation (e.g., need for travel/commuting).
   f. Information that will be recorded and how it will be recorded (e.g., on paper, by photographs, videotape, audiotape).

4. Description of the likelihood of any discomforts and inconveniences associated with participation, and of known or suspected short- and long-term risks.

5. Explanation of who will have access to data collected and to the identity of the evaluation's participants (i.e., level of anonymity or confidentiality of each person's participation and information) and how long the data will be stored.

6. Description of how the data will be made public (e.g., final evaluation report, scholarly presentation, printed publication). An additional consent is required for publication of photographs, audiotapes, and/or videotapes.

7. Description of other evaluation projects or other people who may use the data.

8. Explanation of the participants' rights:
   a. That they may terminate or withdraw from the evaluation study at any point.
   b. That they may ask for clarification or more information throughout the evaluation effort.

BOX 9.1 CONTINUED

c. That they may contact the appropriate administrative body if they have any questions about the conduct of the individuals doing the evaluation or the evaluation's procedures.

Designing an Ethical Evaluation

A necessary precaution before beginning an evaluation is to ensure that it is designed in an ethical manner. One of the more useful research designs involves separating participants into control and experimental groups, and providing a treatment to the experimental group but not to the control group.

The essential dilemma here is whether or not it is ethical to withhold a treatment, assumed to be beneficial, from participants in the control group. Even if control-group participants are on a waiting list and will receive the treatment at a later date, is it right to delay service in order to conduct the evaluation?

Proponents of this evaluation design argue that people on a waiting list will not receive treatment any faster whether they are involved in the evaluation study or not. Furthermore, it is only *assumed* that the treatment is beneficial; if its effects were known for sure, there would be no need to do the evaluation study. Surely, social workers have an ethical responsibility to test such assumptions through evaluation studies before they continue with treatments that may be ineffective or even harmful.

As mentioned before, the same kind of controversy pertains to an evaluation design in which clients are randomly assigned to two different groups, each receiving a different treatment intervention. Proponents of this design argue that no one is sure which treatment is better—that is what the evaluation study is trying to discover—and so it is absurd to assert that a client in one group is being harmed by being denied the treatment offered to the other group. Social workers, however, tend to have their own ideas about which treatment is better. Ms. Gomez's worker, for example, may believe that she will derive more benefit from behavioral than from existential therapy, and that it will be harmful to her if random assignment happens to put her in the existential group.

Informing Others About an Evaluation's Findings

Another ethical consideration in an evaluation is the manner in which its findings are reported. It may be tempting, for example, to give great weight to positive findings while playing down or ignoring altogether negative or disappointing findings. There is no doubt that positive findings tend to be more enthusiastically received; but it is obviously just as important to know that two variables (i.e., the program and its outcomes) are not related as to know that they are.

All evaluation studies have limitations, because practical considerations make it difficult to use the costly and complex designs that yield the most certain results. Since evaluation studies with more limitations yield less trustworthy findings, it is important for us to be honest about an evaluation's limitations and for other social workers to be able to understand what the limitations imply.

Sometimes, the sharing of results will be a delicate matter. Staff may be reluctant to hear that the program is less effective than they thought. It will also be difficult, and often inadvisable, for us to share with research participants results that show them in an unfavorable light. For example, it may be honest to tell Mr. Yen that he scored high on the anxiety scale, but it may also be extremely damaging to him. Workers wrestle every day with the problems of whom to tell, as well as how, when, and how much. The same difficulties arise in social work evaluation.

[AGENCY LETTERHEAD]

Ms. Blackburn, MSW
Intake Worker II
City Social Services
Dallas, Texas 75712

Dear Ms. Blackburn:

As discussed on the phone, burnout among child protection workers is an issue of concern not only to child protection workers like yourself but to management alike. Research Services is asking you to voluntarily participate in our study. We will need this signed informed consent form before our interview can begin. We are deeply appreciative of your willingness to voluntarily participate in the department's research project.

Our interview will be held in your office and should last no more than one hour. Our objective is to elicit your views on the nature of the stresses (if any) that you face on a day-to-day basis. We may be discussing politically sensitive issues from time to time, and you have our assurance that we will maintain absolute confidentiality with respect to views expressed by you.

We will be asking you to complete a standardized measuring instrument that assesses a worker's degree of burnout before our interview begins. This task should take no more than ten minutes. All research materials will be kept in a locked file, and the identity of all workers interviewed for this study will be safeguarded by assigning each a number, so that names do not appear on any written materials.

With respect to any research or academic publications resulting from this study, specific views and/or opinions will not be ascribed either to you or to your organization without your prior written consent.

Your signature below indicates that you have understood to your satisfaction the information regarding your participation in our research project. Should you decide not to participate for whatever reason, or should you wish to withdraw at a later date, this will in no way affect your position in the agency. If you have any further questions about our study, please contact Research Services and we will address them as quickly as possible.

Sincerely,

Beulah Wright, MSW
Director, Research Services

YES: I AM WILLING TO PARTICIPATE IN THE RESEARCH PROJECT

Signature_____   Today's Date:_____

FIGURE 9.1   Example of a Simple Consent Form

research procedures; consequently, applicable professional and institutional ethical standards for conducting research should be met.

Finally, the propriety standards address completeness and fairness. These standards seek to ensure that a complete, fair, and balanced assessment of the program being evaluated results from the process. As we have seen in Chapter 4, evaluation is only a representation. This means that there are multiple possible pictures of a program, each representing a different perspective. Evaluators are responsible for creating a fair and balanced representation that can take into account all reasonable perspectives. Often this means that no single picture will emerge as the result of an evaluation and that evaluators will need to explain how the several perspectives fit together and how they relate to the overall social, economic, political, and professional context in which the program operates.

Accuracy

The final set of standards address accuracy. This has to do with the technical adequacy of the evaluation process and involves such matters as validity and reliability, measurement instruments, samples, comparisons, and research designs. These standards make clear the evaluator's responsibility for maintaining high technical standards in all aspect of the process. The evaluator is also responsible for describing any methodological shortcomings and the limits within which findings can be considered to be accurate.

OTHER STANDARDS

While the Joint Committee standards are the oldest and probably best known, there are other sources for evaluation standards too. As evaluation is becoming increasingly professionalized, a variety of national and regional evaluation associations now exist, and several of these have issued their own standards and guidelines. Most important among existing evaluation associations are the American Evaluation Association, Canadian Evaluation Association, European Evaluation Association, and Eurasian Evaluation Association.

The American Evaluation Association (1994) has issued what it calls "Guiding Principles For Evaluation," which act, essentially, as a set of standards. The basic principles enunciated by the American Evaluation Association are displayed below. The full document, in which these standards are elaborated further, is available through the web site of the American Evaluation Association.

— **Systematic Inquiry:** Evaluators conduct systematic data-based inquiries about whatever is being evaluated.
— **Competence:** Evaluators provide competent performance to stakeholders.
— **Integrity/Honesty:** Evaluators ensure the honesty and integrity of the entire evaluation process.
— **Respect for People:** Evaluators respect the security, dignity, and self-worth of the respondents, program participants, clients, and other stakeholders with whom they interact (see Box 9.1).
— **Responsibilities for General and Public Welfare:** Evaluators articulate and take into account the diversity of interests and values that may be related to general and public welfare.

PRINCIPLES OF EVALUATION PRACTICE

The discussion in this chapter has addressed a variety of matters ranging from technical approaches to evaluation to appropriate uses of the resulting products. We conclude by providing some guidelines for effective evaluation practice. These guidelines result in high-quality, principled practices that can ensure that political influences are kept to a minimum and the integrity of the evaluation process is maintained.

Principle 1:
Evaluation and Service Delivery
Activities Should Be Integrated

Evaluation and service delivery activities should be integrated to the extent possible. When evaluation is regarded as part of the service delivery process, it is much more likely that data collection will be focused on relevant issues and carried out conscientiously. As well, it is much more likely that the resulting information will be used as feedback for development rather than as evidence for judgment. Integrating evaluation with service delivery tends to ground evaluation activities and lessens the chance that evaluation will become a political tool or weapon.

While the idea that "evaluation and service delivery go hand in hand" is easy enough to grasp intellectually, it is practiced much too rarely. Evaluators must make a special effort to advocate this position and help administrators and workers alike to see the benefits of it. There are a number of things an evaluator can do to increase the likelihood that the concept of evaluation as an integral part of its service delivery structure is accepted.

First, the "evaluation-practice integration" message may need to be sent repeatedly. Successfully incorporating evaluation into client service delivery involves educating staff members at all levels, from the line to management. The message needs to be included in training and repeated as necessary. Second, helping administrators and staff use evaluation products effectively is a powerful strategy; once they see the how data from evaluation can help inform decision making, support for integrating evaluation activities is sure to increase. Finally, data collection protocols should ensure that only those data that are truly needed are collected, and in a manner that imposes as little burden on staff members as is possible. Data collection has costs associated with it; the benefits of collecting any data should clearly outweigh the costs of collecting it, and should be perceived to do so by staff.

Principle 2:
Involve from the Beginning as Many
Stakeholder Groups as Possible

Because of the different points of view represented by various stakeholder groups, and because of the possibility that some group or groups may wish to use the evaluation to promote their agenda—hidden or open—it is important to involve members from relevant stakeholder groups early in the evaluation process. The benefit of including as many stakeholder groups as possible is that the evaluation plan will be open to scrutiny from a diverse range of perspectives and therefore the interests of the different groups are likely to be balanced.

The downside of course is that "too many cooks spoil the broth." Thus, while it is important to include as many stakeholder groups as possible, it is not necessary to involve everyone in all aspects of the evaluation effort. Stakeholder groups can be invited to periodic review meetings where updates are provided and the main interests and concerns of stakeholder groups are aired and discussed. Between formal meetings, stakeholder groups can be kept involved in other ways. For example written information, perhaps in the form of an insert to the program newsletter, can be circulated about the status of the evaluation, describing current evaluation activities, results, and decisions. Responses can be invited, thereby ensuring ongoing stakeholder feedback.

Principle 3: Involve All Levels of Staff in the Evaluation Process

A constructive environment is one in which all levels of staff are involved in the evaluation process. A frequent mistake is to make the assumption that only senior-level staff members need to be involved in planning the evaluation and that only they should receive the findings derived from an evaluation. In well-functioning programs, decisions are made at all levels. Consequently, it is important that the evaluation system serve the needs of staff members at all levels, providing information for high-quality decision making throughout the program. Making decisions on the basis of evaluation findings is, as we have seen, a matter of making effective use of feedback. Depending on the extent to which a program's objectives are being achieved, decisions can be made to continue existing activities, to modify them, or to switch to new ones.

When staff members at any level in the organization are required to operate without adequate feedback, the effectiveness of their contributions will be decreased. In the process, the entire organizational performance suffers.

Principle 4: Make Explicit the Purpose of the Evaluation

The purpose of an evaluation should be clearly spelled out to all those who are asked to participate, as well as to those who will be affected by the findings. Purpose includes information about who initiated and is funding the evaluation, as well as the types of decisions to be based on the findings. This is a time for clarity and frankness. If the purpose of an evaluation is to develop information (via reliable and valid data) that can help in making decisions about funding, this should be clearly spelled out. If specific aspects of program functioning are the primary concern and it is hoped that evaluation results will shed light on relevant procedures and practices, this, too, should be explicitly stated.

Although this guideline may seem obvious, it is sometimes violated. For example, it is sometimes claimed that the purpose of an evaluation is to obtain data for program development, but it subsequently turns out that it was actually commissioned to provide data for a funding decision. It is clearly unethical for evaluators to knowingly engage in evaluations with hidden agendas; if evaluators discover such a situation in the course of the work, they have a responsibility to make known their concerns and find appropriate remedies. These remedies may include discussions to resolve the concern, formal dissent in the form of a cover letter, refusal to sign the report, or resignation (American Evaluation Association, 1994).

Principle 5:
Provide a Balanced Report and Disseminate Early and Regularly

The manner in which findings are reported and disseminated is an important matter of evaluation practice. The need to tailor reports to the audience and to report in a clear, comprehensible manner has already been discussed in this chapter. The contents of reports is another matter for attention; it is important that reports be balanced and fair. It may be tempting, for example, to give great weight to positive findings while playing down or ignoring disappointing findings. While positive findings tend to be more enthusiastically received, it is obviously just as important to know when results fall short of expectations. Moreover, evaluation studies, like any research, have limitations: It is important to describe such limitations in a way that decision makers are able to understand what the limitations imply.

Sometimes, the dissemination of reports will become controversial. Because information is a source of power in our world, some stakeholders may seek to further their political objectives by manipulating dissemination— withholding, delaying, or selectively circulating reports. Such manipulative tactics can be short-circuited if evaluators pay attention to establishing procedures for dissemination early in the process, well before results are in. The most equitable practices are those that provide for dissemination to all stakeholder groups through regularly scheduled reports, in the case of a monitoring evaluation, and through early dissemination, in a project type evaluation.

SUMMING UP AND LOOKING AHEAD

This chapter presented various considerations that should be taken into account when evaluating a social service program. Because programs take place in the real world, politics and political influence are often unavoidable. As well, because they are complex entities, technical decisions can often influence the course of the evaluation, as well as its results. Evaluators have a responsibility to ensure that their work provides accurate, fair, and complete information to decision makers and that it is used in an open, constructive decision-making process.

Professional standards, ethical guidelines for conducting research, and evaluation practice principles provide guidance to evaluation practitioners that will help them to ensure that their evaluations are constructive, ethical, and of the highest quality. Chapter 10 builds on the ethical and professional issues discussed in this chapter, in that it presents diversity issues that must be addressed in an evaluation.

KEY TERMS

Accuracy: A standard of evaluation practice that requires technical adequacy of the evaluation process; includes matters of validity, reliability, measurement instruments, samples, and comparisons.

Ethics: The moral practice of evaluation or the "code of right and wrong" for deciding how to handle data, how to interact with clients, and how to proceed in politically charged situations.

Fairness: A standard of evaluation practice that requires evaluations to be conducted in a fair and ethical manner; includes the dissemination of evaluation results.

Feasibility: A standard of evaluation practice that requires evaluations to be conducted only under conditions that are practical and economically viable.

Informed Consent: Procedures in which clients, or evaluation subjects, are told in advance about the major tasks and activities they will perform during an evaluation study; clients then participate in the evaluation study only if they are willing to engage in these activities.

Performance Appraisal: The process of evaluating the efficiency and effectiveness of a staff person's work; a possible misuse of evaluation practice.

Utility: A standard of evaluation practice that requires evaluations to be carried out only if they are considered potentially useful to one or more stakeholders.

STUDY QUESTIONS

1. Select one of the outcome evaluations presented in Box 3.3 (pages 80-81). Assess the evaluation procedures of the case study according to the standards for evaluation practice in the areas of utility, feasibility, fairness, and accuracy. Explain your answer in detail.

2. In your own words, list the factors that can influence evaluation outcomes.

What strategies can you offer to minimize the bias that these factors may introduce into evaluation outcomes?

3. Discuss the process of obtaining informed consent from a client via Box 9.1. What level of detail would you use to explain the client's participation in the evaluation? Would your approach to receiving informed consent from a client be formal or informal? Explain your answer in detail.

4. Discuss the differences between internal and external uses of evaluation data. Provide a specific example of each.

5. Many workers fear and resist program evaluation as a formal part of client service. What strategies can you suggest to increase their level of comfort with the notions of accountability and evaluation?

6. What strategies can you suggest to minimize the misuse of program evaluation in human service agencies? Explain your answer in detail.

7. In groups of four, create a code of ethics to guide human service workers in conducting evaluations. Develop brief guidelines focused on the following themes: purpose of evaluation, informed consent, evaluation design, and dissemination of results. Compare your code of ethics with Box 9.1.

8. In groups of five, choose a program-level human service intervention. Clearly identify a purpose, or reason, for evaluating the intervention. How does defining the purpose of the evaluation affect the choice of evaluation design, sampling procedures, data collection, data analysis, and dissemination of results? What other purposes of evaluation can you identify? How do different purposes influence the design and procedure of the evaluation?

9. A coworker maintains that evaluation of interventions and programs always produce the same result. Comment.

10. You argue that the selection of objectives affects the outcome of an evaluation at the case and program levels. Outline the main points of your argument.

11. You also maintain that the timing of data collection may also affect evaluation outcomes. How do you support your position?

12. You argue that sample selection and interpretation of results affect evaluation outcomes. Why?

13. Given that evaluation is a social activity, why is ethical evaluation practice so important?

14. Ethical guidelines and principles for social workers indicate that the purpose of the evaluation should be clearly spelled out for all those who participate. Why is this important?

15. Ethical guidelines also require informed consent for participation in evaluations. Why?

16. How is confidentiality a paramount component of ethical evaluation? How can the confidentiality of participants be ensured? Discuss in detail. Provide a social service example throughout your discussion.

17. How do ethical considerations affect the selection of evaluation designs at the case and program level? Discuss in detail. Provide a social service example throughout your discussion.

18. How do ethical considerations affect the dissemination of results at the case and program level? Discuss in detail. Provide a social service example throughout your discussion.

19. In a county agency, an evaluation has been commissioned to justify decisions about budget cuts that have already been made. In what ways is this an inappropriate use of evaluation? Discuss in detail. Provide a social service example throughout your discussion.

20. How can an evaluation be used to distract attention from negative publicity? Discuss in detail. Provide a social service example throughout your discussion.

21. How can evaluation data be used appropriately to guide internal decision making? Discuss in detail. Provide a social service example throughout your discussion.

22. How can evaluation data be used appropriately to guide external decision making? Discuss in detail. Provide a social service example throughout your discussion.

23. The establishment of a constructive context for evaluation begins with making a commitment to internal, continuous, self-directed evaluation. What practices must be adopted to accomplish this? Discuss in detail. Provide a social service example throughout your discussion.

REFERENCES AND FURTHER READINGS

American Evaluation Association. (1994). *Guiding Principles for Evaluators*. Magnolia, AR: Author. Retrieved October 11, 2000, from the World Wide Web: http://www.eval.org.

Gabor, P.A., & Grinnell, R.M., Jr. (1994). *Evaluation and quality improvement in the human services*. Boston: Allyn & Bacon.

Gabor, P.A., Unrau, Y.A., & Grinnell, R.M., Jr. (1997). *Evaluation and quality improvement in the human services* (2nd ed.). Boston: Allyn & Bacon.

Gabor, P.A., Unrau, YA., & Grinnell, R.M., Jr. (2001). Program-level evaluation. In R.M. Grinnell, Jr. (Ed.), *Social work research and evaluation: Quantitative and qualitative approaches* (6th ed., pp. 481–509). Itasca, IL: F.E. Peacock Publishers.

Gilchrest, L., & Schinke, S. (2001). Research ethics. In R.M. Grinnell, Jr. (Ed.), *Social work research and evaluation: Quantitative and qualitative approaches* (6th ed., pp. 55–69). Itasca, IL: F.E. Peacock Publishers.

Joint Committee on Standards for Educational Evaluation (1994). *Program evaluation standards* (2nd ed.) Beverly Hills, CA: Sage.

Unrau, Y.A., & Gabor, P.A. (2001). Evaluation in action. In R.M. Grinnell, Jr. (Ed.), *Social work research and evaluation: Quantitative and qualitative approaches* (6th ed., pp. 510–526). Itasca, IL: F.E. Peacock Publishers.

Weinbach, R.W. (2001). Research contexts. In R.M. Grinnell, Jr. (Ed.), *Social work research and evaluation* (6th ed., pp. 41–54). Itasca, IL: F.E. Peacock Publishers.

Williams, M., & Grinnell, R.M., Jr. (1990). *Social work research: A primer*. Itasca, IL: F.E. Peacock Publishers.

Williams, M., Tutty, L., & Grinnell, R.M., Jr. (1995). *Social work research: An introduction* (2nd ed.). Itasca, IL: F.E. Peacock Publishers.

Williams, M., Unrau, Y.A., & Grinnell, R.M., Jr. (1998). *Introduction to social work research*. Itasca, IL: F.E. Peacock Publishers.

10

Chapter Outline

Carol Ing

Culturally Appropriate Evaluations

OUR VILLAGE HAS GROWN to encompass the world. Faster means of transportation, the expansion of trade, and the human desire to seek a better life have created societies that no longer find their roots in one cultural tradition and their voice in one common language. Rather, migration trends and globalization activities have laid the foundations for complex, culturally diverse societies with representation from several racial, ethnic, and cultural groups. Diversity is reflected throughout society: in schools, in the workplace, and within all types of formal organizations. Social service organizations are no exception; there is increasing diversity both among staff and also among service recipients. Of course, diversity also has an impact on the field of evaluation; the challenge for evaluators is to work effectively in culturally diverse settings.

As is made clear throughout this book, evaluation is more than the technical practice of organizing and implementing data collection activities, analyzing data, and reporting findings. Although these are important evaluation activities, evaluation also involves working effectively with a variety of stakeholders in a wide range of organizations. The tasks include working with people to clarify expectations, identify interests, reconcile differences, and win cooperation.

Evaluators must therefore be adept in establishing interpersonal and working relationships in addition to bringing technical expertise to the evaluation process. When working with different cultural groups or in different cultural settings, evaluators must be culturally competent and also have the ability to adapt the technical processes of evaluation so that they are appropriate for the setting.

In this chapter, a brief overview of culture and cultural competence is provided, followed by a discussion of key issues in culturally competent evaluation practice. As the issues are discussed, we will make use of examples of world view, perceptions, communications, and behaviors that may be characteristic of particular cultures. These are intended only as examples of cultural patterns and not to suggest that any characteristics describe all members of the group. We fully recognize that cultures are not monolithic and that a variety of cultural patterns may exist within broadly defined cultural groups. The descriptions provided within this chapter are for illustrative purposes only and are not meant to be stereotypical of the members of any culture.

We also know that each individual is unique and we recognize that, within any culture, a wide range of individual perceptions, communications, and behaviors may exist. In evaluation, as in any other human interactive process, there is no substitute for meeting each person with openness and acceptance—regardless of cultural background.

THE IMPACT OF CULTURE

Culture is many things: a set of customs, traditions, and beliefs, and a world view. They are socially defined and passed on from generation to generation (Porter & Samovar, 1997). Culture is manifested in perceptions through which we view our surroundings and patterns of language and behaviors through which we interact with others. Culture exists at two levels: at the micro level and at the macro level. Micro-level culture is found with individuals and is reflected in their personal values, beliefs, communication styles, and behaviors. Macro culture exists at the level of organizations, institutions, as well as communities; it is manifested in mandates, policies, and practices.

Fundamentally, culture acts as a filter through which people view, perceive, and evaluate the world around them. At the same time, it also provides a framework within which people process information, think, communicate, and behave. Because different cultures establish different frameworks for perceiving and judging, as well as for thinking and acting, misperceptions, miscommunications, and conflicts are not only possible but likely. Where people are unaware of how culture filters thinking, actions, perceptions, and judgments, the likelihood for misunderstanding is even greater.

The Japanese, for example have traditionally used bowing as a form of greeting, in North America hand shakes are prevalent; in certain European countries hugging and kissing are customary. It is easy to see that what is meant as a friendly gesture in one culture may be viewed as an intrusion in another. In a meeting, for example, a statement that is meant as a hypothetical example in one culture may be viewed as a firm commitment in another.

Moreover, what is valued in one culture may not be nearly as important in another. In North America, for example, there is considerable emphasis on the "bottom line," which, in evaluation, translates to outcomes. Thus, evaluations are often concerned with assessing the outcomes of a social service program. In some cultures, however, the fact that a program has been created, it operates, and it provides employment for community members may be viewed as at least as important as the actual results of the services.

BRIDGING THE CULTURE GAP

Under the principle "respect for people" enunciated by the American Evaluation Association (1994), evaluators are expected to be aware of and respect differences among people and to be mindful of the implications of cultural differences on the evaluation process. Evaluators thus need: (1) a clear understanding of the impact of culture on human and social processes generally and on evaluation processes specifically; and (2) skills in cross-cultural communications to ensure that they can effectively interact with people from diverse backgrounds.

Cultural Awareness

As the previous discussion makes clear, culture provides a powerful organizing framework that filters perceptions and communications and also shapes behaviors and interactions. To practice effectively in different cultural settings, evaluators need a general awareness of the role that culture plays in shaping our perceptions, ideas, and behaviors. Further, evaluators need fundamental attitudes of respect for difference, a willingness to learn about other cultures, and a genuine belief that cultural differences are a source of strength and enrichment rather than an obstacle to be overcome. In particular, evaluators need to be on guard that their perceptions, communications, and actions are not unduly influenced by ethnocentrism, enculturation, and stereotyping—processes that act as barriers to effective communications and relationships.

Because our own history is inevitably based in our own culture, and because we generally continue to be immersed in that culture, a natural human tendency is to judge others and other cultures by the standards of our own beliefs and values. This is known as ethnocentrism; it leads to defining the world in our own terms. Thus, we might tend to view as normal that which is typical in our own culture; different practices, structures, or patterns that may be typical in other cultures, are likely then to be viewed as "abnormal" or even problematic (Neuliep, 2000).

Among some social groups, for example, child rearing is viewed as a community responsibility, with extended family and other community members taking an active role when necessary. This is seldom typical in urban North American culture, where high mobility often places families in communities without extended family or other support networks. Thus, while in a large urban setting an appropriate outcome for family preservation programs may be that the family remains intact, in communities located in rural or remote areas or on Native American reservations, a more appropriate outcome might be that suitable care-giving arrangements are identified within the family's kinship or community network. In short, an ethnocentric evaluator might, however, unwittingly identify mainstream North American values for a Native American family preservation program; this would clearly result in a distortion in the evaluation process.

Enculturation is a related process, which refers to the fact that, as children, we learn to behave in ways that are appropriate to our culture. We also come to adopt a variety of core beliefs about human nature, human experience, and human behavior. This process teaches us how to behave, interact, and even think. Of course, other cultural groups will have different ways of thinking, behaving, and interacting. In some Asian cultures, for example, people value discussion, negotiation, and relationship, while in North America, people tend to be more direct and task-oriented (Hall 1983). Similarly, some cultures such as the Swiss and Germans emphasize promptness, while in some Southern cultures, a meeting is seldom expected to start at the appointed time, but only after everyone has arrived (Lewis 1997).

The differences in behavior patterns and interactions are real; however, it is important for evaluators to recognize that others' patterns are as legitimate and appropriate as their own. Where evaluators are unable to do this, stereotyping may occur, resulting in misunderstanding and misjudgment. An evaluator, for example, may become frustrated because it is difficult to start meetings on time in a community or because it is not possible to keep to a tight schedule, and she may begin to stereotype the group she is working with as uninterested, noncooperative, and disorganized. Obviously, such stereotypes will have the effect of creating additional barriers to communications and interactions and will hinder the evaluation process.

Intercultural Communications

While awareness of the impacts of culture is important, it is the actual communications upon which effective relationships depend. Because evaluation is as much a relationship process as a technical matter, effective communications are always important, and particularly so in communications across cultures.

There are many models of intercultural communications; one of the more useful one is offered by Porter and Samovar (1997). In this model, perceptions are regarded as the gateway to communications; they are the means by which people select, evaluate, and organize information about the world around them. Perceptions, of course, depend in large part upon an individual's world view, which is, in part, formed as a result of his or her cultural experiences. Perceptions help us select, organize, and interpret a variety of external stimuli, including the communications that others direct toward us.

After we process the communications that are directed toward us, we usually respond. Different cultures support different communications patterns and styles and thus our response is also shaped and formed, at least in part, by our cultural background. Communications, then, are inextricably bound with culture. The opportunity for misunderstanding, ever present in any communication, is even greater when individuals from different cultural backgrounds interact.

Intercultural communication takes place at both the nonverbal and verbal levels. Anyone who interacts with members of another culture needs an understanding of both nonverbal and verbal communications patterns typical in that culture. We will briefly look at communications at each of these levels.

An important part of human communications takes place nonverbally. Facial expressions, time, use of space, and gestures convey much information and are deeply based in culture. Without an understanding of the meaning of nonverbal communications symbols used by a culture, it is all too easy to misinterpret signs.

For example, a hand gesture that has virtually no meaning in one culture may be a vulgar symbol in another culture. For example, the "OK" sign, widely used in North America, is a circle, formed by the thumb and the first finger; this sign is considered to be offensive and unacceptable in Brazil, and to mean money in Japan (Morrison, Conway, & Borden 1994).

Positioning oneself in relation to another may result in an inadvertent message of disinterest or aggression. North Americans usually feel comfortable standing at a distance of about two and half to four feet from others. However, members of some cultures, among them Arabic, for example, prefer to stand much closer when engaged in a conversation (Hall, 1983). An evaluator who positions himself at a North American distance may be perceived as cold, aloof, and disinterested by members of such cultures.

Similarly, the use of eye contact carries culturally specific meaning. In European-based cultures, eye contact is used extensively to demonstrate interest and to confirm that one is listening. Many other cultures, however, do not use eye contact extensively, and may perceive it as disrespectful and even threatening. For example, prolonged eye contact in cultures such as that of the Japanese is considered to be rude (Samovar, Porter, & Stefani, 1998).

On the verbal level, words also derive much of their meaning through culture. As language is the primary means through which a culture communicates its values and beliefs, the same words may have different meanings within different cultures. For example, the Japanese use the word "hai," meaning "yes," to indicate that they have heard what was said and are thinking about a response. Since, in many circumstances, it is considered impolite to openly express disagreement, "hai" is used even when the listener is actually in disagreement with what is being said (Koyama, 1992). Thus the meaning assigned to "yes" is quite different than that commonly understood by North Americans, who consider "yes" to mean that the listener is in agreement.

As the evaluation process involves extensive transmission of information through communications, it is obviously vital that communications be accurate and effective. Without an understanding of intercultural communications generally, and an ability to understand the specific patterns used by the group with whom the evaluator is dealing, communications problems may arise and derail the evaluation process.

CULTURAL FRAMEWORKS

As we have seen, culture often defines a group's values and beliefs, and creates its communications patterns. In addition, culture also provides frameworks for other complex structures and processes. Different cultural groups, for example, have different methods of gathering information and of making decisions. An understanding of these patterns is essential to ensure that data collection and analytical processes are appropriate and reports are practical and relevant. This section briefly looks at cultural frameworks regarding data, decision making, individualism, tradition, the pace of life, and concepts of time.

Orientation to Information

Some cultures thrive on "hard" data and greatly value processes, such as research, that produce data which can then be considered and acted upon (Lewis, 1997). These cultures, which include the North American mainstream culture, are considered data oriented. On the other hand, some cultures such as Middle Eastern and Latin American cultures, are viewed as dialogue oriented, in that they pay more attention to relationships and process than to data (Lewis, 1997). These groups tend to view statistics and data with some suspicion and regard it as only part of a picture. Such cultures consider relationships and context as more important than numbers.

Decision Making

In many Western cultures, logic and rationality are highly valued and used extensively in making decisions about important matters (Lewis, 1997; Hoefstede, 1997). The research approaches, upon which evaluation processes are based, are examples of this style of "scientific" thinking. However, some cultures are less impressed by science and prefer intuition or more subjective, personal approaches to thinking and decision making. When evaluators prepare a report for people whose culture supports a scientific orientation to thinking, quantitative data with statistical analyses is quite appropriate; however, if the users are people who come from a culture that prefers more subjective and intuitive approaches to decision making, a report organized around the presentation of quantitative results will be less useful and comprehensible.

Individualism

Although most cultures support both individualistic and collectivistic tendencies, there is, in each culture, a bias toward one or the other (Hoefstede, 1997). In individualistic cultures, such as the mainstream North American culture, people work toward individual goals, and initiative, competition, and achievement are highly valued. In collectivistic cultures, people are group oriented; loyalty, relationships, and overall community development are valued while individual goals are downplayed. In such cultures, the family, organizations with which people are affiliated (including the workplace), and the community are particularly important.

Keeping in perspective an organizations' cultural view on individualism versus collectivism is important in understanding the behaviors, the interactions, the work processes, and the structures that may be found in the course of an evaluation. What may appear, from an individualistic perspective, as an unwieldy work process involving too many people may, in fact, be explained by a culture-based desire not to leave anyone out and to create as wide a network of involvement as is possible.

Tradition

Some cultures are more traditional and value the status quo and conformity while others encourage innovation and view change as necessary if progress is to be made (Dodd, 1998). Change-oriented cultures, such as mainstream North American society, encourage experimentation, risk taking, and innovation. They consider change as an opportunity to improve. In other cultures, however, such as with some traditional Asian cultures, values are centered around tradition and continuity. The young are expected to give way to the wishes of the older generation, and new ideas are not encouraged because they might disrupt the structure of society.

The reader will readily recognize that evaluation, as a change and improvement oriented activity, is grounded in Western cultural values. As such, the concept of evaluation itself may seem alien to those steeped in more traditional cultures. After all, evaluation is concerned with identifying areas for improvement, and therefore implies change, while traditional cultures value stability and continuity. Inevitably, evaluators will sometimes work with organizations that are based in a tradition-oriented culture. In such circumstances, evaluators need to be sensitive to the fact that there may not exist a common understanding even about the basic premises of the evaluation process.

Pace of Life

In North America, especially in larger cities, we live our lives at an accelerated pace. Our schedules are jammed with many activities; agendas are overloaded and there is an expectation that everything is a priority and must be done immediately. Time is viewed as linear and rigid; we live with the sense that if we miss an event, it is forever gone. In such cultures, which are called monochronic, people tend to organize their lives by the clock (Hall, 1983). Clearly in such cultures, it is important to be on time for meetings to meet deadlines and to stay on schedule (Samovar, Porter & Stefani, 1998). In a sense, time is so central that members of the culture are hardly aware of its importance, but all things, including personal relationships, take second place to successful time management.

On the other hand, in polychronic cultures, life is lived at a slower pace, activities grind to a halt on weekends, during rest times, as well as during festivals and important celebrations. Slower-paced cultures—for example, those in Latin America, the Middle East, and Indonesia—tend to be less aware of time and hold less of a concept of it as a commodity that must be managed. Time is seen as circular and flexible; the Indonesians even refer to it as "rubber time" (Harris & Moran, 1996).

Time is not nearly as important an organizing force in people's lives as it is in monochronic cultures; if the scheduled start time passes without the event taking place, people are not unduly disturbed as another appropriate start time can be set. "Time is money" could not have arisen as a central idea in these cultures, which focus on relationships and interactions. Time management and business come second (Hall, 1983). In such cultures, it is vital to establish a personal relationship before conducting business.

Obviously evaluators need to have a good understanding of the concept of time held within the setting where they conduct their work. Tight schedules that provide few opportunities for cementing working relationships and disregard widely observed rest periods, holidays, and celebrations are obviously unrealistic and will be unsuitable in polychronic cultures. Attempting to impose such a schedule will be regarded as thoughtless and will impede rather than facilitate the evaluation process.

Further, in assessing the achievement of milestones and other accomplishments, evaluations need to take into account the concept of time and the pace of life prevalent in the particular culture. In setting up a new social service program, for example, planning, procedure, policy development, initial staffing, and other preparatory activities may be accomplished in a much briefer period of time in one setting than in another. Both the concept of time and the pace of life might be, in fact, equally appropriate when cultural orientation toward time is taken into account.

PUTTING IT TOGETHER:
THE PRACTICE OF CULTURALLY COMPETENT EVALUATION

Although some evaluators come from minority backgrounds, many do bring a mainstream North American cultural orientation to their work. This orientation will result in part form their own cultural background and in part from their formation and education as evaluators. The methods of evaluation are, to a large degree, based in a Western or North American cultural tradition. Inevitably, evaluators will bring their own culturally based beliefs, values, and perspectives as well as their culturally based tool kit to the work.

More and more evaluations are conducted in settings that are culturally different from mainstream North American culture. Evaluations are conducted at reservations, at women's shelters, at organizations serving immigrants, and at agencies that grew from the needs and aspirations of minority communities and reflect the cultures of those communities.

Evaluators who undertake work in culturally different settings or among people from different cultural backgrounds require the skills to effectively conduct their work and to make the evaluation process meaningful within those settings. The essential competencies are: (1) cultural awareness, (2) intercultural communication skills, (3) specific knowledge about the culture in which they hope to work, and (4) an ability to appropriately adapt evaluation methods and processes.

Cultural Awareness

To be effective in intercultural work, evaluators need a degree of cultural awareness that will provide them with an understanding of the impact of culture on all human values, attitudes, and behaviors, as well as interactions and processes. They need to understand how culture filters communications and how evaluation itself is a culture-based activity. Further, evaluators should have an understanding of concepts such as ethnocentrism, enculturation, and stereotyping—all of which may subtly, or not so subtly, raise barriers to effective communications and relationships.

In addition, evaluators need to bring attitudes of openness and acceptance to their work, as well as a genuine belief that cultural differences need not pose barriers but can strengthen and enrich the evaluation process. Evaluators who wish to practice in diverse settings also need a high degree of self-awareness, as well as understanding of their own cultural values and experiences, and the impact of these values and experiences on their communications patterns, relationships, and professional work.

Cultural awareness increases through contact with other cultures through experiencing differences. Travel, work in culturally different settings, and living in diverse communities are ways in which evaluators can develop their awareness and attitudes.

Intercultural Communication Skills

The ability to approach others with openness and acceptance is foundational to the effective communications, regardless of setting; in intercultural communications it is particularly important. However, effective intercultural communications also requires specific knowledge of the other culture and its communication symbols. As we now know, the meaning of nonverbal or verbal symbols is culturally defined. It is, therefore, important to know the meaning of common nonverbal and verbal communications symbols in an attempt to ensure accuracy, in both the transmission as well as the reception of messages.

Evaluators can prepare for their work by reading novels set in the culture, watching high-quality movies, and perusing books and guides that describe prevailing communications patterns. The use of cultural guides, to be discussed in the following section, is also helpful in learning to understand the meaning of common communication symbols.

Developing Specific Knowledge About the Culture

In the previous section, the importance of developing specific understanding about prevailing communications patterns in a specific culture was discussed. However, more than communication patterns need to be understood by an evaluator who wishes to be effective in a culturally different setting. Specific knowledge about various details of the culture are important to ensure that effective relationships can be established, the work is planned in a realistic manner, and the resulting products will have utility.

Among other things, it is important to have some sense of the history of the group who comprise the culture in which the evaluation will be conducted. On Native American reservations, for example, the history of oppression and dislocation is vitally important and helps to frame values, attitudes, and beliefs. Among certain immigrant groups, escape from oppression is a dominant theme, and newly found freedoms and opportunities help to frame a highly individualistic and achievement-oriented culture.

Beyond history, specific values, beliefs, and perspectives that shape individuals' and groups' perceptions and communications are vital to understand, as are the cultural structures, processes, and frameworks that are characteristic of the group. For example, in working with Native American groups on reservations, it is customary to include elders on advisory committees and to listen with respect to the ideas and opinions that are expressed by elders. Further, meetings begin with a prayer to the Creator and not with a review of the agenda, as is the case in most Western-oriented institutions. Concepts of time have been discussed previously; it is sufficient to say that the scheduled starting time for meetings may or may not be firmly fixed, depending on the setting.

There are a myriad of other details about culture, some of which may be important to understand in order to work successfully in the setting. For example, one of the authors of this book once conducted an evaluation on a reservation; the work included observing a restorative justice circle in action. The program had been conceived carefully with extensive use of traditional symbols. One of these symbols was the circle itself, which symbolized a teepee; a convention had developed over time that participants entered and left the circle in one particular place that symbolized the entry to the teepee. Entering or leaving in any other place was regarded as the equivalent of walking through the walls of the teepee.

Of course, an evaluator coming from the outside would not have been aware of this and would inevitably have committed a cultural *faux pas* at some point during the process. Happily, this was averted in this case because a member of the evaluation project, who was from the community itself, served as a cultural guide, and briefed the evaluator on the meaning of the cultural symbols involved as well as regarding appropriate behaviors.

In general, specific cultural knowledge can be obtained through the same methods as suggested for understanding the specifics of communications patterns: travel, reading guidebooks and histories by authors from the culture, and watching movies. Engaging collaborators from within the cultural group, although not necessarily from within the organization itself is, perhaps, the most effective way of learning about values, beliefs, traditions, behavior patterns, and the detailed texture of another culture.

Adapting Evaluations

Developing cultural awareness, intercultural communications skills, and specific knowledge of the culture of the group with which an evaluator is involved are foundational to conducting effective evaluations. The final set of skills involves adapting the evaluation processes and methods so that they will be appropriate and meaningful within the culture of the organization where the evaluation is being conducted. Adapting evaluations involves: (1) working with stakeholders, (2) ensuring that the work processes are appropriate, and (3) ensuring that the products are meaningful and useful.

Working with Stakeholders

As is discussed throughout this book, a variety of groups, including funders, staff members, program participants, and community members may have an interest in how a program performs and, consequently, in evaluation results. As discussed throughout this book, different groups of stakeholders are likely to have different interests; this will particularly be true in the case of evaluations conducted in settings with culturally different stakeholders.

Generally, funders represent powerful institutions such as governments and foundations within mainstream society. They will therefore articulate their interests from a North American or Western cultural perspective. In practice, funders will likely be interested in data that shed light on the extent to which the program is delivering the services that had been contracted and with what effect.

Further, they will prefer to have the data packaged as a formal report, replete with quantitative data and statistics as well as specific recommendations for change and improvement. On the other hand, if the setting is based in a different culture, staff members, service recipients, and community members may be more interested in understanding the role that the program is playing within the community. If they come from a dialogue-oriented culture, for example, they may be interested in descriptions of the service process, service recipients' stories about their experiences with the service, and its impacts on their family. They will be looking not so much to receive data for the purpose of making changes but rather to develop broader and deeper understanding of the program and its place in the community.

Evaluators need to work at understanding each stakeholder group's perspectives, expectations, and interests and realize that these may be fundamentally different from one another. Therefore, a culturally competent evaluator must be committed to accommodate within the evaluation process the different perspectives and interests of diverse stakeholders.

Adapting Processes

Evaluation work always involves obtaining the cooperation of staff members and other stakeholder groups in carrying out the required evaluation procedures—particularly data collection. This is especially true when a monitoring system of quality improvement is put into place; the effectiveness of such a system depends on staff members carrying out their assigned roles in the evaluation process in a knowledgeable and consistent manner. It is therefore very important that the work processes be designed so that they are congruent with the culture within the organization.

For example, evaluators need to take into account the cultural meaning of time in the organization. If the organization is polychronic and operates at a relatively relaxed pace, the scheduling of evaluation events and activities must take this into account. A schedule that may be appropriate in an organization that operates from a monochronic cultural perspective may be totally unfeasible within a polychronic culture. Attempting to impose such a schedule will create tensions and stresses and is likely to result, at best, in very inconsistent implementation of evaluation activities. At worst, the entire evaluation enterprise may be discredited and collapse.

It is thus important that evaluators design work processes in a manner that is congruent with the cultural meaning of time. Scheduling should take into account the concept of time and orientation to time, not impose a burden that would be regarded by the culture as unduly stressful or inappropriate, and should ensure that holidays, community celebrations and festivals, are taken into account in the setting of schedules.

Similarly, data collection activities need to take into account the cultural orientation of the staff members, who are likely to collect the data, and service recipients, who are likely to provide it. In dialogue-oriented cultures, the collection of highly quantitative data involving the use of standardized measures, rating scales, and structured surveys may be inappropriate and result in inconsistent data collection at best. At worst, service recipients and staff members will go through the motions of providing and collecting data without really understanding why the data are needed or how they are to be used. The reliability and validity of such data, of course, are likely to be low, compromising the entire evaluation effort.

Data collection protocols and procedures need to take into account whether evaluation participants are orientated to data or dialogue and should be designed to be as meaningful and culturally appropriate as is possible. In dialogue-oriented cultures it may not be entirely possible, or advisable, to avoid the collection of quantitative data, but such data collection methods should be used sparingly. Ample explanations and support should also be provided to evaluation participants so they can find meaning in these tasks and carry them out effectively.

Providing Meaningful Products

Ultimately, evaluations are undertaken to generate information products that stakeholders will find useful. It is particularly important that evaluation products be appropriate to the culture of stakeholders. As discussed earlier, funders are likely to find reports useful when they address the extent to which the program meets its contractual obligations for providing services and describe the outcomes of those services. Further, funders will look for quantitative data and statistical analyses that support the findings of the report. Managers who regularly deal with funders may also favor reports of this type.

However, other stakeholder groups may not find such products useful or understandable. This will be especially the case if stakeholders come from cultural backgrounds that are dialogue oriented. Reports with descriptions, stories, illustrations, and even pictures are likely to prove more meaningful to such stakeholders.

Culturally competent evaluators should accommodate all stakeholder groups who have a legitimate interest in evaluation results. Tailoring reports to funders' needs alone represents poor evaluation practice and is unlikely to result in meaningful program change. Program development necessarily comes from the inside and is based, primarily, on the initiative of the managers and staff. Evaluation products should support the efforts of managers and staff to develop the program by providing data that are meaningful, practical, and useful.

It is usually the case that quantitative and qualitative approaches can be combined within an evaluation. While matters that interest funders are more likely to be more suited to quantitative data collection and analyses, increased understanding can result from including descriptively oriented material that focuses on contextual matters. Statistics describing the demographic makeup of service recipients, for example, can be supplemented by providing more detailed descriptions of a few selected service recipients. Often this can be accomplished by providing people the opportunity to tell their stories in their words.

As described in Chapter 9, the Joint Committee on Standards for Educational Evaluation (1994) calls for the implementation of utility standards, intended to ensure that an evaluation will serve the information needs of intended users. Clearly, this underscores the responsibility of evaluators to understand the intended audience for evaluations and to ensure that evaluation products are culturally appropriate and therefore comprehensible, meaningful, and useful.

SUMMING UP AND LOOKING AHEAD

Conducting evaluations is a complex endeavor; undertaking evaluations that involves stakeholders from different cultural backgrounds adds considerable additional complexity.

This chapter presented the challenges of applying evaluation methods in culturally diverse settings. Part IV presents the utility of evaluation.

KEY TERMS

Collectivism: A cultural value that attaches importance to group process, loyalty, relationships, and community development; common to many Eastern cultures.

Cultural Awareness: The understanding of the role that culture plays in shaping our perceptions, ideas, and behaviors.

Culture: A set of customs, traditions, and beliefs, and a worldview that are social defined and passed on from one generation to the next; exists at micro levels within individuals and at macro levels in organizations, institutions, and communities.

Enculturation: the process of learning to behave in ways that are appropriate to a particular culture; the process of acquiring core beliefs about human nature, experience, and behavior.

Ethnocentrism: Judging others and other cultures by the standards of our own beliefs and values; defining what is "normal" in the world in our own cultural point-of-view.

Individualism: A cultural value that attaches importance to individual goals as well as initiative, competition, and achievement; common to mainstream North American culture.

Intercultural Communication: Verbal and nonverbal transmission of ideas and messages that takes place between persons of different cultures. Includes such things as facial expressions, time, use of space, gestures, eye contact, words, and other signals that intentionally or unintentionally convey a message to another person.

Monochronic Culture: Views time as linear and rigid; people in these cultures tend to organize life by the clock and live with the sense that if an event is missed, it is gone forever—for example, mainstream North American culture.

Polychronic Culture: Gives less value to clock time and instead views time as circular and flexible; relationships and interactions are more highly valued for organizing life than is time—for example, Indonesian culture.

STUDY QUESTIONS

1. Pick a social problem such as child abuse, domestic violence, homelessness, or teen pregnancy. Identify 10 value or belief statements that you have about the social problem that you picked. Share your statements with a person of a different culture than yours. Does the person agree or disagree with your views?

2. List the different cultural groups that are part of your local community. Identify what you know about the customs, traditions, beliefs, and worldview of each.

   Is what you believe about different cultures in your community based on cultural truths or stereotypes?

3. Which of the different cultural groups in your community are you least comfortable with? Identify patterns of communication in your culture and this other culture. Discuss how the differences in communication patterns might impact your understanding of service needs in this other culture.

4. "It is important that social workers are aware of their ethnocentric beliefs and behaviors." Discuss why you agree or disagree with this statement.

5. You are a social worker who has been hired to evaluate a family support program in a culture that is different from yours. Discuss steps that you could take to ensure that intercultural communications between you and program stakeholders are accurate.

6. Imagine that you are the lead evaluator of a social service program that serves people in a culture that values personal approaches to decision making over "scientific" data collected from a group. Identify strategies to measure the impact of the program on clients served that are congruent with the values and beliefs of the program.

7. Discuss the ways in which different cultural orientations to information, individualism, tradition, and time can impact the planning of an evaluation for a social service program.

8. Discuss how reading a novel about a different culture might assist you with increasing intercultural awareness. What are the dangers of relying solely on novels to teach you about other cultures?

9. Visit a social service agency that serves clients from a culture that is different from yours. Discuss with the worker the knowledge and skills needed to be successful with helping clients from that particular culture.

10. Discuss the advantages and disadvantages of adapting evaluation procedures to fit the unique characteristics of one particular culture.

11. Develop a plan for yourself that will protect you from judging others from your ethnocentric world view. Specifically, identify names of people that could be your cultural guides and steps that you can take to reflect on your words and behaviors as you work with people from other cultural groups.

REFERENCES AND FURTHER READINGS

American Evaluation Association. (1994). Guiding Principles for Evaluators. Magnolia, AR: Author. Retrieved October 11, 2000, from the World Wide Web: http://www.eval.org

Dodd, C. (1998). *Dynamics of intercultural communication* (5th ed). New York: McGraw Hill.

Hall, E.T. (1983). *The dance of life: Other dimensions of time.* New York: Doubleday and Company.

Harris, P.R., & Moran, T. 1996). *Managing cultural differences: Leadership strategies for a new world business* (4th ed). London: Gulf.

Hoefstede, G. (1997). *Cultures and organizations: Software of the mind.* New York: McGraw Hill.

Koyama, T. (1992). *Japan: A handbook in intercultural communication.* Sydney, NSW: National Center for English Language Teaching and Research.

Lewis, R.D. (1997). *When cultures collide: Managing successfully across cultures.* London: Nicholas Brealey

Morrison, T., Conway, W.A., & Borden, G.A. (1994). *Kiss, bow, or shake hands: How to do business in sixty countries.* Holbrook, MA: Adams Media Corporation.

Neuliep, J.W. (2000). *Communication: A contextual approach.* New York: Houghton Mifflin.

Porter, R.E., & Samovar, L.A. (1997). An introduction to intercultural communication. In L.A. Samovar & R.E. Porter, *Intercultural communication: A reader* (8th ed., pp. 5–26) New York: Wadsworth.

Samovar, L.A., & Porter, R.E. (1997). *Intercultural communication: A reader* (8th ed.) New York: Wadsworth

Samovar, L.A., Porter, R.E., & Stefani, L.A. (1998). *Communication between cultures* New York: Wadsworth.

Part *IV*

Utility of Evaluation

11

Chapter Outline

Developing a Data
Information System

A S WE KNOW FROM CHAPTERS 3 AND 4, data collection is not an indiscriminate activity. In short, it is not undertaken in the hope that the data collected will somehow be useful to someone in some place at some time. Data collection procedures must reflect a careful analysis of information needs at all levels within the social service program and should provide for the collection of useful data in the least disruptive, most economical, and efficient manner possible.

The data collected for evaluations of all kinds can be characterized as a data information system. Within this system, specific data are collected, analyzed, and reported. Of course, systems of any kind may function well or not so well. Some evaluations are inadequately planned, resulting in a lack of coherence in data collection, analyses, and reporting. Others are well planned using the approaches described in Chapter 4. These systems function well in that they collect the right data in a form so they can be readily analyzed and subsequently reported to the stakeholders.

The concept of a data information system applies whether the evaluation process involves a project approach or monitoring approach to quality improvement. In a project type of situation, the information system will usually be active for a shorter period of time—the duration of the project. As well, project evaluations tend to be concerned with fewer variables, usually program outcomes, resulting in smaller information systems. Conversely, in a monitoring situation, the evaluation system will be active on an open-ended basis; it will also usually be concerned with a larger number of variables, resulting in a larger information system. In particular, monitoring types of evaluations are more likely to include a larger number of process issues than are project evaluations.

Whether an information system is created for a monitoring or project evaluation, it should be designed in a way that data collected at any stage are demonstrably relevant to the decisions to be made. Data collected by front-line workers, for example, should bear upon, in the first instance, decisions they are required to make. In other words, the data collected by workers must guide clinical decision-making. At the same time, these data must be capable of being aggregated in a manner that is relevant to administrators and other stakeholders interested in outcomes.

Essentially, an effective information system should:

1. Recognize that different data needs exist among different stakeholders
2. Be capable of delivering needed information to all levels of stakeholders in a timely manner and in a format usable at that level

Because we have emphasized the benefits of a monitoring approach to quality improvement throughout this book, this chapter provides illustrations and examples from monitoring situations. However, the discussion and illustrations do apply in project type evaluations as well.

STAFF MEMBERS' ROLES IN DEVELOPING
A DATA INFORMATION SYSTEM

Designing, developing, and maintaining an effective information system is not only a technical matter; human and social issues also need consideration. Staff members, as human beings, may have reactions that range from skepticism to resistance when faced with the introduction of an information system. These reactions are related not only to the personality and experience of the individual but also to the collective experience of the work group and of the organization as well. Where recent experience includes reorganization, restructuring, and questionable use of previous evaluation results, staff members will understandably react with suspicion, if not outright hostility (Gabor & Sieppert, 1999).

Establishing and maintaining an information system requires the cooperation of all program staff, from line-level workers through senior administrators. Inevitably, much of the burden of data collection falls on the line-level workers. Involving them in the planning and design of the information system helps to ensure that information needs at the direct-service level will be met and that data can be collected without undue disruption to service provision. Moreover, the involvement of line-level workers helps to secure their cooperation and commitment to the evaluation process.

Administrators must contribute by committing the necessary resources for the implementation of the system, including providing training and support. The design and implementation of an information system is expensive. Computer hardware and software may have to be purchased and consultation fees and training costs will probably be incurred. Providing adequate training and support to professional and staff is a vital consideration. Training is particularly necessary if the new system introduces computerization. Often, administrators will not hesitate to spend tens of thousands of dollars on equipment but will skimp on training the personnel who are to use it. This is shortsighted; as a general rule, administrators should expect to spend at least one dollar for training for every dollar spent on equipment.

It is very important that an evaluation be carried out within an organizational culture that acknowledges that social service programs inevitably fall short of perfection. The purpose of an evaluation is not to assign blame; it is to provide better services by identifying strengths and limitations so that the former can be reinforced and the latter corrected. An attitude of continuous learning and developing is the essence of the learning organization; the information system generates feedback that facilitates the process. When the objective is improvement and development, and workers can see the contribution of an effective information system to that objective, they are more likely to cooperate and contribute to the effective functioning of that information system.

Establishing an Organizational Plan

As discussed in Chapter 4, effective information systems are the result of careful planning and design, as well as negotiation and compromise. Early involvement in the planning of the system by front-line workers, administrators, and other relevant stakeholders is important. Any data collection plan must take into account at least three sets of needs:

— First, data collection must meet case-level decision-making needs, serving decisions to be made immediately as well as those made throughout the client's progress within the program. Certain data, for example, are required at client intake in order to decide whether to accept the referral. Once accepted, the client may go through a formal assessment procedure, at which point further data will likely be collected. Other stages of service provision will require still further data. The case-level information system should be designed to take advantage of, and build on, existing data collection.

— Second, the system must be designed to accommodate the program-level decision-making responsibilities of the administrators and other stakeholders. To avoid the creation of parallel evaluation systems at the case and program levels, the latter should be designed to make as much use of data collected for case-level evaluation as is possible. This often entails the aggregation of case-level data.

— Third, technical requirements of the system must also be considered. The system will require certain types of data, formats, data collection procedures, and analytic capabilities.

CASE-LEVEL DATA COLLECTION

Perhaps the best way to decide what data are needed at the case level is to follow a client through the program by way of a client case-flow analysis. Figure 11.1 presents an example of a case-flow chart illustrating the sequence of events in a child protection program.

The beginning of the process is the referral. Suspected neglect or abuse may be reported by a variety of people, including relatives, teachers, neighbors, and health care workers. All referrals are immediately directed to the Screening Unit. Because every allegation of child abuse must be looked into, at this point the two most relevant pieces of data are the age and place of residence of the alleged victim. Within a short period, a screening worker normally contacts the referring source as well as the family to verify the complaint and to obtain further details. Based on this information, the worker decides whether a full investigation is warranted. If so, an investigating worker will likely interview the alleged victim and will probably also interview relevant others.

As with every activity, each interview has a specific purpose. The purpose of interviewing the alleged victim is fourfold:

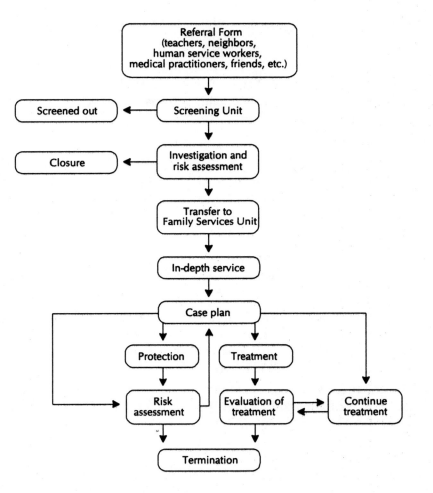

FIGURE 11.1   Flow Chart for a Child Protection
                    Program

— to verify that the alleged abuse has in fact occurred
— to ensure the immediate safety of the child
— to determine whether treatment is needed, and if so,
— what treatment would be best to inform the child and others connected
  to the case about what will happen next

The investigating worker will conduct this interview on the basis of data collected by the screening worker and will need data in the following general areas:

— the specific circumstances of the alleged abuse
— the specific circumstances in which it was disclosed
— data about the child
— data about the family

The screening form thus must be designed to incorporate these different data needs. From a case-level perspective, then, the data collected at screening serves two broad purposes:

1. to make a decision about whether further investigation is warranted
2. to provide the investigating worker with initial information data

Since a monitoring system is intended to provide needed and timely data to staff members, and since front-line workers themselves will be in the best position to know what data they need to help them in their decision making, front-line workers should be involved in designing forms.

When the investigation is complete, the data are used to assess the degree of continuing risk to the child. On this basis, the worker determines whether further services are required. Continuing cases are transferred from the Screening Unit to the Family Services Unit, where a worker is assigned to the family to coordinate protection and treatment functions. The Family Services Unit worker then conducts a full assessment based on the data provided by the investigating worker in the Screening Unit, as well as any additional data collected. The purpose of assessment is to develop an in-depth understanding of the situation and of child and family needs so that an appropriate intervention plan can be established. In other words, data collected during assessment are used in making decisions about the client's case plan.

As Figure 11.1 indicates, the case plan formulated may have both a protection component and a treatment component. Practice objectives are established in relation to both of these components, and data collected during service provision are used to assess the degree to which interventions are achieving practice objectives. Case-level data will also be needed subsequently, in aggregated form, for program evaluation purposes. Thus, it is important to take into consideration program evaluation needs, when determining what data are to be collected for case-level evaluation.

Termination criteria for protection and treatment often differ. Protection workers are likely to focus on the continuing safety of the child, whereas treatment workers may focus on family functioning. The family may therefore still be undergoing treatment when protection services have been discontinued. Ultimately, when the decision to terminate all services is made, the case can be closed.

As is evident, data collection is not a matter of randomly assembling whatever data come to hand. The data collected in each phase should be fully and firmly linked to the objectives of the particular phase, the decisions to be made during the phase, and the data needs of subsequent phases. Insufficient data lead to poor decision making; overly profuse and irrelevant data result in a lack of clarity and unnecessary costs.

To ensure that there is adequate congruence between the data collected and the decisions to be made, a data collection analysis can be undertaken. This analysis lists, in chronological order:

— the decisions to be made
— the data needed to make each decision
— the actual data collected

If there is a discrepancy between what is needed and what is being collected, data collection protocols need to be revised.

PROGRAM-LEVEL DATA COLLECTION

Data collection at any program stage must be designed to fulfill the data needs of both line-level workers and administrators alike. From the perspective of a multiprogram agency, for example, it is often useful to identify the main data collection events for each program. Typically, a program collects data at intake, at every contact with a client, as well as at termination. Other data collection events may be planned, depending on circumstances and needs.

A specific plan for identifying the key data collection events for a family service agency, for example, across five of its programs is presented in Figure 11.2. As you can see, the agency has five programs. It has: an Information Program, an Education Program, a Parent Support Program, a Counseling Program, and a Mediation Program. Each cell marked with an "X" represents a major data collection event for which a corresponding data collection

Forms	Information	Education	Parent Support	Counseling	Mediation
• Registration	X	X	X	X	X
• Assessment				X	X
• Contact notes			X	X	X
• Termination			X	X	X
• Outcome:					
Self-report		X	X	X	X
• Outcome:					
Measures				X	X
• Satisfaction	X	X	X	X	X

FIGURE 11.2   Example of a Data Collection Plan

instrument (or form) can be designed. In the case of this agency, the four major data collection events are registration, assessment, client contacts, and termination. In addition, data relating to satisfaction and outcomes are also desired. Once the information needs are identified, data collection forms can be designed for each of these purposes.

To illustrate this point, consider the counseling program operated by the agency. The service is funded by the Department of Social Services (DSS) to provide counseling services to DSS clients with psychosocial problems who need more help than the brief instrumentally oriented counseling that can be provided by the DSS. Figure 11.3 shows part of an intake form that new clients might complete in the center's office while they are waiting for a first interview.

Data Collection at Intake

The intake form is usually the first document in the client's file. Of course, different programs need different or additional data. A job-training program, for example, will likely ask about jobs previously held, previous income, reason for present unemployment, and participation in other job-training programs.

An individual intake form provides data for a case record, but it is not very useful for program evaluation purposes unless the data are aggregated with

Name: _____

Current Address: _____

_____

_____ Zip Code: _____

Home Telephone Number: _____

- TYPES OF SERVICE SOUGHT (circle one number below):

    1. Individual counseling
    2. Couple counseling
    3. Family counseling
    9. Other (please specify _____)

- SEX (circle one number below):

    1. Male
    2. Female

- BIRTH DATE _____

- REFERRAL SOURCE (circle one number below):

    1. Self
    2. Friends, family
    3. Physician
    4. Clergy
    5. Department of Social Services
    6. Other agency
    9. Other (please specify _____)

- REASONS FOR SEEKING SERVICES (circle one number below):

    1. Marital problems
    2. Family problems
    3. Problems at school
    4. Problems at work
    5. Parent-child problems
    6. Health problems
    7. Substance abuse
    8. Personal adjustment problems
    9. Other (please specify _____)

FIGURE 11.3   Example of a Client Intake Form

Sex of Client

Sex	Number	Percent
Male	90	45
Female	110	55
Totals..........	200	100

Age of Clients

Age Ranges	Number	Percent
10–19	30	15
20–29	78	39
30–39	42	21
40–49	28	14
50–59	12	6
60 +	10	5
Totals..........	200	100

Referral Sources of Clients

Sources	Number	Percent
Self	8	4
Friends, family	12	6
Physicians	8	4
Clergy	10	5
DSS	126	63
Other agencies	28	14
Other	8	4
Totals..........	200	100

Reasons Clients Requesting Services

Presenting Problems	Number	Percent
Marital problems	18	9
Family problems	40	20
Problems at school	28	14
Problems at work	12	6
Parent-child problems	30	15
Health problems	20	10
Substance abuse	22	11
Personal adjustment	20	10
Other	10	5
Totals..........	200	100

FIGURE 11.4   Excerpts from a Monthly Intake Report for January 2001 (from Figure 11.3)

other intake forms. Figure 11.4 provides four simple tabular reports on the counseling service compiled by aggregating the data from 200 individual client intake forms for the month of January 2001. These reports are examples of information related to client characteristics, discussed in Chapter 4.

Figure 11.4 shows at a glance that 200 new clients were accepted into the program during the month of January, 63 percent of whom were referred by DSS. The program is thus able to document the degree to which it is achieving one of its maintenance objectives: providing services to clients referred by DSS. Equally important, if referrals from DSS fall short of objectives, staff members will be able to spot this trend immediately and take steps to better meet the program's mandate, or perhaps to negotiate an adjustment of this mandate if new circumstances have arisen. The point of importance is that monitoring provides ongoing feedback that helps to ensure continuing achievement of a program's mandate—to see clients referred by DSS.

Contrast this with the situation of a program that undertakes occasional evaluations. By the time data indicating a problem with DSS referrals are analyzed and reported, the problem will have existed for a period of time and is likely to have serious consequences. In all likelihood, the program's reputation among the DSS workers will have suffered. DSS may even have concluded that because this program is not providing adequate service, alternative services should be contracted.

The report also provides other useful data. Tables reporting the frequency distribution of the sex and age of new clients provide the data required to ensure that the program is attracting the type of clients for whom it was established. Assume that another one of the program's maintenance objectives is to attract 100 adolescents and young adults each month. Figure 11.4 indicates that 54 percent of new clients are 29 years of age or under. This kind of data indicates that the program is on the right track.

On the other hand, if an objective had been to provide services to a large number of senior citizens, data revealing that only 5 percent of new clients are 60 years of age or over would be cause for concern (Figure 11.4). A program is unlikely to undertake extensive changes on the basis of data for one month, but if several consecutive monthly reports were to indicate that older people constitute only a small percentage of new clients, staff may well conclude that a problem exists and needs to be addressed.

Data Collection at Client Contact

The course of service provision can be followed by completing, after each session, a Client Contact Form, such as the one illustrated in Figure 11.5. The form is designed to provide workers with the information they need to maintain a record of services provided and also to provide data to the information system for evaluation purposes. The form is designed for easy completion, using primarily check-box formats for entering the data. At the end of the form, there is a space for the workers' anecdotal notes, which may be made in the manner preferred by each worker. All but the anecdotal information is designed to be ultimately transferred into the information system. After identifying data for the client and worker are entered, the type of service and service location are specified.

As discussed in Chapter 4, these are the types of data that make it possible for service statistics to be compiled and reported on a regular basis. In this case, counseling is the service provided. Because the data are captured at this point it will later be possible to track the number of counseling sessions provided to the client. The record also makes it possible to track the total number of counseling sessions provided within the program and the agency. Similarly, noting the service location, or whether the service was provided by telephone, will make it possible to generate a description of services provided by location.

In Chapter 4, quality standards were also identified as one possible focus of evaluation. The present Client Contact Form records data about whether the service was provided to an individual or a larger unit within the family and also whether community resource suggestions were made. These data can later be compiled to provide a profile of the client system to which services are provided, as well as the number of community resources suggested in this case. It will be recalled that the agency had set objectives regarding these standards; by capturing the data on the Client Contact Form, the extent to which these standards have been met can be tracked.

On this contact form, the provision is also made for recording the length of the session and the length of preparation, including travel time and paper work. These data reflect administrative needs. Management was desirous of tracking the costs associated with moving services out of the center and decided that, for a period of time, data should be collected that would provide information about such costs. By tracking time spent in travel and preparation, the additional costs related to moving services out of the center can be easily determined.

Finally, the Client Contact Form records the results of any measurements that were completed during service provision. In this case, a practice objective

- Date: January 15, 2001
- Worker: Mary Carnes
- Client Name: Jane Harrison
- ID Number: 144277
- Type of Service:
  __ Family support
  __ Mediation
  X_ Counseling
  __ Interactive Play
  __ Other: _____
- Service Location:
  __ Phone
  __ Center
  X_ School
  __ Other
- Type of Contact:
  __ Individual: parent
  __ Individual: child
  __ Family
  __ Couple
  X_ Parent-child dyad
  __ Collateral: _____
- Community resources suggested:
  1. None
  2. _____
  3. _____
- Length of session, in minutes: 40
- Length of travel, in minutes: 25
- Measures:

Objective	Measure	Score
Self-esteem	Index of Self-esteem	39
	(See Figure 6.1)	

- Notes:

FIGURE 11.5   Excerpts from a Client Contact Form

was self-esteem improvement, and Hudson's Index of Self-Esteem was used as the measure (see Figure 6.1). The current week's score on the instrument, 39, is recorded for this practice objective. There is a provision for recording other

Client's Name: _____   Date (M-D-Y)   ___ ___ ___

Client Identification Number   _____

- CLOSURE DECISION WAS:

  1. Mutual
  2. Client's
  3. Worker's
  9. Other (specify _____)

- REASON FOR CLOSURE:

  1. Service no longer needed
  2. Further service declined
  3. Client stopped coming
  4. Client moved
  5. Referred elsewhere
  9. Other (specify _____)

- PRACTICE OBJECTIVES:

Objective	*Score*	*Measuring Instrument*
1._____	____	_____
2._____	____	_____
3._____	____	_____
4._____	____	_____

- IS FOLLOW-UP REQUIRED?

  1. Yes (if so, why _____)
  2. No (if so, why not _____)

FIGURE 11.6   Example of a Client Termination Form

Cases Terminated

Method of Termination	Number	Percent
Mutual consent	25	50
Client's decision	18	36
Worker's decision	7	14
Totals.......	50	100

Average of Clients' Practice Objectives

Practice Objectives	Beginning	End	n
Self-esteem	61	42	12
Peer relations	57	37	4
Depression	42	27	4
Marital satisfaction	51	48	6
Clinical stress	47	41	9
Alcohol involvement	40	31	4
Partner abuse	52	42	1
Sexual satisfaction	66	60	5
Anxiety	52	41	5
Total..........			50

Note: All practice objectives are measured with Hudson's Scales as reported in Nurius and Hudson, 1993. High scores = higher levels of problem.

FIGURE 11.7   Excerpts from a Monthly Summary
                              Report of Closed Cases

scores, as well. These data can be used to follow changes in practice objectives during the course of the intervention and, as well, can be aggregated into monthly summaries (as shown at the bottom of Figure 11.7) and, ultimately, into a pretest-posttest group evaluation design.

Data Collection at Termination

When the case is closed, a termination form is completed. On this form, data regarding the nature of termination, as well as the final level of outcomes, can be recorded. Moreover, the need for any follow-up can also be noted. An example of a Client Termination Form is provided in Figure 11.6. Data from client terminations can also be aggregated and summarized.

Figure 11.7 provides excerpts from a summary report of cases closed in the counseling unit during one recent month. These data are the result of aggregating data from clients' intake and termination forms. Aggregating data in this manner provides information that is very useful in understanding program functioning. We can readily see, for example, that over a third (36 percent) of the clients who terminated did so unilaterally.

Depending on the program's norms, expectations, and past experiences, these data may be considered problematic. If the data are further analyzed to learn more about the termination process, program staff can determine whether unilateral termination is characteristic of any particular client group, such as males, older clients, or clients with specific practice objectives. Such data are invaluable in diagnosing the problem and deciding on program adjustments and modifications. Data from subsequent reports will then shed light on the success of the measures adopted.

Data pertaining to specific client practice objectives are also useful. Comparing the average practice objective score at the beginning with the average score at termination for a group of clients provides data about net change achieved with respect to each practice objective. Doing so takes the form, in research terms, of a one-group, pretest-posttest design. As shown in Chapter 8, such designs make it possible to describe change but allow only limited inferences about the cause of that change.

Of course, data in themselves do not tell the whole story. They are very useful indicators, but their full interpretation requires careful attention to contextual variables and issues. For instance, it is possible that the relatively modest results achieved with clients experiencing marital and family problems is attributable to factors other than the way in which the program is designed and delivered. It may be that two of the more experienced workers have been on leave for the past several months.

Perhaps one of these positions was covered by temporarily reassigning a less-experienced worker, while the other one was left vacant. Thus, during the preceding several months, fewer marital counseling and family therapy hours may have been delivered, and by less experienced staff: This could obviously have affected client outcomes. In general, interpreting the data resulting from evaluation requires consideration of contextual variables and cannot be done purely on the basis of quantitative results.

Data Collection to Obtain Feedback

As discussed in Chapter 4, satisfaction with a social service program often becomes a focus for evaluation. Thus, staff members depicted in the illustrations above have determined that it would be useful to obtain feedback from program participants regarding various aspects of their satisfaction. Consequently, a satisfaction survey was developed, which clients are asked to complete at the time of service closure. An example of a very simple satisfaction survey instrument is provided in Figure 11.8.

Again, such data are most useful when aggregated across clients. An excerpt from such analysis is provided in Figure 11.9. As may be seen, a large majority of clients consider the services helpful and the staff members supportive, and think themselves better off as a result of services. As well, two thirds would recommend the services to others and about 68 percent indicate a high or very high level of overall satisfaction with the agency.

Staff members may react to summaries such as those shown in Figures 11.7 and 11.9 in a number of ways. They may resent the fact that their work is being scrutinized, particularly if the monthly summary has been newly instituted. Where the results suggest that there is room for improvement (which is often the case), they may be uncertain of their own competence and, perhaps, feel that they are being judged. Alternatively, or perhaps in addition, they may be alerted to the fact that they need to modify their approaches to improve results.

Which one of these feelings predominates depends to some extent on the way the information system was introduced to the practitioners. Workers who were consulted about the system's development, informed about its advantages, and involved in its design and implementation are more likely to regard the monthly summaries as useful feedback. Staff who were neither consulted nor involved are likely to regard them with apprehension and resentment.

Equally important in shaping attitudes to monitoring is how the agency's management uses, or abuses, the data generated. If the data are used in a judgmental, critical manner, staff are likely to remain skeptical and defensive about the monitoring process. Where the data are regarded as useful feedback and are used in a genuine, cooperative effort to upgrade and further develop services, workers will likely welcome such reports as tools that can help them—and the agency—improve.

Please provide us with feedback on our services by completing the following brief questionnaire. For each question, circle one response.

- The services received were helpful:

    Strongly Disagree   Disagree Agree   Strongly Agree

- Staff members were supportive:

    Strongly Disagree   Disagree Agree   Strongly Agree

- I am better off as a result of these services:

    Strongly Disagree   Disagree Agree   Strongly Agree

- I would recommend these services to others:

    Strongly Disagree   Disagree Agree   Strongly Agree

- My overall satisfaction with these services is:

    Low   Moderate   High

- Comments or suggestions:

FIGURE 11.8   Example of a Client Satisfaction Survey

These considerations suggest that administrators should view evaluation data as a means of assisting them in identifying areas for improvement and in identifying factors in problems and difficulties. Obviously, this approach is far more likely to evoke a positive response than one in which undesirable results signal the beginning of a search to apportion blame.

Administrators' responsibilities do not, however, end here. To foster a truly positive environment for evaluation, administrators should not only be concerned with pinpointing potential trouble spots, but should also be

The services I received were helpful.

	Number	Percent
Strongly Disagree	22	11
Disagree	36	18
Agree	94	47
Strongly Agree	48	24
Totals......	200	100

Staff members were supportive.

	Number	Percent
Strongly Disagree	18	9
Disagree	38	19
Agree	88	44
Strongly Agree	56	28
Totals......	200	100

I am better off as a result of these services.

	Number	Percent
Strongly Disagree	30	15
Disagree	46	23
Agree	98	49
Strongly Agree	26	13
Totals......	200	100

I would recommend these services to others.

	Number	Percent
Strongly Disagree	40	20
Disagree	30	15
Agree	74	37
Strongly Agree	56	28
Totals......	200	100

My overall satisfaction with these services is....

	Number	Percent
Low	24	12
Moderate	40	20
High	90	45
Very High	46	23
Totals......	200	100

FIGURE 11.9   Program Level Report of Results from a
Client Satisfaction Survey (from data
collected via the form in Figure 11.8)

committed to supporting workers' efforts to improve program effectiveness. These are key roles for an administrator of any social service organization.

DATA MANAGEMENT

Effective evaluation systems are powered by information gleaned from the data. As programs become more complex, and as evaluation becomes an increasingly important function, organizations require increasingly sophisticated data management capabilities. Data management includes collection and recording; aggregation, integration, and analyses; and reporting. These functions may be carried out manually, through the use of computers, or through a combination of manual and computer-based methods.

Manual Data Management

Not long ago, most data management functions were undertaken manually. Data collection forms were designed, completed in longhand or by typewriter, and filed, usually in case files. The need to produce specific data—for example, looking at the referral sources of all new cases in the last six months—usually entailed a manual search of all new case files, as well as manual aggregation and analyses of the data. While such a system could unearth the required data, the process was cumbersome and labor-intensive.

As organizations found that they were called upon to generate certain types of data on a regular basis, they developed methods for manually copying specific data (e.g., referral sources, age and sex of client, presenting problem) from client records onto composite forms or spreadsheets. In this way, manually searching files for the required data could be avoided. However, the composite forms or spreadsheets were still analyzed manually. While an improvement, such a system was limited not only because manual analyses were time-consuming but also because they could provide only the data that had been identified for aggregation. A need for data other than that which had been included on the spreadsheet still entailed a manual search of all relevant files.

Obviously, manual methods are labor-intensive and costly. They are also limited in their flexibility and in their capacity to quickly deliver needed data. It is not surprising that, with the ready availability of powerful desktop computers, social service organizations have increasingly turned to computer-based data management systems.

Computer-Assisted Data Management

Computers can be used in both case- and program-level evaluations. Because they increase the capacity for data management and make the process more efficient, their use in recent years has dramatically increased.

Even so, at this time, few social service organizations rely entirely on computers for data management. Usually, data management systems are a combination of manual and computer-based methods. Manual functions, however, are decreasing and, correspondingly, computer-based functions are increasing. The trend is clear: Computers are becoming increasingly important in evaluation. Typically, data are collected manually through the completion of forms and measuring instruments. At this point, the data are often entered into the computer, which maintains and manages the data and carries out the required aggregation and analyses.

The computer can easily assist, for example, with the aggregation and analysis of case-level monitoring data. Figure 11.7 illustrated this process, using the example of an agency where workers routinely use standardized measuring instruments to track changes in clients' practice objectives. As may be seen, the computer has selected all clients who had practice objectives related to self-esteem during a specified period of time and calculated the average initial and final self-esteem scores for those clients. There were 12 clients in the group, and the average score for the group dropped from 61 at the beginning of service to 42 at termination, a considerable decline in problems with self-esteem. In this instance, the data management capabilities of the computer readily allowed a one-group pretest-posttest evaluation design to be carried out.

Further analyses can be conducted on these results to determine if the decline is statistically significant. A variety of computer programs can rapidly carry out such analyses. This represents a major advantage over manual data analyses, as most statistical computations tend to be complex, cumbersome, and time-consuming. With today's statistical software packages, the required computations can be easily and accurately accomplished; indeed, more sophisticated procedures, prohibitively time-consuming when done by hand, also become possible.

Similarly, the computer analysis can readily provide data on other points of focus: service data, client characteristics, quality indicators, and client satisfaction. As in the case of the outcome data discussed above, computers can refine analyses to provide data not only about the entire group but to answer more specific questions. A computer can easily select clients who received services in conjunction with other family members (a quality indicator described in Chapter 4) and compare their outcomes to those who received individual services. Similarly, data pertaining to two or more operating periods can be compared. These are just two examples of powerful analyses that become possible through computers; the result is information that allows deeper understanding of programs and services.

There is a potential danger in the ready availability of such analytical power; people who have little knowledge or understanding of data analyses or statistics can easily carry out inappropriate procedures that may serve to mislead rather than inform. Nevertheless, when used knowledgeably, such statistical power makes more incisive analyses possible.

Another group of software programs, known as *relational databases,* are also increasingly being used in data management. As the name suggests, these programs enable the linking of disparate data in a way that makes it possible to look at and understand data in different ways. Through linking the data contained on client contact forms with information on intake and termination forms, for example, it may be possible to analyze the relationship between initial presenting problems, the course of service provision, and client outcomes. A virtually unlimited flexibility in analyzing data is provided by such programs, which leads to an increasingly more sophisticated understanding of programs, services, and their specific elements. Gabor and Sieppert (1999) provide a detailed example of one such system.

Reporting

Regular reports provide continuous feedback, which is the essence of monitoring. Essentially, reports provide the same data, updated for new cases, on a regular basis. Examples of such reports are provided in Figures 11.4, 11.7, and 11.9.

As with other data management, computers are particularly useful in generating such reports. Software packages used to conduct statistical analyses or to maintain relational databases usually have provisions for repeating the same analyses. Basically, once a data analysis is specified, it can be run over and over again using updated data and producing updated reports. Moreover, formats for reports, whether tables, graphs, or charts, as well as headings and labels, can also be specified in advance. Using computers, there is little limit to the number of reports that can be generated, making it possible to provide timely information, tailored to the needs of staff members at all organizational levels. This, in turn, makes possible an ongoing, organization-wide quality improvement process.

A Look to the Future

It is probably safe to predict that over the next few years computers will play an increasingly important role in data management. With the ready availability of more powerful computer hardware and software programs, it is likely that many organizations will attempt to automate as much of their data management processes as is possible.

One prominent area for automation is the data entry process. Laptop computers make direct data entry possible and feasible. Workers and clients will increasingly use electronic versions of forms, instruments, and questionnaires, entering data directly into laptop computers. Although it may be hard to picture workers and clients in the social services engaging in such activities, they are quite common in the business world. It is only a matter of time until most people will have sufficient familiarity with computers to feel comfortable in interacting with and entering data into them. Already, many people are doing so through automatic tellers, voice mail, and electronic travel reservations.

Data entered directly into laptop computers will be electronically transferred into the organization's data management system, eliminating the need for completing paper copies and manually entering data into the system. This development will not only make data management more accurate and efficient but will also make possible the creation of larger, more powerful systems.

Such developments are probably inevitable. Though some might regard them with suspicion, computer-based information systems can be powerful tools in the service of quality-improvement efforts. Ultimately, the technology represented by computerization is, in itself, neither good nor bad. Like any technology, it can be used well but it can also be misused. Clearly, evaluators and social service professionals alike will need to keep a close eye on such developments and ensure that computer use is congruent with professional values and ethics.

SUMMING UP AND LOOKING AHEAD

This chapter stressed that the development of an information system in an existing social service program requires the full cooperation of both line-level workers and administrators. Front-line workers have an important role to play in the design and development of the system. Administrators must be prepared to provide training, support, and resources in addition to demonstrating that the monitoring system is intended to improve the program, not to assign blame.

The following chapter builds upon this one in that it presents how decisions can be made with objective and subjective data.

KEY TERMS_____

Client Contact Form: A uniform program document completed by workers; records aspects of service delivery such as when client was seen, for how long, nature of client-worker activities, and case notes.

Data Information System: A manual or computerized bank of data that stores client and program information. Data in the system are used to address questions raised by different stakeholders.

Data Management: A process that involves data collection and recording, data aggregations, integration and analysis, and data reporting; can be manual or computer assisted.

Intake Form: A uniform program questionnaire that is used to collect basic demographic and background data from clients upon entry to the program; usually the first document placed in a client's file and typically completed by a worker during an interview with the client.

STUDY QUESTIONS_____

1. Data information systems contain data that ultimately will answer questions raised by various stakeholder groups. Identify five generic questions that might be asked of a social service program. Given your questions, what data (or variables) must be included in a program's data information system?

2. Imagine that you are the evaluator hired to set up a data information system for your social work education program. Name the different stakeholder groups that you would consult. Identify key data (or variables) that each stakeholder group would likely insist on including in the system. (*Hint: think of likely questions that would be of interest for each stakeholder group.*)

3. Review the list of stakeholder groups that you identified in the question above. Rank the groups in order, starting with the group that you believe should have the most "say-so" with respect to what data ought to be included in the data information system. What rationales can you offer for your rankings? Do other students in your class agree or disagree with your rankings and rationales?

4. This chapter stresses that program-level and case-level data information systems ought to parallel each other in any given program. How do parallel systems benefit program administrators, program workers, and clients? What problems are likely to occur for each of these stakeholder groups when

program and case-level data information systems are unrelated?

5. Look at the flow chart presented in Figure 11.1. Identify a case-level question at each step in the chart that would assist you in monitoring an individual client's progress. Identify a program-level question at each step in the chart that would assist you in monitoring overall client progress (i.e., all clients).

6. Intake forms are common to most social service programs. Identify generic data (or variables) that would likely appear on such a form. What case-level decisions could you make with these data, if any? What program-level decisions could you make with these data, if any?

7. A social worker exclaims "There is no point in collecting data from clients at termination because the feedback will not be used to benefit their individual case." Explain why you agree or disagree with this statement. Compare your answer with those of other students in your class.

8. Look at the excerpt from a summary report presented in Figure 11.7. What questions does the information presented in the figure raise for you? Is it possible to make recommendations for program development based on the numbers presented? Why or why not? Discuss your answers with other students in your class.

REFERENCES AND FURTHER READINGS

Gabor, P., & Sieppert, J. (1999). Developing a computer supported evaluation system in a human service organization. *New Technology in the Human Services 12,* 107–119.

Nurius, P.S., & Hudson, W.W. (1993). *Human services: Practice, evaluation, and computers.* Belmont, CA: Brooks/Cole.

12

Chapter Outline

Decision Making with
Objective and Subjective Data

IDEALLY, ALL PROFESSIONAL DECISIONS should be arrived at via a rational process based on the collection, synthesis, and analysis of relevant, objective, and subjective data. Objective data are obtained by an explicit measurement process that, when carefully followed, reduces bias and increases the data's objectivity. Subjective data, on the other hand, are obtained from impressions and judgments which, by their very nature, incorporate the values, preferences, and experiences of the individuals who make them.

It is our position that objective data, *when combined with* subjective data, offer the best basis for decision making. The best practice- and program-relevant decisions are made when we understand the advantages and limitations of both objective and subjective data and are able to combine the two as appropriate to the circumstances.

OBJECTIVE DATA

The main advantage of using objective data when making decisions is in the data's precision and objectivity. At the program level, for example, an agency may receive funding to provide an employment skills training program for minority groups. If appropriate data are kept, it is easy to ascertain to what degree the eligibility requirement is being met, and it may be possible to state, for example, that 85 percent of service recipients are in fact from minority groups. Without objective data, the subjective impressions of community members, staff members, funders, and program participants would be the sources of the data. Individuals may use descriptors such as "most," "many," or "a large number" to describe the proportion of minority people served by the employment-skills training program. Obviously, such subjective judgments are far less precise than objective data, and they are, also, subject to biases.

Objective data, however, are not without their own limitations. Among these are:

1. Some variables are difficult to measure objectively.
2. Data may be uncertain or ambiguous, allowing conflicting interpretations.
3. Objective data may not take all pertinent contextual factors into account.

Although considerable progress has been made in recent years in the development of standardized measuring instruments, not all variables of conceivable interest to social workers are convenient and feasible to measure. Thus, objective data may not be available to guide certain practice and program decisions. In the same vein, even if a variable can be measured, data collection plans may not call for its measurement—or, the measurement may have been omitted for any of a variety of reasons that arise in day-to-day professional activity. Consequently, objective data are not always available to guide practice and program decision making.

Where objective data are available, their meaning and implications may not always be clear. At the case level, a series of standardized measures intended to assess a 10-year-old's self-esteem may yield no discernable pattern. It would thus be difficult, on the basis of such objective data alone, to make decisions about further interventions and services. At the program level, objective data may indicate that, over a three-month period, people participating in a weight-loss program lose an average of five pounds a person. Although the results seem favorable, the average weight loss is not very great, making it unclear whether the program should be continued as is, or whether modifications should be considered.

Finally, objective data seldom provide contextual information—although the context relating to them is important in their interpretation. In the example of the weight-loss program, the average five-pound loss would probably be considered inadequate if the clientele were known to be a group of people who, for medical reasons, needed to lose an average of sixty pounds each. On the other hand, if the clientele were known to be a group of skiers preparing for the ski season, the program could be considered quite successful.

SUBJECTIVE DATA

Although it might seem desirable to base all decisions on logically analyzed objective data, such information on all factors affecting a given practice or program decision is seldom available. Consequently, objective data are often supplemented by more subjective types of data, such as the workers' impressions, judgments, experiences, and intuition.

As human beings, we assimilate subjective data continuously as we move through our daily life; competent social work professionals do the same, noting the client's stance, gait, gestures, voice, eye movements, and set of mouth, for example. At the program level, an administrator may have a sense of awareness of staff morale, history and stage of development of the organization, external expectations, and the ability of the organization to absorb change. Seldom are any of these subjective data actually measured, but all of them are assimilated. Some subjective data are consciously noted; some filter through subconsciously and emerge later as an impression, opinion, or intuition. Clearly, such subjective data may considerably influence case and program decision making.

At the case level, for example, perceptions, judgments, and intuition—often called clinical impressions—may become factors in decision making. A worker may conclude, based on body language, eye contact, and voice, that a client's self-esteem is improving. Further case-level decisions may then be based on these subjective impressions.

At the program level, objective data may suggest the need to modify the program, in the face of inadequate results. The administrator, however, may put off making any modifications, on the basis of a subjective judgment that, because several other program changes had recently been implemented, the team's ability to absorb any more changes is limited.

To the extent that subjective data are accurate, such a decision is entirely appropriate. The main limitation of subjective data, however, is that impressions and intuition often spring to the mind preformed, and the process by which they were formed cannot be objectively examined. By their nature, subjective data are susceptible to distortion through the personal experience, bias, and preferences of the individual. These may work deceptively, leaving workers unaware that the subjective data upon which they are relying actually distort the picture.

In reality, case- and program-level decision making uses a blend of objective and subjective data. Together, the two forms of data have the potential to provide the most complete information upon which to base decisions. Ultimately, the practitioner will have to use judgment in reconciling all relevant sources of data in order to arrive at an understanding of the situation. In building an accurate picture, it is important not only to consider all sources of data but also to be aware of the strengths and limitations of each of these sources. Quality case and program decisions are usually the result of explicitly sifting through the various sources of data and choosing those sources in which it is reasonable to have the most confidence under the circumstances.

Having considered decision making in general, we now turn to an examination of the process at the case and program levels, specifically.

CASE-LEVEL DECISION MAKING

If high-quality case level decisions are to be reached, the social worker should know what types of decisions are best supported by objective data and what types will likely require the use of subjective data.

A helping relationship with a client is a process that passes through a number of stages and follows logically one from the other. There are essentially four stages: (1) the engagement and problem-definition phase, (2) the practice objective–setting phase, (3) the intervention phase, (4) the termination and follow-up phase. In practice, these phases are not likely to follow a clear sequence. Engagement, for example, occurs most prominently at the beginning of the professional relationship, but it continues in some form throughout the entire helping process. Problem definition is logically the first consideration after engagement, but if it becomes evident during intervention that the client's problem is not clearly understood, the problem-definition and objective-setting phases will have to be readdressed. Nevertheless, discernible phases do exist. The following describes how case-level decisions can be made in each phase.

The Engagement and Problem-Definition Phase

Suppose a married couple, Mr. and Ms. Wright, come to a family service agency to work on their marriage problems and have been assigned to a worker named Maria. From Ms. Wright's initial statement, the problem is that her partner does not pay enough attention to her. In Maria's judgment, Ms. Wright's perception is a symptom of yet another problem that has not been defined. The client's perception, however, is a good starting point, and Maria attempts to objectify Ms. Wright's statement. In what ways, precisely, does her partner not pay enough attention to her? Ms. Wright obligingly provides data: Her partner has not gone anywhere with her for the past three months, but he regularly spends three nights a week playing basketball, two nights with friends, and one night at his mother's.

Mr. Wright, protestingly brought into the session, declares that he spends most nights at home and the real problem is that his partner constantly argues. Further inquiry leads Maria to believe that Mr. Wright spends more nights away from home than he reports but fewer than his partner says; Ms. Wright, feeling herself ignored, most likely is argumentative; and the underlying problems are actually poor communication and unrealistic expectations on the part of both.

A host of other problems surfaced subtly during the interview and cannot be addressed until the communications problem is solved; communication, therefore, should be the initial target of the intervention—the first practice objective.

A second practice objective could be to reduce the Wrights' unrealistic expectations of each other. Let us consider that the Wrights have these two practice objectives that are specifically geared toward the program objective, "to increase their marital satisfaction." Maria believes that the attainment of the two practice objectives will increase the Wrights' marital satisfaction—the main purpose for which they are seeking services. Remember, the Wrights want a happier marriage (that is why they sought out services); they did not seek out help with their dysfunctional communication patterns and unrealistic expectations of one another. Thus, to increase their marital satisfaction becomes the program objective, and communications and expectations become the two practice objectives.

So far, Maria's conclusions have been based on her own impressions of the conflicting data presented by the Wrights. Unless the problem is straightforward and concrete, the engagement and problem-definition phase often depends more on the worker's subjective judgment, experience, and intuition than it does on objective data. Even when standardized measuring instruments are used to help clients identify and prioritize their problems, the choice of the problem to be first addressed will largely be guided by the worker's subjective intuition and judgment. Once intuition has indicated what the problem might be, however, the magnitude of the problem can often be measured with more objectivity through the use of standardized measuring instruments.

In the Wrights' case, Maria has tentatively decided to formulate a practice objective of increasing the Wrights' communication skills. In order to confirm that communication skills are problematic, she asks Mr. and Ms. Wright to independently complete a 25-item standardized measuring instrument designed to measure marital communications skills. The instrument contains such items as, "How often do you and your spouse talk over pleasant things that happen during the day?" with possible responses of "very frequently," "frequently," "occasionally," "seldom," and "never." This instrument has a range of 0 to 100, with higher scores showing better communication skills. It has a clinical cutting score of 60, indicating effective communications above that level, and it has been tested on people of the same socioeconomic group as the Wrights and may be assumed to yield valid and reliable data.

The introduction of the measuring instrument at this stage serves two basic purposes. First, the scores will show whether communication is indeed a problem, and to what degree it is a problem for each partner. Second, the scores will provide a baseline measurement that can be used as the first point on a graph in whatever case-level design Maria selects (see Chapter 7).

The Practice Objective–Setting Phase

In the Wrights' case, the program objective is to increase their marital satisfaction. Thus, a related practice objective (one of many possible) is to increase the couple's communication skills to a minimum score of 60, the clinical cutting score on the standardized measuring instrument. The practice objective–setting phase in this example thus relies heavily on objective data: It is framed in terms of a change from very ineffective communication (score of 0) to very effective communication (score of 100).

The same process applies in cases where the standardized measuring instrument selected is less formal and precise. Maria, for example, may ask each partner to complete a self-anchored rating scale indicating his and her level of satisfaction with the degree of communication achieved. The scoring range on this instrument could be from 1–6, with higher scores indicating greater levels of satisfaction and lower scores indicating lesser levels of satisfaction. If Mr. Wright begins by rating his satisfaction level at 3 and Ms. Wright indicates hers at 2, the practice objective chosen may be to achieve a minimum rating of 4 for each partner. Here again, practice objective–setting is based on objective data collected at the beginning of Maria's intervention.

The Intervention Phase

The selection of the intervention strategy itself will be based on objective and subjective data only to a limited degree. Perhaps Maria has seen previous clients with similar practice objectives and also has objective evidence, via the professional literature, that a specific treatment intervention is appropriate to use in this specific situation. But even though the intervention is chosen on the basis of data accumulated from previous research studies and past experience, each intervention is tailored to meet the needs of the particular client system, and decisions about strategy, timing, and its implementation are largely based on subjective data—the worker's experience, clinical judgment, and intuition.

Although objective data may play only one part in the selection of an intervention strategy, once the strategy is selected, its success is best measured on the basis of consistently collected objective data. Ideally, objective data are collected using a number of different standardized measures. In the Wrights' case, for example, the scores from repeated administrations of the standardized instrument that measures the degree of communication will comprise one set of objective data for one particular practice objective.

Frequency counts of specifically selected behaviors may comprise another set: for example, a count of the number of conversations daily lasting at least five minutes, or the number of "I" statements made daily by each partner. The self-anchored rating scale, described in the previous section, could be a third source of data. These sets of data together provide considerable information about whether, and to what degree, progress is being made.

Maria is also likely to come to a more global opinion about how the couple are doing in regard to their communication patterns. This opinion will be based on a variety of observations and impressions formed as she works with the couple. The process by which such an opinion is formed is intuitive and—depending on the worker's skill, experiences, and the circumstances—may be quite accurate. The method by which it is arrived at, however, is idiosyncratic and is, therefore, of unknown validity and reliability. For this reason, relying on clinical impressions exclusively is inadvisable.

On the other hand, as we saw in Chapter 6, objective measures may have their own problems of validity and reliability. The best course is a middle one: Determination of a client's progress should be based on a combination of objective data *and* subjective data. Where objective and subjective data point in the same direction, Maria can proceed with considerable confidence that she has a clear and accurate picture of her clients' progress. Where objective and subjective data diverge, Maria should first attempt to determine the reasons for the difference and ensure that she has a good understanding of her clients' problems and needs. When Maria is satisfied that she has an accurate grasp of her client system's progress, she is ready to proceed to decisions about the most appropriate treatment intervention to use.

These decisions are guided by changes in the practice objective. Three patterns of change are possible: (1) deterioration, or no change; (2) insufficient, or slow change; and (3) satisfactory change.

Deterioration, or No Change

Suppose that Ms. Wright scored a 40 on the first administration of the standardized measuring instrument that measures the degree, or level, of communication patterns, scores a 41 on the second, a 43 on the third, and a 42 on the fourth (see Figure 12.1). In addition, Mr. Wright scores 50, 51, 53, and 52 respectively. How would Maria analyze and interpret such data?

First, Maria will want to consider what the other available sources of data indicate. Let us assume that, on the self-anchored communication satisfaction scale, Ms. Wright still rates her satisfaction at 2 and that, during the sessions, she avoids eye contact with Mr. Wright and tries to monopolize the worker's attention with references to "he" and "him." In this situation, the data all seem to point to the same conclusion: There has been virtually no change or progress. Under such circumstances, it is reasonable to place considerable reliance on the data contained in Figure 12.1

As Figure 12.1 also indicates, the slope of the line connecting the measurement points is virtually flat—that is, it is stable, indicating neither improvement nor deterioration. Moreover, the level of the problem is well below the desired minimum score of 60. Such data would normally lead Maria to conclude that a change in the intervention is warranted—resulting in a *BC* design.

Here qualitative considerations may also enter the case-level decision-making process. Maria, for example, may be aware of disruptions in the lives of Mr. and Ms. Wright. Perhaps Mr. Wright received a lay-off notice during the second week of the intervention. Maria may now need to consider whether the effects of the intervention might not have been counteracted by these adverse circumstances. Ultimately, she will need to decide whether to continue the intervention in the hope that, once the couple have dealt with the shock of the impending lay-off, the intervention will begin to have the desired effect.

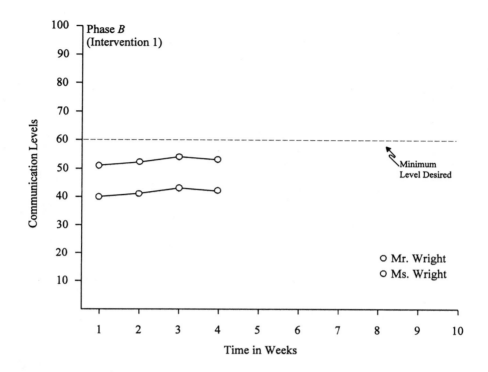

FIGURE 12.1   *B* Design: The Wrights' Communication
Levels Over Time, Indicating No Change

It is also possible that the intervention is known to have a delayed impact. This characteristic could have been determined from the professional literature or from Maria's previous experience with using the intervention. Under such circumstances it may, again, be reasonable to maintain the intervention for some time longer and see whether movement toward the practice objective begins.

How long it is sensible to continue an intervention in the absence of documented progress is a matter best left to Maria's and the couple's judgment. As long as there is reason to believe that an intervention may yet have the desired impacts, it is justified to pursue that intervention. If there is no evidence of change for the better, however, the intervention will need to be changed. Note that data will provide objective evidence supporting the need for a change in the intervention, but they will not indicate what future intervention strategies might be used instead. Formulation of a new intervention strategy will again call upon Maria's and her clients' judgment.

Insufficient, or Slow Change

Insufficient or slow change is a familiar scenario in the social services. A gradual but definite improvement in the communication scores may be noted, indicating that Mr. and Ms. Wright are slowly learning to communicate. Their relationship continues to deteriorate, however, because their communication scores are still below 60—the minimum level of good communication; progress needs to be more rapid if the marriage is to be saved.

In general, many clients improve only slowly, or improve in spurts with regressions in between. The data will reflect what is occurring—what the problem level is, and at what rate and in what direction it is changing. No data, however, can tell a worker whether the measured rate of change is acceptable in the particular client's circumstances. This is an area in which subjective clinical judgment again comes into play.

The worker may decide that the rate of change is insufficient, but just marginally so; that is, the intervention is successful on the whole and ought to be continued, but at a greater frequency or intensity. Perhaps the number of treatment sessions can be increased, or more time can be scheduled for each session, or more intensive work can be planned. In other words, a B design will now become a B_1B_2 design (as illustrated in Figure 12.2) or, if baseline data have been collected, an AB design will become an AB_1B_2 design. If, on the other hand, the worker thinks that intensifying the intervention is unlikely to yield significantly improved results, a different intervention entirely may be adopted. In this case, the B design will become a BC design (illustrated in Figure 12.3), or the AB design will become an ABC design.

Sometimes improvement occurs at an acceptable rate for a period and then the client reaches a plateau, below the desired minimal level; no further change seems to be occurring. The data will show the initial improvement and the plateau (see Figure 12.4), but they will not show whether the plateau is temporary, whether it is akin to a resting period, or whether the level already achieved is as far as the improvement will go. Again, this is a matter for clinical judgment. The worker and client system may decide to continue with the intervention for a time to see if improvement begins again. The exact length of time during which perseverance is justified is a judgment call. If the client system remains stuck at the level reached beyond that time, the worker and client system will have to decide whether to apply the intervention more intensively, try a new intervention, or be content with what has been achieved.

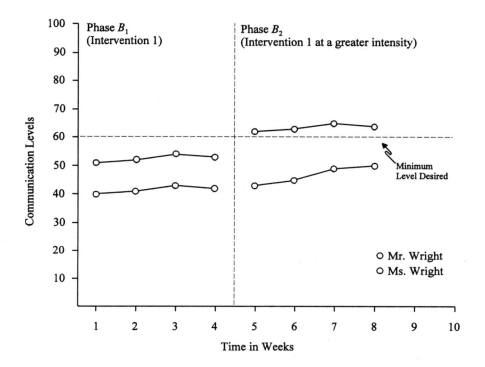

FIGURE 12.2 B_1B_2 Changing Intensity Design: The Wrights' Communication Levels Over Time, Indicating Insufficient Change at B_1 Followed by a More Intensive B_2

Satisfactory Change

Frequently objective data will show an improvement. At times the improvement will be steady and sustained, and at other times an overall trend of improvement will be punctuated with periods of plateau or even regression. This latter scenario is illustrated in Figure 12.5. Essentially, continuation of the treatment intervention is justified by continuing client progress, although Maria may wish at times to make minor modifications in the intervention.

It is important to keep in mind that not all case-level designs permit the worker to conclude that the intervention has caused the change for the better (see Chapters 7 and 8). In the case of many designs that are likely to be used in the monitoring of human service interventions, it is possible to conclude

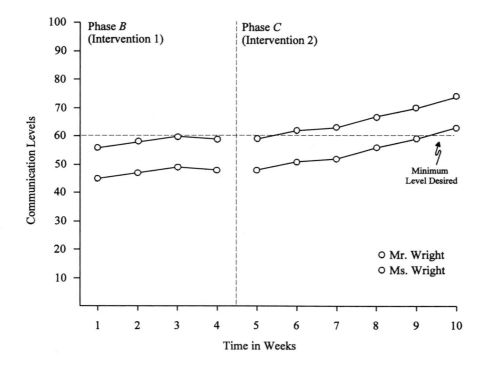

FIGURE 12.3   *BC* Design: The Wrights' Communication Levels Over Time, Indicating Insufficient Change at the *B* Intervention Followed by a *C* Intervention

only that the client's practice objective has changed for the better. This is the situation in the *B* design shown in Figure 12.4 where Mr. Wright has obtained communication scores over 60 but Ms. Wright has yet to reach the minimum acceptable level of 60. From a service perspective, however, evidence that Mr. and Ms. Wright are improving is sufficient justification for continuing the intervention; it is not necessary to prove that the intervention is causing the change.

When the data show that a client has reached the program or practice objective, the worker will, if possible, initiate a maintenance phase, perhaps gradually reducing the frequency of contact with a view to service termination, but also trying to ensure that the gains achieved are not lost. If other practice objectives need to be resolved, the maintenance phase for one objective may coincide with the baseline or interventive phase for another. It is quite possible

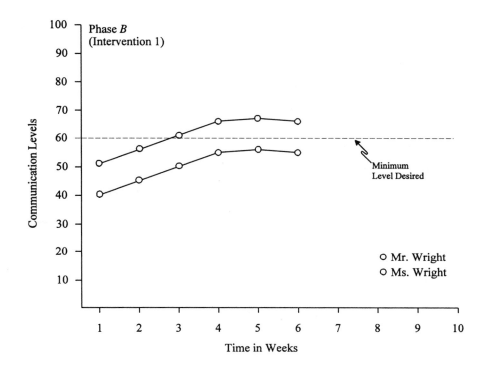

FIGURE 12.4   *B* Design: The Wrights' Communication Levels Over Time, Indicating an Initial Improvement Leveling Off to a Plateau

to engage in a number of case-level designs at the same time with the same client; because client practice objectives are usually interrelated, data obtained in one area will often be relevant to another.

The maintenance phase is important, ensuring that the practice objective really has been satisfactorily resolved. Assume that data show a steady improvement, culminating at a point above the target range (as in Figure 12.3). One measurement below the minimum desired level means only that the practice objective was not at a clinically significant level when that measurement was made. Subsequent measurements may show that a significant problem still exists. A number of measurements are required before Maria can be confident that the practice objective has stabilized at the desired level. Similarly, where the trend to improvement included plateaus and regressions, measurements must continue beyond the achievement of the practice objective to ensure that the objective has indeed stabilized in the desired level and direction.

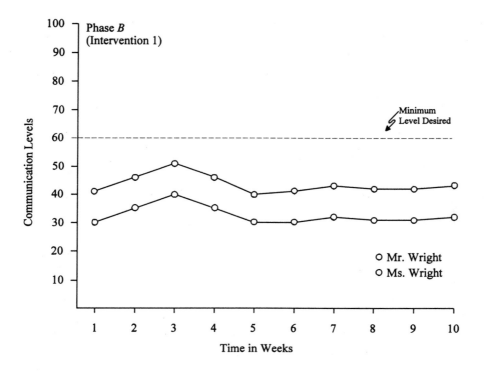

FIGURE 12.5   *B* Design: The Wrights'
Communication Levels Over Time,
Indicating Some Improvement with
Periods of Plateaus and Regressions

The Termination and Follow-Up Phase

Once it is decided that the program objective (not the practice objective) has been accomplished, the next step is termination and follow-up. The termination decision is straightforward, in theory: When the data show that the program objective has been achieved, via the attainment of practice objectives, and the objective level is stable, services can be terminated. In reality, however, other factors need to be taken into account, such as the number and type of support systems available in the client's social environment and the nature and magnitude of possible stressor events in the client's life. We must carefully weigh all these factors, including information yielded by objective and subjective data, in making a decision to end services.

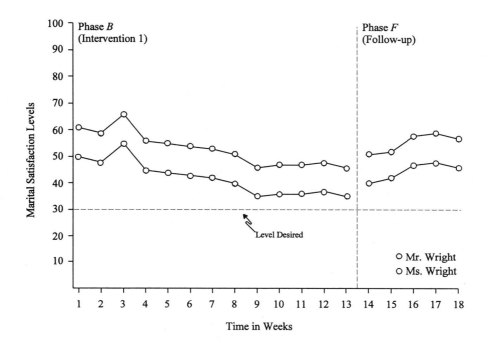

FIGURE 12.6   *BF* Design: The Wrights' Marital Satisfaction Levels During Treatment (*B*) and After Termination (*F*), Indicating Maintained Improvement After Termination

Ideally, the follow-up phase will be a routine part of the program's operations. Many social work programs, however, do not engage in any kind of follow-up activities, and others conduct follow-ups in a sporadic or informal way. If the program does conduct routine follow-up, decisions will already have been made concerning how often and in what manner the client should be contacted after the termination of services. If no standardized follow-up procedures are in place, we will have to decide whether follow-up is necessary and, if so, what form it should take.

Data can help decide whether a follow-up is necessary. If data reveal that a client has not reached a program objective, or has reached it only marginally, a follow-up is essential. If data show a pattern of improvement followed by regression, a follow-up is also indicated, to ensure that regression will not occur again.

The follow-up procedures that measure program objectives may be conducted in a number of ways. Frequently used approaches include

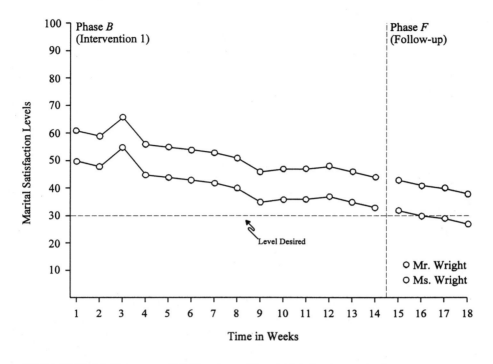

FIGURE 12.7   *BF* Design: The Wrights' Marital
Satisfaction Levels During Treatment (*B*)
and After Termination (*F*), Indicating a
Deterioration After Termination

contacting former clients by letter or telephone at increasingly longer intervals
after the cessation of services. A less frequently used approach is to continue
to measure the program objectives that were taken during the intervention
period. As services to the Wrights are terminated, Maria could arrange to have
them each complete, at monthly intervals, the Marital Satisfaction Scale (the
measure of the program objective). Maria could mail the scale to the Wrights,
who, because they have already completed it during the course of the
intervention, should have no problem doing so during follow-up. The inclusion
of a stamped, self-addressed envelope can further encourage them to complete
this task. In this manner, Maria can determine objectively whether marital
satisfaction gains made during treatment are maintained over time.

At a minimum, collecting program-level data (not case-level data) during
follow-up results in a *BF* design, as illustrated in Figures 12.6 and 12.7. If an
initial baseline phase had been utilized, the result would be an *ABF* design.

Where follow-up data indicate that client gains are being maintained, a situation illustrated in Figure 12.6, termination procedures can be completed. Where follow-up data reveal a deterioration after termination, as illustrated in Figure 12.7, Maria is at least in a position to know that her clients are not doing well. Under such circumstances, complete termination is not warranted. Instead, Maria should consider whether to resume active intervention, provide additional support in the clients' social environment, or offer some other service. The follow-up data will not help Maria to decide what she should do next, but they will alert her to the need to do something.

It should be noted that Figures 12.6 and 12.7 provide data for marital satisfaction scores (the lower the score the better the marital satisfaction) and do not represent the couple's communication scores, as in Figures 12.1–12.5 (the higher the score the better the communication). This is because follow-up data are concerned with program objectives (in this case, marital satisfaction), not practice objectives (in this case, communication and expectations of one another).

PROGRAM-LEVEL DECISION MAKING

The primary purpose of the monitoring approach at the program level is to obtain feedback on the program in an ongoing manner so that the services provided can be continually developed and improved.

In the first instance, the program may be assessed with regard to the achievement of process objectives. Process objectives are analogous to facilitative practice objectives; their achievement makes it more likely that program objectives will also be achieved. In a sense, they speak to the effectiveness and efficiency of the service operation. Process objectives, for example, might address the type of clientele to be served, indicating that a minimum of 75 percent should come from minority backgrounds.

Or, these objectives could speak to the length of waiting lists, specifying that no one should have to wait longer than two weeks prior to the commencement of services. Other process objectives could deal with the number of continuing education hours provided to staff members, premature termination of cases, service hours provided, and similar other matters.

The actual program objectives may be assessed in various ways. Success rates may vary with problem type. A particular social service program, for example, may achieve good success with children who have family-related problems but less success with children whose problems are primarily drug-related. Or perhaps desirable results are achieved with one type of client but not another: A drug rehabilitation program may be more successful with adults than it is with adolescents. Or, again, a particular program within an agency may achieve its program objectives better than another program within the same agency. A child welfare agency, for example, may successfully operate an adolescent treatment foster-care program but have less success with its adolescent group-care program. If several residential programs are operated, one may achieve its program objectives to a higher degree than another.

Finally, the agency must be considered as a whole. How successful is it when all of its programs are assessed together? What might be done on a general organizational level to improve the agency's effectiveness and efficiency?

A picture of results can be readily achieved through the collection and analysis of objective and subjective data. The kinds of data collected and analyses performed will depend on the program being considered. This section begins with a few words about process evaluation and then deals in detail with outcome evaluation.

Process

Usually, data can be readily gathered on matters of interest in a process evaluation. Collecting data, for example, on the demographic characteristics of clients, the length of time spent on waiting lists, the types of services provided, and the total number of hours of each is a relatively straightforward matter. In the monitoring approach, these and similar data are collected continuously and analyzed on a regular basis. Reports available to staff members make clear to what degree process objectives are being met. Process objectives usually pertain to good and desirable practices that are thought to lead to desired results. A more in-depth discussion of process evaluations is found in Chapter 3.

Outcome

Outcomes can be classified into three nonmutually exclusive areas: (1) problems and cases, (2) program, and (3) agency.

Problems and Cases

Many human service agencies offer services to people with a variety of needs: pregnant teens, disabled seniors, preadolescents with self-esteem problems, couples seeking help with their marriages, and people who are trying to stop smoking. The agency will be interested in knowing, and is usually required by funders to document, to what degree its programs are helping people with particular types of social problems.

The results achieved by any one client, satisfactory or not, do not say much about the general effectiveness of the program as a whole. Program effectiveness is determined only by examining data from groups of clients, often using simple aggregation methods that are described shortly.

Assume, for example, that during a six-month period of a smoking cessation program, the program served 80 clients, 40 male and 40 female. Using the case-level monitoring techniques previously described, data will be available showing the number of cigarettes smoked by each client at the beginning and at the end of the intervention. Aggregating the individual client results indicates that the average number of cigarettes smoked daily at the beginning of the intervention was 34, and the average number smoked at the end of the program was 11. Thus, the clients smoked, on the average, 23 fewer cigarettes after they completed the stop-smoking program. These aggregated data, after analysis, provide a method of assessing the outcome of the program. The aggregated data and the results of the analysis for all 80 clients are presented in Table 12.1.

The analysis presented in Table 12.1 is a simple one—the calculation of the difference between beginning and ending average number of cigarettes smoked. The analysis could be extended to determine whether this difference might have come about by chance alone. This is what is meant by the term "statistical significance." Detailed treatment of statistical procedures is beyond the scope of this text but is readily available in any introductory statistics book.

To return to our example, the decline in smoking can be documented as a net change of 23 cigarettes, on the average, per client. Although the data available in this situation permit documentation of the program's objective, or outcome, it is not possible to attribute this change to the intervention. The particular evaluation design used was the descriptive one-group pretest-posttest design, and, as we saw in Chapter 8, such descriptive designs do not support inferences about causality. Nevertheless, this type of design enables staff members to document the overall results of their services.

Further analyses of these data may provide additional and more specific information. Suppose, for example, that program staff had the impression that they were achieving better results with female smokers than with male

TABLE 12.1   Average
Number of Cigarettes Smoked at
the Beginning and End of the
Smoking Cessation Program
($N = 80$)

Beginning	–	After	=	Difference
34		11		23

smokers. Examining the results of males and females as separate groups would permit a comparison of the average number of cigarettes each group smoked at the end of the program. The data for this analysis are presented in Table 12.2. Note that the average number of cigarettes smoked at the beginning of the program was exactly the same for the males and females, 34. Thus, it could be concluded that there were no meaningful differences between the males and females in reference to the average number of cigarettes they smoked at the start of the intervention.

As Table 12.2 shows, at the end of the program males smoked an average of 18 cigarettes daily and females an average of 4 cigarettes. On the average, then, females smoked 14 fewer cigarettes per day than did males. Essentially, this analysis confirms workers' suspicion that they were obtaining better results with female smokers than with male smokers.

The information obtained via the simple analysis presented above provides documentation of outcomes, a vitally important element in this age of accountability and increased competition for available funding. There is,

TABLE 12.2   Average Number of
Cigarettes Smoked at the Beginning and End
of the Smoking Cessation Program by Sex
($N = 80$)

Sex	Beginning	–	After	=	Difference	n
Males	34		18		16	40
Females	34		4		30	40
Totals	34		11		23	80

however, a further advantage to compiling and analyzing evaluation data. By conducting regular analyses, social work administrators and workers can obtain important feedback about program strengths and weaknesses. These data can be used to further develop services. The data discussed above, for example, may cause the services to be modified in ways that would improve effectiveness with male clients while maintaining effectiveness with female clients. This would not only improve services to the male client group but would also boost overall program outcomes.

Program

As we know from Chapter 1, a program is a distinct unit, large or small, that operates within an organization. An agency, for example, may comprise a number of treatment programs, or a child welfare agency may operate a treatment foster-care program and a residential child abuse treatment program as part of its operations. The residential program itself may comprise a number of separate homes for children of different ages or different problem types.

These programs should be evaluated if the agency as a whole is to demonstrate accountability and provide the best possible service to its clientele. A thorough evaluation will include attention to needs, process, and outcomes as well as efficiency. Since the greatest interest is often in outcome, however, this section focuses on outcome evaluation (Chapter 4), where the question is, "To what degree has a program succeeded in reaching its program objectives?"

If this question is to be answered satisfactorily, of course, the program's objectives must be defined in a way that allows them to be measured (Chapter 6). Let us assume that one of the objectives of the residential child abuse treatment program is to enable its residents to return to their homes. The degree of achievement of this program objective can be determined through a simple count: What percentage of the residents returned home within the last year?

If the agency includes several programs of the same type, in different locations, lessons learned from one can be applied to another. In addition, similar programs will likely have the same program objectives and the same ways of measuring them, so that results can be aggregated to provide a measure of effectiveness for the entire agency. If the programs are dissimilar—for example, a treatment foster-care program and a victim-assistance program—aggregation will not be possible, but separate assessment of program outcomes will nevertheless contribute to the evaluation of the agency as a whole.

Agency

Outcome evaluation, whether in respect to an agency, a program, or a case, always focuses on the achievement of objectives. How well has the agency fulfilled its mandate? To what degree has it succeeded in meeting its goal, as revealed by the measurement of its program objectives? Again, success in goal achievement cannot be determined unless the agency's programs have well-defined, measurable program objectives that reflect the agency's mandate.

As seen in Chapter 2, agencies operate on the basis of mission statements, which often consist of vaguely phrased, expansive statements of intent. The mission of a sexual abuse treatment agency, for example, may be to ameliorate the pain caused by sexually abusive situations and to prevent sexual abuse in the future. Although there is no doubt that this is a laudable mission, the concepts of pain amelioration and abuse prevention cannot be measured until they have been more precisely defined.

This agency's mandate may be to serve persons who have been sexually abused and their families living within a certain geographical area. If the agency has an overall goal, "to reduce the trauma resulting from sexual abuse in the community," for example, the mandate is reflected and measurement is implied in the word "reduce." The concept of trauma still needs to be operationalized, but this can be accomplished through the specific, individual practice objectives of the clients whose trauma is to be reduced: The primary trauma for a male survivor may be fear that he is homosexual, whereas the trauma for a nonoffending mother may be guilt that she failed to protect her child.

If logical links are established between the agency's goal, the goals of the programs within the agency, and the individual practice objectives of clients served by the program, it will be possible to use the results of one to evaluate the other. Practice objective achievement at the case level will contribute to the success of the program, which will in turn contribute to the achievement of the agency's overall goal.

USING OUTCOME MONITORING DATA
IN PROGRAM-LEVEL DECISION MAKING

Just as a program outcome for any client may be acceptable, mixed, or inadequate, evaluation results can also be acceptable, mixed, or inadequate, reflecting the degree to which its program objectives have been achieved.

Acceptable Results

Before a result can be declared "acceptable," it is necessary to define clearly what counts as an acceptable result for a specific program objective. Let us return to the example of the residential program, where one of the program's objectives included enabling residents to return home: If 90 percent of residents succeed in making this move within six months of entry into the program, has the program's objective been achieved to an acceptable degree? What if 80 percent of residents return home within six months and a further 10 percent return home within a year? Or suppose that 100 percent return home within six months but half of the adolescents are eventually readmitted to the program.

Evidently, an acceptable result is largely a matter of definition. The program administrators and funders must decide what degree of objective achievement can reasonably be expected given the nature of the problems, the resources available, and the results of similar programs. Are the results for the smoking cessation program, for example, shown in Tables 12.1 and 12.2, indicative of success? If the program comprises a number of subprograms, the same considerations apply with regard to each.

Defining criteria for success should be done in advance of obtaining results, to avoid politicizing the results and to make it possible to set relevant program objectives.

Once the standards for an acceptable level of achievement have been set, evaluation becomes a matter of comparing actual outcomes against these standards. Where standards are met, program personnel can, with some degree of confidence, continue to employ existing procedures and practices. If a monitoring approach to evaluation is used and outcomes are analyzed on a regular basis, workers will be able to see not only whether program objectives are being achieved to an acceptable degree, but also whether the level of achievement is rising or falling. Any persistent trend toward improvement or decline is worth investigating so that more effective interventions and processes can be reinforced and potential problems can be detected and resolved.

Mixed Results

Occasionally, the results of an outcome evaluation will show that the program is achieving its objectives only partially. A program may be successful in helping one group of clients, for example, but less successful with another. This was the situation in the smoking cessation program presented above: Female clients were being helped considerably, but male clients were obtaining much less impressive results (Table 12.2). Similarly, an evaluation may reveal seasonal variations in outcomes: At certain times of the year a program may achieve its program objectives to an acceptable degree, but not at other times. Clients in farming communities, for instance, may be able to participate in the program in the winter more easily than during the growing season, when they are busy with the tasks of farming. This factor alone may result in reduced achievement at both the case and program levels. It is also possible that one program within an agency is achieving its objectives to a greater degree than another similar program.

In such situations, staff members will undoubtedly wish to adjust practices and procedures so that the underperforming components can be upgraded. In making any adjustments, however, care must be taken not to jeopardize those parts of the operation that are obtaining good outcomes. In the case of the smoking cessation program, for example, the workers may be tempted to tailor several sessions more to the needs of male clients. Although this may indeed improve the program's performance with male clients, the improvement may come at the expense of effectiveness with females.

A preferable strategy might be to form separate groups for males and females during some parts of the program, leaving the program unchanged for female clients but developing new sessions for male clients to better meet their needs. Of course, it is impossible to predict in advance whether changes will yield the desired results, but ongoing monitoring will provide feedback about their efficacy.

Inadequate Results

One of the strengths of a program-level monitoring system is that it takes into account the entire program process, from intake to follow-up. A low level of program objective achievement is not necessarily attributable to the interventions utilized by the workers with their clients. It is possible that the problem lies in inappropriate eligibility criteria, unsatisfactory assessment techniques, inadequate staff training, or a host of other factors, including unforeseen systematic barriers to clients' involvement in the program.

If an outcome evaluation shows that results are unsatisfactory, further program development is called for. To diagnose the problem or problems, the program administrator and workers will want to examine data concerning all the stages that lead up to intervention as well as the intervention process itself.

Once they have ideas about the reasons for suboptimal performance, they are in a position to begin instituting changes to procedures and practices—and monitoring the results of those changes.

SUMMING UP

One of the most important reasons for monitoring is to obtain timely data on which further decisions about intervention plans or program development can be based. At the case level, the worker will continually monitor changes in the client problem; at the program level, data relating to needs, processes, and outcomes can help staff make informed decisions about program modifications and changes.

STUDY QUESTIONS_____

1. Explain the difference between empirical and subjective data.

2. In your own words, briefly outline the limitations of empirical data. Compare your list with those identified in this chapter.

3. In your own words, briefly outline the limitations of subjective data. Compare your list with those identified in this chapter.

4. What is meant by the phrase "Garbage in, garbage out" in monitoring evaluations? What suggestions can you offer for workers to avoid the "Garbage in, garbage out" scenario?

5. Suppose a worker intuitively feels that her client is at risk for experiencing more serious episodes of loneliness. What suggestions can you offer to assist the worker in obtaining empirical data to support her subjective conclusion?

6. What is meant by the "clinical significance" of data? How does the clinical significance of data affect decision making for social service workers?

7. What options for program development might an administrator have when program results prove to be inadequate? What ethical considerations must be addressed?

8. In groups of four, agree on a social service problem and the criteria for client termination. Identify four different methods of measuring the problem that will assist you in deciding whether or not the client is ready for termination. To what degree will the information obtained from each of these methods be consistent? Will the decision to terminate client services tend to rely more on empirical or subjective data? Present your findings to the class.

9. In groups of five, develop a hypothetical social service program, complete with a mission statement, a goal, objectives, activities, and measurements of the program objectives. Choose an exploratory design to monitor and appraise case-level client outcomes, and identify the type of data to be collected for various practice objectives. Suppose the data obtained indicate

mixed results. What adjustments would you make to the interventions to increase client success? Review your list of adjustments and prioritize them according to order of implementation. Present your discussion to the class.

10. Human service decision making is based upon two different types of data. What are they? As you briefly describe each type, explain how they guide the decision-making process.

11. What are the advantages of using empirical data in decision making? Justify your response. Be specific and clear. Use a social service example throughout your discussion.

12. What are the limitations of using empirical data in decision making? Justify your response. Be specific and clear. Use a social service example throughout your discussion.

13. Under what conditions do workers use subjective data in decision making? When is the use of subjective data useful to the decision-making process? Justify your response. Be specific and clear. Use a social service example throughout your discussion.

14. Identify and discuss the major drawback to using subjective data in decision making. Justify your response. Be specific and clear. Use a social service example throughout your discussion.

15. How do practitioners make decisions at the case level? How are the highest-quality decisions reached? Justify your response. Be specific and clear. Use a social service example throughout your discussion.

16. What phases exist in a helping relationship in which decisions have to be made?

17. You are currently working with a client named Jennifer who wants to lose weight. You also see her mother, Irene, who is having problems with her boss at work. What types of decisions do you make with each of these clients in the engagement and problem definition phase of intervention? On what types of data are these decisions based? Justify your response. Be specific and clear.

18. Define a practice objective for Irene. To what degree does this phase rely on empirical data? Justify your response. Be specific and clear.

19. In what ways are your intervention strategies with clients like Jennifer and Irene based on empirical data? Justify your response. Be specific and clear.

20. How would your success with Irene be measured on the basis of consistently collected data? On what basis should you determine Irene's progress? Justify your response. Be specific and clear.

21. You realize your intervention decisions regarding Irene are based of her progress and your interpretation of her progress. How would you interpret a deterioration or no change in Irene as she works toward her practice objective? How would you interpret an insufficient or slow change in Irene's progress? Justify your response. Be specific and clear.

22. What kind a£ data would you take into account when deciding when Irene should be terminated? How can data aid your decision about whether to follow up with Irene? Justify your response. Be specific and clear.

23. What is the purpose of using a monitoring approach to quality improvement at the program level? How can program progress be assessed? Justify your response. Be specific and clear.

24. What kinds of data must be collected and analyzed when measuring the outcomes of a particular program? How is an evaluation of program outcomes conducted? Justify your response. Be specific and clear. Use a social service example throughout your discussion.

25. Suppose a program-level evaluation indicated *acceptable* results. How would such a result affect staff and administrative behavior? Justify your response. Be specific and clear. Use a

social service example throughout your discussion.

26. Suppose a program-level evaluation indicated *mixed* results. How would such a result affect staff and administrative behavior? justify your response. Be specific and clear. Use a social service example throughout your discussion.

27. Suppose a program-level evaluation indicated *inadequate* results. How would such a result affect staff and ad-ministrative behavior? Justify your re-sponse. Be specific and clear. Use a human service example throughout your discussion.

28. In your own words, discuss in depth why program objectives are measured at follow-up and not practice objectives. What is the rationale behind this? What are the limitations of follow-up data if practice objectives are not being measured? Under what cir-cumstances would the measurement of practice objectives be justified for fol-low-up data? Justify your answer. Use one common social service example throughout your discussion.

29. How would you determine the success of the smoking program via the data contained in Tables 12.1 and 12.2? Do you feel the program achieved its pro-gram objective of reducing the smoking behavior of its clientele to zero? Dis-cuss in detail. Justify your response.

30. Table 12.2 presents a breakdown by sex of the data contained in Table 12.1. Construct five hypothetical tables that are similar to Table 12.1 using the vari-ables age, referral source, ethnicity, extent of previous smoking behavior, and socioeconomic status. What would these other tables tell you in reference

to the stop-smoking program? Discuss in detail. Justify your answer.

31. Reread Chapter 7 on case-level evalua-tions. As you know, all exploratory, descriptive, and explanatory case-level evaluation designs can be used in case-level decision making. Discuss how each one of these designs can be utilized in a monitoring approach to quality improvement by highlighting what case-level decisions can be made with each design. Provide one common social service example throughout your discussion.

32. Reread Chapter 8 on program-level evaluations. As you know, all explor-atory, descriptive, and explanatory pro-gram-level evaluation designs can be used in program-level decision making. Discuss how each one of these designs can be utilized in a monitoring approach to quality improvement by highlighting what program-level deci-sions can be made with each design. Provide one common social service example throughout your discussion.

33. As we have seen in this chapter, some standardized measuring instruments are constructed where a higher score means there is *more* of a problem than a lower score (e.g., Figures 12.6 and 12.7, marital satisfaction levels). Some are designed where a higher score means that there *is less* of a problem than a lower score (e.g., Figures 12.1 through 12.5, communication levels). Discuss the implications that these two kinds of instruments have for you in reference to interpreting scores from them. Go to the library and find an ex-ample of each.

Credits

Box 1.1: Adapted from: "The generation of knowledge," by Grinnell, R.M., Jr., in R.M. Grinnell, Jr. (Ed.), *Social work research and evaluation: Quantitative and qualitative approaches* (5th ed). Copyright © 1997 by F.E. Peacock Publishers; and "Research in social work," by Grinnell, R.M., Jr., Rothery, M., & Thomlison, R.J., in R.M. Grinnell, Jr. (Ed.), *Social work research and evaluation* (4th ed.). Copyright © 1993 by F.E. Peacock Publishers.

Box 1.2: Adapted from: Council on Social Work Education (2000). *Baccalaureate and masters curriculum policy statements.* Alexandria, VA: Author.

Box 1.3: National Association of Social Workers (1999). *Code of ethics.* Washington, DC: Author.

Box 5.3: Adapted from: "Utilizing existing statistics," by Sieppert, D.J., McMurtry, S.L., & McClelland, R.W., in Grinnell, R.M., Jr. (Ed.), *Social work research and evaluation: Quantitative and qualitative approaches* (6th ed.). Copyright © 2001 by F.E. Peacock Publishers.

Box 9.1: Adapted from: Gabor, P.A., & Grinnell, R.M., Jr. *Evaluation and quality improvement in the human services.* Copyright © 1994 by Allyn & Bacon; Gabor, P.A., Unrau, Y.A., & Grinnell, R.M., Jr. *Evaluation and quality improvement in the human services* (2nd ed.). Copyright © 1997 by Allyn & Bacon; Grinnell, R.M., Jr., & Williams, M. *Research in social work: A primer.* Copyright © 1990 by F.E. Peacock Publishers; Williams, M., Tutty, L.M., & Grinnell, R.M., Jr. *Research in social work: An introduction.* Copyright © 1995 by F.E. Peacock Publishers; "Research contexts," by Williams, M., Grinnell, R.M., Jr., & Tutty, L., in R.M. Grinnell, Jr. (Ed.), *Social work research and evaluation: Quantitative and qualitative approaches* (5th ed.). Copyright © 1997 by F.E. Peacock Publishers; and Williams, M., Unrau, Y.A., & Grinnell, R.M., Jr. (1998). *Introduction to social work research.* Copyright © 1998 by F.E. Peacock Publishers.

Figure 3.1: Adapted from: "Designing measuring instruments," by Mindel, C., in R.M. Grinnell, Jr. (Ed.), *Social work research and evaluation: Quantitative and qualitative approaches* (6th ed.). Copyright © 2001 by F.E. Peacock Publishers.

Figure 5.1: Adapted from: "Survey research," by McMurtry, S.L., in R.M. Grinnell, Jr. (Ed.), *Social work research and evaluation: Quantitative and qualitative ap-*

proaches (6th ed.). Copyright © 2001 by F.E. Peacock Publishers.

Figure 5.2 Adapted from: *Social research methods: Qualitative and quantitative approaches* (3rd ed.), by Neuman, W.L., Copyright © 1997 by Allyn & Bacon.

Figure 6.1: Adapted from: Hudson, W.W. Copyright © 1993 by WALMYR Publishing Company, Post Office Box 2629, Tallahassee, Florida, 32314.

Figure 6.2: Adapted from: Reid, P.N., & Gundlach, J.H., "A scale for the measurement of consumer satisfaction with social services," *Journal of Social Service Research, 7, 37-54.* Copyright © 1983 by P.N. Reid and J.H. Gundlach.

Figure 6.3: Adapted from: Dunst, C.J., Jenkins, V., & Trivette C. (1990). Family support scale: Reliability and validity. *Journal of Individual, Family, and Community Wellness, 1,* 45-52.

Figure 6.4: Adapted from: Alter, C., & Evens, W. (1990). *Evaluating your practice. A guide to self-assessment.* New York: Springer.

Figures 7.1-7.7: Adapted from: Grinnell, R.M., Jr., & Williams, M. *Research in social work: A primer.* Copyright © 1990 by F.E. Peacock Publishers; Williams, M., Tutty, L.M., & Grinnell, R.M., Jr. *Research in social work: An introduction.* Copyright © 1995 by F.E. Peacock Publishers; and Williams, M., Unrau, Y.A., & Grinnell, R.M., Jr. *Introduction to social work research.* Copyright © 1998 by F.E. Peacock Publishers.

Figure 9.1: Williams, M., Tutty, L.M., & Grinnell, R.M., Jr. *Research in social work: An introduction.* Copyright © 1995 by F.E. Peacock Publishers; "Research contexts," by Williams, M., Grinnell, R.M., Jr., & Tutty, L., in R.M. Grinnell, Jr. (Ed.), *Social work research and evaluation: Quantitative and qualitative ap-*

proaches (5th ed.). Copyright © 1997 by F.E. Peacock Publishers; and Williams, M., Unrau, Y.A., & Grinnell, R.M., Jr. (1998). *Introduction to social work research.* Copyright © 1998 by F.E. Peacock Publishers.

Chapter 8, Boxes 8.1, 8.2: Adapted from: Gabor, P.A., & Grinnell, R.M., Jr. *Evaluation and quality improvement in the human services.* Copyright © 1994 by Allyn & Bacon; Gabor, P.A., Unrau, Y.A., & Grinnell, R.M., Jr. *Evaluation and quality improvement in the human services* (2nd ed.). Copyright © 1997 by Allyn & Bacon; "Group research designs," by Grinnell, R.M., Jr., in R.M. Grinnell, Jr. (Ed.), *Social work research and evaluation* (4th ed). Copyright © 1993 by F.E. Peacock Publishers; "Research designs," by Grinnell, R.M., Jr., & Stothers, M., in R.M. Grinnell, Jr. (Ed.), *Social work research and evaluation* (3rd ed.). Copyright © 1988 by F.E. Peacock Publishers; Grinnell, R.M., Jr., & Williams, M. *Research in social work: A primer.* Copyright © 1990 by F.E. Peacock Publishers; "Group designs," by Grinnell, R.M., Jr., & Unrau, Y., in R.M. Grinnell, Jr. (Ed.), *Social work research and evaluation: Quantitative and qualitative approaches* (5th ed.). Copyright © 1997 by F.E. Peacock Publishers; Williams, M., Tutty, L.M., & Grinnell, R.M., Jr. *Research in social work: An introduction.* Copyright © 1995 by F.E. Peacock Publishers; Williams, M., Unrau, Y.A., & Grinnell, R.M., Jr. (1998). *Introduction to social work research.* Copyright © 1998 by F.E. Peacock Publishers; "Group research designs," by Grinnell, R.M., Jr., & Unrau, Y., in R.M. Grinnell, Jr. (Ed.), *Social work research and evaluation: Quantitative and qualitative approaches* (6th ed.). Copyright © 2001 by F.E. Peacock Publishers.

Index

EVALUATION IN THE HUMAN SERVICES
Edited by John Beasley
Production supervision by Kim Vander Steen
Cover design by Jeanne Calabrese Design, River Forest, Illinois
Internal design and composition by Grinnell, Inc., Dallas, Texas
Printed and bound by Victor Graphics, Baltimore, Maryland